Choosing Our Future

First Published in 1992, *Choosing Our Future* presents a personal but highly rigorous account of the environmental problems facing us and of the ways in which they can be tackled. Ann Taylor's approach centres on the traditional values of democratic socialism, establishing their inherent compatibility with modern concerns of sustainable economic development and environmental protection. She argues that people and the planet are interdependent and that ensuring a balance between the needs of both is the historic role of the Labour Party.

Lucid and topical, this book will appeal to anyone who is interested in realistic, hard- headed solutions to environmental problems. It will be of interest to general readers and to members of the Labour movement, environmentalists and professionals in environmental management and regulation. It will also be useful to students of politics and development.

Choosing Our Future

A Practical Politics of the Environment

Ann Taylor

Routledge
Taylor & Francis Group

First published in 1992
by Routledge

This edition first published in 2024 by Routledge
4 Park Square, Milton Park, Abingdon, Oxon, OX14 4RN

and by Routledge
605 Third Avenue, New York, NY 10017

Routledge is an imprint of the Taylor & Francis Group, an informa business

Publisher's Note
The publisher has gone to great lengths to ensure the quality of this reprint but points
out that some imperfections in the original copies may be apparent.

Disclaimer
The publisher has made every effort to trace copyright holders and welcomes
correspondence from those they have been unable to contact.

A Library of Congress record exists under LCCN:

ISBN: 978-1-032-63826-3 (hbk)
ISBN: 978-1-032-63831-7 (ebk)
ISBN: 978-1-032-63830-0 (pbk)

Book DOI 10.4324/9781032638317

Choosing our future

A practical politics of the environment

Ann Taylor

ROUTLEDGE

London and New York

First published 1992
by Routledge
11 New Fetter Lane, London EC4P 4EE

Simultaneously published in the USA and Canada
by Routledge
a division of Routledge, Chapman and Hall, Inc.
29 West 35th Street, New York, NY 10001

Typeset by LaserScript, Mitcham, Surrey
Printed and bound in Great Britain by Mackays of Chatham PLC,
Chatham, Kent

British Library Cataloguing in Publication Data
A catalogue record for this book is available from the British Library

0–415–07945–4 Hb
0–415–07946–2 Pb

Library of Congress Cataloging in Publication Data
Taylor, Ann, 1947–
  Choosing our future: a practical politics of the environment/
Ann Taylor.
  p. cm.
Includes bibliographical references and index.
  ISBN 0–415–07945–4 (hb). – ISBN 0–415–07946–2 (pb)
  1. Economic development – Environmental aspects. 2. Environmental
  protection. 3. Human ecology. I. Title.
HD75.6T39 1992
333.7 – dc20   91-42951
                                                                      CIP

For Andrew and Isabel

Contents

Foreword

Gro Harlem Brundtland
Prime Minister of Norway

> In the middle of the 20th century, we saw our planet from space for the first time. . . . From space, we see a small and fragile ball dominated not by human activity and edifice but by a pattern of clouds, oceans, greenery and soils. Humanity's inability to fit its doings into that pattern is changing planetary systems fundamentally. . . . This new reality, from which there is no escape, must be recognized – and managed.

This passage is taken from the overview of 'Our Common Future', the report of the World Commission on Environment and Development which was presented in 1987. But the observation remains valid even five years later. Global interdependence is growing, and the need for a better management of this interdependence increases with it.

Since we presented our report, we have made some progress in dealing with regional and local environmental problems such as air pollution, water and waste management. Globally, the agreements to protect the ozone layer and the start of negotiations on a world climate convention are signs of progress.

But these encouraging developments have not been sufficient to offset the general trend towards global environmental deterioration. There is growing scientific evidence that the scope of human activities on Earth will soon surpass the carrying capacity of nature. Precious natural resources such as fossil fuels, fertile topsoil and biodiversity are being rapidly depleted. We may be approaching critical thresholds in nature's ability to absorb the waste products of human civilization.

How do we maintain and strengthen world order in a situation of rapid global change? How can we move from the stage of merely trying to cope with global change to a better, more long-term and strategic management of interdependence?

When the World Commission on Environment and Development was established in 1983, our challenge was to address vital global issues and to propose a strategy for dealing effectively with them. The United Nations General Assembly gave us, in fact, the mandate to formulate a global agenda for change.

Our dream was of a world worth living in both for present and for future generations. Sustainable development – defined as a process of change which can satisfy the needs of the present generation without compromising the ability of future generations to meet their needs – became our vision for our common future. Sustainable development is the only viable strategy for global change. It means that we must aim at nothing less than a shift in the overall direction of the world economy. It means creating a new kind of growth and that we must change the way economic decisions are made.

There is today a growing recognition of the important complementary roles of the public and private sectors in development. Support is rising for a more market-friendly approach to development.

But the war against hunger, disease, poverty, or ecological degradation cannot be left to the market to fight. We will never see the day when the market alone brings about sustainability on the global level.

There should be no mistake about the role of politics and governments. Business and industry must be given a clear sense of direction, defined through democratic government and accountable government.

With greater freedom for the market comes greater responsibility. Those who live by the market, must face the challenge of ensuring that we do not all die by the market. A quest for growth and profit alone is no longer enough, economic activities must also become sustainable to justify their existence in the global market place of the twenty-first century.

To achieve the transition to sustainable development, we must focus on the positive incentives for change. We need to find the right mix between government regulations, government incentives and industry's self-control and corporate strategies.

Governments must establish the framework conditions which can accelerate the development and dissemination of environmentally benign technology. The market mechanisms must be adjusted so that prices reflect the true environmental costs of what we do and how we consume.

More active use of economic instruments to benefit the environment will also require international harmonization of rules. We must avoid distortions of international trade relations. Closer international cooperation is necessary to establish standardized charges. Political authorities must strengthen networks of international cooperation to regain their ability to deal with these problems.

We need to build a strong international public sector. We must pool our sovereignties and share the responsibility for peace, human rights and sustainable development. To meet the challenges of environmental degradation, we must develop a new generation of international agreements, based on cost-effectiveness and on equitable burden-sharing.

In our focus on global environmental issues, a key task is to promote sustainable development in the South. This is where the real battle to save our common future will be won – or lost. More than 80 per cent of the world population already lives in the Third World, and this percentage is increasing. Paradoxically, population growth is usually most rapid where poverty is great and where health and education services are weak.

Whereas the rich world is beginning to cope with the first generation of environmental problems, these same problems are still very much on the increase in the Third World. In the countryside, poverty leads to greater pressure on marginal lands, thus increasing the rate of deforestification. In cities, the explosive rate of urbanization will lead to staggering pressures on local governments to provide basic management. Urban decay is too often overlooked in our discussions on environmental problems.

The World Commission focused on human resource development as a crucial requirement not only to build up technical knowledge and capabilities, but also to create new values to help individuals and nations cope with rapidly changing social, environmental and development realities.

A strategy for global change must include women and women's issues in policy-making at all levels. Women in developing countries are among those suffering most from the deterioration of the environment. Although there are economic, social and cultural differences between women in different parts of the world, many of the challenges facing women are universal.

Women comprise more than 50 per cent of the world's population and they constitute one third of the world's labour force. But they do not have the political representation and power according to their number and participation in production and economic activities. Women are the most homebound part of the population, they raise children, they provide for the family, they run the social networks and they do the greater work in the health and social services. They recognise the importance of the environment for the well-being of a society and for the future of their children. But women do not have the power to make priorities in production and trade. Their access to land and water has diminished, and they own less than one hundredth of the world's total wealth.

Women's participation is a prerequisite for global change. Not only because women should have the opportunity to influence and control their own lives and living conditions for their children and family. Women's experiences and qualities are also vital in our efforts to combat poverty and inequality, and to safeguard our common future. Participation in the democratic process will strengthen women's self-esteem. We need women as part of a conscious public opinion that can keep democratic pressure on political decision-making, to set new targets to increase environmental accountability and to ensure a better future.

Sustainable development is an ambitious concept. It implies that we must seize control of our common future through a new and more active management of global change. This will not be an easy task. To succeed, we must be able to bridge the gap between the developing and the industrialised countries, between the poor and the rich. In this process, the participation of women is of vital importance.

February 1992

Acknowledgements

Credit for convincing me that this book could be written and was not just a fanciful idea must go to David Wheeler and Abigail Melville, who helped and encouraged this project from the start. My thanks also to Nick Young for his considerable assistance throughout and to Nick Sigler and John Newbigin for their time and constructive comments. Andrea Bonsey and Verity Lambert gave much background assistance as did Alan Jinkinson, Dave Prentice and Dick Barry. My apologies must go to those in my office whose normal work was often disruped by 'the book'; and last, but obviously not least, to my family for yet another commitment which demanded my time.

Introduction

Two facts about the twentieth century have challenged our view of the earth, our way of managing it, and our way of dividing its fruits. The first is a massive increase in the rate of resource depletion and pollution, caused by increased economic activity. The second is the revolution in information technology, which has effectively 'shrunk' the world, giving us almost instant access to the data, and even television pictures, of human and environmental disasters as they happen. We have no excuse for ignorance or inaction.

Hundreds of books, pamphlets, newspaper articles, radio and television programmes have, rightly, focused on the first of these points, drawing attention to the environmental problems and constraints we face: from great and threatening issues like global warming to more local, but nonetheless important and keenly felt, issues like contamination of water supplies, despoliation of the beauty of our countryside, and the dehumanisation of our cities and towns. In this book I aim to address these issues, not so much with a view to identifying or publicising problems – for many experts, in many fields, have already done that – but with the specific objective of identifying ways we can and should begin to tackle them. This, I believe, is the proper approach for a politician: and it is an essentially practical approach.

I also believe, as a practical politician, that we now have an opportunity, and a duty, to make decisions and choices of a kind that we have never really contemplated before. This should be done in a spirit of hope and determination, not in a spirit of despair. Environmental concern has often been closely associated with doom-mongering, and with dire warnings about the terrible future our children will endure. But this can be turned around: if environmental protection is about protecting our future – and it is – then we should be able to see, in the environmental choices we make now, an opportunity for providing our children with a better future and a better quality of life. And perhaps the greatest challenge of all is working out what we mean by a 'better quality of life'. Do we mean an increase in private wealth, an increase in the level of consumption of material goods, and ever more sophisticated ways of exploiting the planet's resources? Or do we mean fairer distribution of existing wealth, more control of government structures by ordinary people, a greater sense of community and an understanding that our well-being is linked to that of others? In this sense, thinking about environmental protection means thinking about the kind of values that should guide our decision making.

From this, it should be clear that the environment is not, and never could be, a 'non-political issue'. Some environmentalists have wanted to depoliticise environmental debate because they feel – rightly – that the problems concern each and every one of us, and cannot be resolved by political parties that they see as representing only sectional interests. But this feeling has led some to a rather simplistic belief – summed up in the slogan originally devised by the German Greens, 'neither left nor right but forward', – that environmentalists should reject, or transcend, more conventional political analysis.

Yet many, perhaps most, environmental problems are intimately bound up with questions such as the distribution of power and wealth. Consider, for example, the plight of millions of peasant farmers in Third World countries who are obliged to plant on steep, previously wooded slopes. Such people invariably know that after two or three rainy seasons the topsoil will be washed away, leaving the ground barren and the rivers swollen with silt. But if, as is very often the case, all the best land is occupied by large scale producers growing crops for export, the small farmers have no choice but to scratch a living where they can, even though this causes soil erosion. Clearly, this is not a purely technical problem, and there will be limits to what can be achieved with technical remedies (such as changing crops or introducing high yield varieties). For the most basic problem is political; and so the solution, as with many environmental and development problems, must also be political.

This is the sort of issue, specifically in connection with development, that I consider in more detail in Chapter 2. But the same kind of analysis, showing the political dimension of environmental issues, applies equally to Britain. In a sense, indeed, all environmental problems are fundamentally political, because they are the result not of external causes but of the way that our society is organised, the way that resources are distributed and put to use, and the kinds of economic and social goals we pursue, individually and collectively.

This political dimension can be seen clearly in specific issues, such as the recent privatisation of the water industry and energy utilities. On the most generous interpretation, this was a logical implementation of seriously held Conservative political ideology: the belief that private profit is not just reconcilable with public interest, but actually in some way guarantees it. In vigorously rejecting this view, in arguing that public health can be jeopardised by attempts to maximise returns to water shareholders, in pointing out that the narrow objective of making money will almost certainly prejudice moves towards clean, efficient energy generation, my colleagues and I were not just taking environmental concerns on board. We were offering a different political analysis, one that has a less cynical view of human motivation and seeks to meet needs through democratic participation, cooperation and planning, rather than through blind faith in the market place. Again, the questions are all to do with values. What's more important: providing dividends to shareholders, or supplying safe drinking water to the public? What matters most: making money out of selling plenty of electricity now, or making the country a cleaner place and leaving our children with sufficient energy reserves to meet their future needs?

I make no apology for placing the welfare of children at the centre of my understanding of environmental issues. On a daily and personal basis, my first instinct in considering environmental matters is to think of my own children: what may harm them, now or in the future; what may blight their health or their prospects? I am sure that the great majority of parents feel and react in very much the same way. There is absolutely nothing wrong with this: nothing unsophisticated, nothing feeble minded, nothing intellectually lacking. On the contrary, as I argue in Chapter 7, this very practical and personal concern is the only reasonable way of interpreting the much vaunted idea of 'sustainability'. And when considering immediate action, protecting the welfare of children is an excellent guide to what must be done. We should remember, for example, that babies wheeled in pushchairs along city streets are at the same level as vehicle exhaust pipes. That thought should dictate what we allow to come out of those exhaust pipes, and where we allow the vehicles to drive. Similarly, and even more specifically, when considering public exposure to toxic substances we should be guided by what infants can tolerate, rather than setting standards, as at present, according to the tolerance levels of adult males.

But before outlining a practical programme for action, as I shall do throughout the book but particularly in the later chapters, there is some groundwork to be done in clarifying the concepts that are regularly used – and sometimes misused – in environmental debate. What, exactly, do we mean when we talk about 'the environment'? What is an 'environmental perspective'? Is such a perspective compatible with a broad range of political outlooks, or does it imply particular moral and political values? These are important questions because their answers will inevitably colour our perception of problems, the kinds of solution that seem acceptable, and our idea of what environmental protection itself amounts to.

As a way into these questions, it will be useful to return to the second point I made at the beginning, about the metaphorical shrinking of the world, because this – quite literally – affects our picture of the planet.

When Caesar sat in Rome the world seemed limitless. The spaces beyond the fringes of Empire were as broad and unknown as the outer reaches of the universe are now unknown to us. Yet 2,000 years later we can, from our armchairs, press a button and watch documentaries about kangaroos in Australia, condors in the Andes or people starving in the Sudan. The difference is not just that the frontiers of exploration and conquest have gradually extended over the whole of the earth's surface. By the beginning of this century the world had been effectively mapped out in all but a few details, but a truly global view was available, if at all, only to a tiny, intellectual élite. Wars could happen in faraway places with the public barely being conscious of them. This was the case, for example, with the American intervention in the Philippines in 1901. Six hundred thousand Filipinos died in the central island of Luzon, but the war was hardly reported back in the United States, let alone in Britain (Constantino, 1978).

The contrast with the Vietnam and Gulf wars could hardly be more striking. In this sense, the development of mass communications media is potentially a great force for good. Public awareness can be both a constraint on the activities of governments and a spur to action. That is why, as I shall argue throughout, it is so important to guarantee access to information on environmental matters. Meanwhile a further, relevant aspect of the communications revolution is the effect it has had not just on the amount of information we receive, but on the way we now tend to view the world.

The space exploration programme of the 1960s and 1970s, however defensible or otherwise the expenditure it involved, had an interesting side effect in bringing into our homes television pictures of our planet spinning delicately in space. This, indeed, turned out to be the most arresting and memorable image of the moonshots. Neil Armstrong, standing with his golfclubs in an eerie moonscape, was completely upstaged by the breathtaking beauty of the earth, viewed as a whole for the first time in human history. As testament to its power, the image has been reproduced in thousands of magazines, posters, even advertisements, so that it is now a visual cliché. With the visual cliché go the verbal ones, coined in an effort to communicate the impact of seeing and considering the earth as a whole: 'spaceship earth'; 'global village'. Already these phrases have an old-fashioned ring; and yet we are the first generation of people ever to have seen, and thought about, our world this way.

It is a truism that travellers often learn more about themselves on their journeying than about the places they visit. Perhaps something of the kind happened vicariously to the millions of viewers who followed the trip to the moon. Instead of looking outwards to the stars and beyond, our attention lingered on this new view of home. What was so striking was its singleness, its unity, its indivisibility. And that, notably, is one of the most important elements of the environmental perspective. The global environment is not a collection of separate parts, it is a highly complex whole, a system. National boundaries drawn on maps are irrelevant to the actions of particles of air, earth and water within that system.

The sight of the earth as viewed from space would not, of course, by itself make people receptive to an ecological point of view. But the world has shrunk in many other ways. Consider, for example, the length of time it would have taken, a hundred years ago, to send a ten page document from Dewsbury to Delhi. Today it can be done almost instantaneously by a variety of different technologies. In many respects, India is no longer so far away.

What would have been the response of a Victorian industrialist to the concept of acid rain? Surely he (for it was invariably a 'he') would have found the whole affair preposterous. He might have been persuaded that smoke from his factory was an unpleasant, local pollutant, but the procedure in such cases was simple. He merely had to build a taller chimney, and the smoke would be dispersed into the skies. The absorptive capacity of the atmosphere was assumed to be unlimited, and the environmental consequences of productive activity to be strictly local. Within such a conceptual framework it would be literally impossible to imagine smoke from a chimney in Dewsbury resulting in acid rain in Scandinavia. If we now know better, it is because our conceptual framework has altered, and this is largely the result of our daily experience of technology. In our world, Scandinavia is not two days away by steamship, it is two seconds away by telefax, fractions of a second away by satellite dish.

It is also true that our conceptual framework has altered because of what scientists have discovered and told us about the world. But scientists themselves don't work in an intellectual void. The research agenda is largely set by the occurrence of concrete problems in the real world, and scientists themselves operate within a conceptual framework that is delineated by the received assumptions and ideas of the day. A scientist growing up in a world of satellite communications and atmospheric damage is likely to reach a different understanding of energy and matter to the scientists of the Renaissance. Which is not to say that the latter, or even the mediaeval alchemists, were stupid, but simply that their starting points were different.

This is not just an academic discussion about the history of ideas: there are important consequences to be drawn out. First, it is clear that we should not be afraid of science and technology *per se*. On these grounds alone, we can immediately distance ourselves from 'deep green' utopianism that would have us live out a pleasantly anarchistic, but recognisably mediaeval, existence (although real mediaeval life was undoubtedly far from pleasant for most people). For far from being 'the problems' in themselves, science and technology are the very instruments by which we have come to an understanding of the limitations of the planet. And, as I argue in Chapter 5, those same instruments, responsibly and democratically used, will certainly have an important part, alongside political interventions, in any 'answers' we may find.

That is not to dismiss high idealism and hope. On the contrary, the second, equally important conclusion to draw is that once our perspective encompasses the problems that productive activity have generated, we are presented with a unique opportunity to do something about them. As I have already said, environmentalists have for too long been identified as prophets of doom. The time is ripe for turning that around, and presenting ourselves as the messengers of real hope.

I mentioned, for example, watching television pictures of people suffering famine in the Sudan. There is little new in famine. Over many millenia of human history, and in every continent, millions of people have died of hunger. What is new is that we, who are in a position to help, can now see them. It would be wrong to be complacent, and suggest that therein lies the solution to all suffering. The problems are complex, and resolving them will inevitably require important shifts in the balance of power and resources. But if, as I believe, a general broadening is taking place in people's perceptions of what is relevant to them, then the prospects for an increased sense of global responsibility are in fact promising.

There are, indeed, indications of an increase not only in public awareness but also in concern about these issues. The generous response of the British public over recent years to emergency aid appeals, 'comic relief' and fundraising concerts may be taken as a case in point. More anecdotal, but in a way no less significant, evidence of changing perceptions was provided a short while ago by the BBC radio soap opera *The Archers*, when the newest member of that family, Ruth, paused over her seed drill to make a direct comparison between her position and that of Sudanese farmers! Would BBC scriptwriters have come up with such a scene 30 years ago when the series started? Surely not. Perhaps we are not so far away from a basic change in the notion of charity, away from patriarchal benevolence and towards solidarity with others who, if not exactly in the same boat, are at least on the same 'spaceship earth'. The idea of 'our common humanity' no longer rests solely on biological definition, but appeals directly to the newly perceived fact that the human race shares a single home and a single destiny.

Unfortunately, the compassion and generosity of the British public over the past decade has not been matched by its government, which has successively cut the overseas aid budget to less than a half of the proportion of GNP recommended by the United Nations. In the same way, environmental policy has lagged behind public awareness and concern as demonstrated, for example, by the rapid growth of campaigning groups and the considerable demand for environmentally benign goods. Far from giving a lead on environmental and development issues, the Conservative government of the 1980s made only token gestures to acknowledge public concern.

In general terms, however, I believe that over the last 30 years the basic 'worldview' of very many of us has changed in a number of significant ways, in no small part because of a change in the way we experience the world through new technologies. We have a greater appreciation of the planet as a single entity, as a whole, and this, combined with the immediacy of communication around the planet, sharpens our understanding that apparently distant problems are of direct relevance to us. So while it is undeniably true that environmental degradation has accelerated dramatically in our lifetimes, it is also the case that we are in a better position than ever before to see what is going on, and therefore to act.

But if this begins to explain a greater, general tendency towards a global perspective, one that is more disposed to see the world as a single system and to appreciate the subtle relations between different elements of that system, it is not yet enough to explain what we count as an 'environmental' issue. This is not a trivial point, and nor is it an easy one to sort out. Most dictionaries follow Einstein's famous remark – 'the environment is everything that's not me' – by defining 'environment' as our 'surroundings', everything that is not a part of us. Can we be more specific than that? And what will an 'environmental perspective' contribute if we can't?

In the first place, it should be clear that the aspect of our surroundings of most fundamental and overriding interest to us is its ability to support human life. We need air to breathe, water to drink, basic shelter, food to eat. Without these, there can be no further discussion about human purposes or the quality of life, because there can be no life at all. So, in a very obvious sense, any change in our surroundings which affects their ability to support us is of immediate and pressing concern. The contamination of air and water, the depletion of natural food stocks, the degradation of soils, and changes in climate or in the physical conditions which enable the sun's energy to be converted into food are, therefore, all primordial 'environmental issues', because they have to do with the environment's capacity to support us. From there, it is only a small step to add that we require our surroundings not just to be capable of supporting human life, but to enable us to live in good health. Any changes which damage our health are therefore clearly also environmental issues. Beyond that, though, things get rather complicated.

Many writers, and most policy makers, have relied upon a broad, intuitive distinction between 'the built' and 'the natural' environment. This distinction is implicit in any appeal to 'nature conservation', and to any argument which attempts to prescribe what our relationship with the rest of nature should be like (as, for example, the common suggestions that we should have 'more respect for nature' or live in 'greater harmony with nature'). Such a rough, working distinction may well be useful, and even necessary, when it comes to actually making policy decisions. And yet we ought to recognise that the distinction is in fact highly imprecise.

A Scottish grouse moor, or a Lake District fell, is, to many people, the epitome of 'wild and natural' beauty. Yet the claims to naturalness of these, and all other British landscapes, must be qualified. Until a relatively short while ago, most of Britain, and indeed Europe, was covered in dense forest, only pockets of which remain. The place names of villages and towns in the English Midlands still bear testament to those destroyed forests. 'Thorpe', for example, means (in Anglo-Saxon) 'clearing in the wood', and the area once covered by Sherwood, in which wild boar were hunted by such recent, historical figures as Henry VIII, is still liberally scattered with Thorpe Abbots, Thorpe Satchvilles and Thorpes by Water. Much of our folklore, too, and the fairy tales we read to our children – from Robin Hood, through Hansel and Gretel to Little Red Riding Hood – remains dense with the metaphor and the crowding presence of dark woods, although now only a few specimen fractions of the woods themselves are left to excite our children's imaginations. It can be instructive to remember our history when condemning the folly of deforestation in Brazil and Cameroon.

Where forests once stood we now have, in non-urban areas, a system of agriculture which itself has undergone several revolutions. The 'peasant poet', John Clare, crafted many a bitter couplet in the 1820s against the enclosure system of agriculture, which replaced the strip farming that itself had replaced the forests. For Clare, the agrarian revolution, that tore down hedges to enlarge the size of fields, was not just a threat to the lifestyle of subsistence farmers and rural communities (sending much of the rural population off to wage labour in factories), it was an attack upon the quality of the countryside, and an attack upon Nature herself.

More than a hundred years later, Clare's anger at interference with the landscape found many echoes in conservationists' dismay at the further industrialisation of agriculture in the post-war period, with its attendant destruction of hedgerows and wildlife. But the interesting fact is that contemporary conserva-tionists have in effect argued for the conservation of a landscape that, to Clare, was modern and unnatural. And the landscape that Clare wanted to conserve was, in turn, a far cry from the original forest cover.

The Scottish Highland clearances were even more dramatic than agricultural enclosure in lowland England. Tourists are often drawn to the Highlands precisely because of their emptiness: because they appear to be amongst the few places left in Europe where Nature is writ large and human habitations are few and far between. Yet, 200 years ago, the Highland valleys were filled with thriving and populous human settlements. A complex clan structure existed on an agricultural base in which cattle were kept in the valleys during the winter and driven up to higher ground in the summer months. In one of the most efficient and brutal operations in agricultural history, these people and their cattle were burned and beaten from their homes in order to make way for large scale, low cost, high profit sheep farming. At first the people were driven towards the coasts, where they were instructed to make a living by fishing. Those who could not adapt to this alien lifestyle were encouraged to go further; and so ended up in disease-ridden ships pointing westwards to the Americas: emigrants as unwilling as the convicts who were pointed eastwards towards Australia.

The Scotland marketed by the tourist boards is thus a relatively new phenomenon. Like the rest of Britain, its appearance and even its ecology have been profoundly altered by economic activity – and it is important to recognise that the presence or absence of human settlements is itself a highly significant factor in the ecology of a region – such that it becomes extremely difficult to say what, in the remaining landscape, is 'natural'. More recently, the story and the landscape have taken another new turn, with the large scale plantation of conifers.

Similar puzzles present themselves when we think about particular elements of our total environment. Common foods such as the tomato and the potato, grown in nearly every British allotment and sold as local produce by nearly every greengrocer, are not native to this country at all. Nature did not bring them here: we did. This transplanting of species is not confined to commercially grown produce. Hundreds of foreign plants have been introduced, particularly by the Victorians, from rhododendrons to flowering cherry trees, and many of them have not only thrived but have become fully integrated into our notion of the typically British conservatory, garden and countryside.

Globally, the picture is even more dramatic. There were no rats in Australia until a couple scuttled off Captain Cook's ship; and the lack of predators there guaranteed the success of rat colonisation, as it did the even more notorious colonisation by rabbits. There were no horses in the Americas until the European conquest. And yet now, Apache Indians riding bareback represent a fundamental part of American mythology of how the west was won. It is indeed true that horses soon spread, in wild herds, across North America, and that indigenous Americans soon incorporated them into their culture. But these were new phenomena: as new as the weapons technology which enabled the cowboys to win all the battles.

In untangling the questions of what, on earth, comes from where, an extremely long history is uncovered of the profound impact on natural ecosystems by human intervention. The selection and development of specialised plant strains and hybrids, long practised for improving crop yields and now given a new twist by the techniques of biotechnology which can genetically modify living organisms, is a further aspect of this intervention, which further complicates our view of nature. Is a bonsai tree, which would never have grown without human intervention, a part of 'nature' or not?

This long history of intervention in itself helps us to see more clearly that the important question now is not whether we should interfere with nature but how we should do so. Our role as major meddlers has long been established, and the problem which now confronts us is to make our meddling less haphazard and less harmful. We are in a far better position than previous generations to predict and understand our impact on local and global ecosystems; and, although our knowledge is still far from perfect, our better understanding places upon us an inescapable responsibility.

But although our historic impact on the natural environment blurs the distinction between the natural and the artificial, we should not go to the extreme of concluding that 'therefore everything is artificial', any more than we should try to wriggle out of the situation by arguing 'we're also part of nature, therefore our interventions are the products of nature, therefore everything is natural'. Such mental gymnastics would be entirely wasted, for we don't in fact have to vote either way: we don't have to describe our environment as basically natural or as basically artificial. It will be more sensible to recognise instead that the dichotomy itself is fundamentally flawed: and this is precisely why it is so hard to say whether a bonsai tree or a field of wheat is natural or not.

A rigid distinction between human beings and nature, between human beings and ecosystems or between human beings and the environment is not possible because we ourselves are part of nature, ecosystems and the environment. We may indeed be unique as a species in terms of the scale of impact we have on our surroundings, but that is not to say that such impact can always or usefully be described in terms of artificiality or unnaturalness. A grouse moor or a lowland field of wheat bounded by hedgerows with a flourishing population of flora and fauna is highly 'unnatural' in the sense that it is entirely the result of human intervention; and yet to the city dweller, come for a day out in the country, to walk through such landscapes may well be to 'commune with nature' or to 'get back in touch with the natural world'.

The important consequence of this is that naturalness and unnaturalness are too unclear to serve, unassisted, as guidelines to environmental protection. Obviously, environmental protection involves making definite choices about what must be protected and conserved. These are complex choices that involve political and ethical judgements, embracing such areas for example as what, if any, rights or values should be accorded to animal species. But such choices cannot simply be made on the basis of wanting to conserve nature, because it is not self-evident what is and what is not natural.

Equally this closes the door on 'ecocentrism' – putting 'the ecosystem' at the centre of our value system, as advocated by 'deep greens' – as a guiding philosophy. For even if it made sense to say that the ecosystem as a whole is more important than the human race, the ecosystem itself is not fixed in time but is something which has changed dramatically throughout prehistory and, through human agency, during our tenure of the planet. So if we agreed in attaching ultimate value to keeping the ecosystem intact, we wouldn't actually be any the wiser as to what to do. It is too late simply to cry 'hands off the ecosystem!' We couldn't release our grip even if we wanted to.

But the baby must not be thrown out with the bathwater. The natural/artifical distinction may be blurred, inadequate and as such an insufficient criterion for policy decisions. But there is a further level to the complexity of our relations with nature that needs to be examined.

Returning to the city dweller walking in the countryside, we can identify a common and familiar need to feel 'in contact with nature'. Many leisure activities reflect the same need. People forsake comfortable homes to go camping in the rain; they spend hours scratching their fingers to pick wild blackberries they could easily afford to buy; they struggle to cook meat over barbecues; they potter in greenhouses or on allotments among tomato seedlings, and grow flowers and houseplants.

It has long been common to talk about the human struggle to dominate nature, but these leisure activities suggest a much more complicated relationship. From a very early age, children are fascinated by animals and insects, and in most healthy adults a large part of that fascination remains. Only the most spiritually impoverished people cannot, at some time, have been filled with awe and wonder at the complexity and immensity of natural phenomena and processes which owe nothing to human design; and when we intervene, by planting bulbs for instance, it is not the gardener's skill that we relish but the beauty of the flowers themselves, which we, of course, are not responsible for.

Iris Murdoch, in her work on ethics, has argued that 'attending to nature' can take people out of their worries and self-absorbing fantasies, making them, literally, if only momentarily, less self-centred. Resentments, conceits, ambitions, financial problems, all of these can be suddenly left behind when one is arrested by the sight of a kestrel hovering, or a hedgehog crossing the lawn, or by noticing that a houseplant has come into flower. Diverting attention away from oneself is, the argument goes, necessary to goodness, and therefore nature can be an instrument of morality.

Without entering that debate, it should at least be conceded that the relationship between nature and individual people is not a trivial matter. Much has been said of the 'amenity' value of the natural environment for leisure purposes, but these can be dangerously belittling phrases: as if natural amenities were somehow on a par with public libraries or swimming pools. That kind of comparison has indeed been implied in some recent attempts to make monetary valuations of environmental amenities. Such attempts fail not just because the environment is much more than an amenity – it is our life support system, too – but because our emotional, and perhaps even moral and spiritual, well-being is deeply embedded in some kind of relationship with nature, however imprecise that term may turn out to be.

We can, for example, imagine the theoretical possibility of human beings living underground, or in outer space, in regulated atmospheres and with adequate food supplies, but without ever seeing, touching or hearing a plant or an animal. We can imagine such a life, perhaps; but almost certainly only as a nightmare. No-one would want, other than out of curiosity, to experience that kind of existence; and, interestingly, people who have come close to it – prisoners, for example – have notoriously become fascinated by, and attached immense value to, such small glimpses of nature as they are afforded: the mouse in the cell, the single tree in the prison courtyard, a cloud scurrying across a tiny patch of sky.

It is, then, if not open to empirical proof, at least intuitively reasonable to suggest that we, collectively and as individuals, need some sense of belonging within a system – 'nature' – which includes 'otherness': species and plants with their own characteristics and purposes. If our surroundings do not meet this need then we are likely, to say the least, to feel distressed and cut off from something important in our own nature: much as the prisoner or the person living underground would feel. Therefore, our basic picture of environmental issues as those which threaten the capacity of our surroundings to support us in good physical health is not adequate in itself. We must have a much broader understanding of human well-being, which is attentive to the *quality* of our surroundings as well as to their life-supporting function. And we must regard issues which touch upon the quality of our surroundings as 'environmental'.

Returning now to the distinction between 'natural' and 'built' environments, it should be pointed out that in an obvious way the built environment is a major, and perhaps the predominant, component of very many people's experience. If, as I have argued, contact with nature is in some way essential to our well-being, then a new element can be discerned in, for example, inner city deprivation. People who are surrounded by concrete, and whose contact with nature is largely confined to experience of the weather, a limited birdlife and perhaps a few plants on the balcony, are clearly and substantially disadvantaged; and it may not be too fanciful to see this kind of deprivation and dislocation as a factor in the breakdown of harmonious community life in our inner cities. Concern for the quality of urban environments, and equity of choice and access to more diverse environments, thus become important issues of social justice.

Seen in this way, it becomes clear that an 'environmental perspective' is an essentially holistic outlook, and one that emphasises the importance, for our own well-being, of our relationship with the whole of our environment, including other forms of life. And yet, especially if the natural/artificial distinction doesn't clarify much, an environmental perspective does not, in itself, tell us how to act. Insofar as it requires us to look hard at the damaging effects of industrial production and consumption, it will tell us a lot about our possible options. But we must do the choosing.

What matters is to decide what kind of world is possible, what kind of world we want to live in, and what kind of world our children are entitled to inherit. Political and ethical judgements are inescapable in this, as they always have been. Describing the environment as a 'non-political issue' is therefore tantamount to rejecting a political approach not just to environmental matters but to all issues. The real challenge is to establish the political and moral values that should inform our environmental decision making.

This book is both a search for and a statement of values. It is natural to begin, as I do in Chapter 1, with a discussion of the socialist tradition, because both the holism of socialist vision and its belief in the possibility of planning the kind of world we want make it receptive to the new, environmental perspective. I separate out different strands of that tradition, acknowledging a centralist and technocratic element, but argue that the important values we need are to be found in the history of the labour movement, and that many of the historic campaigns of labour activists clearly demonstrate what we would today call environmental awareness.

In Chapter 2 I look at global environment and development issues. Emphasising the crucial link between environment and development, I argue that the present structure of the world economy is inimical to sustainable development. Given that the problems are global in nature, I conclude that they can only be resolved by strengthening the role of multinational groupings such as the European Community and United Nations, and by international agreements on resource depletion and pollution levels which implicitly recognise the right and need of the poorer countries to develop.

Returning from a global to a local perspective, in Chapter 3 I consider the contribution that individuals can and should be able to make to environmental protection. My central point is that government should create the necessary framework to make the actions and decisions of individuals count in the way they intend, and to give them the power to play a greater role in planning and policy decisions. In this connection I make a case for a tier of regional government with ecological boundaries, to manage resources and facilitate more democratic planning. I also emphasise the importance of environmental education, and suggest measures for making it more extensive and effective.

The theme of freedom of access to clearly presented environmental information runs throughout Chapters 3, 4 and 5. This is a fundamental issue, which has as much to do with democratic rights as with environmental quality. People are entitled to know what hazards their environment contains (and to be relieved from unnecessary worry about hazards it doesn't contain). Government has a clear responsibility to make such information accessible. I believe that doing so will not only stimulate greater environmental awareness, but also increase public trust in government bodies and pave the way for acceptance of necessary environmental protection measures.

Chapter 4 specifically addresses individual and social perception of environmental hazards and environmental quality, against a background in which government has failed to give a lead in presenting the issues clearly. The danger is that people may opt out of discussion on environmental policy because they feel the debate is too technical and must be resolved by experts. This kind of alienation from the issues can lead to the environmental agenda being set in an undemocratic way, and is likely to hinder environmental enhancement, which will require the participation of us all.

Chapter 5 looks more closely at the social and environmental role of scientific and technological research and development.

Clean technology will play an important part in reducing the environmental impact of industry, so it is vital to take fullest advantage of our considerable research potential. But this also raises questions about how knowledge is directed and applied once it is gained, the role of government in coordinating environmental research, surveillance and management, and the institutional responsibilities of the Department of the Environment. In contrast to the present lack of coordination, I propose mechanisms for establishing a system of integrated pollution control under the umbrella of Labour's Environment Protection Executive. Again, the free flow of information is a linking concept and crucial factor here.

In Chapter 6 I discuss what many feel to be the most thorny and the most important issue: how, in practical terms, to make industrial and commercial activity less polluting, less wasteful and less of a threat to our future prosperity and future options. A clear, regulatory framework will be absolutely necessary: but this should not be thought of as menacing or unduly coercive. For just as, for the whole of society, the costs of pollution – both tangible, financial costs and the costs in terms of reduced quality of life – can significantly outweigh the costs of pollution abatement and prevention, so too, in the case of individual businesses, waste reduction and improved environmental performance can make sound business sense. Indeed, many firms and trade unionists are increasingly receptive to the idea that improving environmental performance will become increasingly necessary to remain competitive, and are concerned about the extent to which we are lagging behind other European countries.

In addition to direct standard setting, I consider the case for the introduction of specific charges on polluters, in the context of a programme of investment in transfer to less damaging technologies. I also discuss the position of natural monopolies – most notably the water industry – and ways in which we can begin to deal with severely contaminated areas.

Much of this overlaps with Chapter 7, in which I discuss the integration of environmental and economic policy. There, I also look at the need for developing alternative economic indicators or re-examining the status of indicators we now use. I examine in some detail, but firmly reject, the case that has been made for basing environmental decisions on cost–benefit analysis that includes monetary valuation of environmental features. One of the many inadequacies of this technique (which tries to put environmental choice in terms of markets and prices, rather than realising that environmental problems themselves reveal the limitations of a market approach) is that it fails to take adequate account of the needs and preferences of people in the future.

I argue that instead we must make an explicit, and an explicitly ethical, commitment to sustainability, in the sense of ensuring equality of opportunity between ourselves and future generations. Enhancing the efficiency of resource use and limiting pollution and environmental stress through strict adherence to precautionary targets makes this a real and practical alternative, without in principle abandoning the possibility of further economic growth.

Chapter 1

The environment and the socialist ethic

Modern wisdom has it that the pressure of environmental collapse has forced upon us a new sense of responsibility towards future generations. This, like many important insights, is a half truth only. It is true that the burden of environmental damage has become so heavy that even the most blithe among us feel uncomfortable about the bill our children will have to pick up. It is not true that concern for future generations is new. On the contrary: such concern has always been the stuff of which socialism is made.

Nuclear waste provides an interesting case. Nuclear waste is rubbish: an unwanted residue. Throughout history we have dealt with unwanted residues by throwing them out. The nastier and more troublesome they are, the further we have thrown them: into middens, rivers and oceans. Even now, we tend to respond to rubbish with a 'chuck it as far as we can' attitude. Toxic chemicals are shipped off to the Third World. Nuclear waste, some have suggested, should be shipped even further: off into outer space.

The problem with nuclear waste is that it is not simply offensive, nor even just dangerous, but that it remains so for many years. Disposal, therefore, affects future generations as much as it affects us, or even more so. We can't simply throw the stuff outside the city gates, or dump it in the oceans and be done with it, because the safety of our children is at stake. This is new; and it also sums up many of the problems of modern pollution. For greenhouse gases are also wastes, rubbish of a different sort that we have thrown away into the atmosphere to the point where waste from our own consumption of energy and goods directly threatens the well-being, and even the prosperity, of future generations.

On an individual level, concern for our children's future has nearly always been a powerful motive in people's behaviour. I can still remember the day my family moved out of my grandparents' small, overcrowded terraced house, complete with outside lavatory, into a brand-new three-bedroomed council house: the space, the garden, the bathroom all seemed incredible luxuries. My parents spent hours decorating, gardening and making curtains with a real sense that they were making life better for their children. But more than that I can remember knowing, feeling, absorbing my parents' feeling that my education should not be curtailed as theirs had been. No-one ever sat down and told me this, it was just understood from the start. My parents made sure that their children had doors opened which, for them, had always remained shut.

My parents were not, of course, unique in this. But just as most working people have always tried, individually, to give their children greater opportunities, so too the whole history of the labour movement can be seen as a history of striving to improve conditions for the future. During the Thatcher years, and particularly among the press that supported her, it became common to castigate workers involved in industrial disputes as short-sighted and selfish, concerned only for their own short term interests; but in most cases this was to turn reality on its head. Anyone who has been involved in a strike knows only too well that to take industrial action is almost always detrimental to the short term interest of individuals, both because of the loss of wages (which might take many months, even years, to recoup) and because of the accompanying stress, in home and workplace. If this was true in the 1980s, how much more so was it in the formative years of the labour movement, when working conditions were so grim, and trade union rights unrecognised?

In organising for the right to unionise, the right to strike, the right to education and social welfare, and the right to tolerable working conditions, early trade unionists were explicitly concerned with securing a better future for their children. In industrial, mining and agricultural communities at the turn of the century, children born into working class families had very slender prospects of breaking away from the lifestyles and the wage labour of their parents; and this remains truer today than is often recognised in complacent talk of a classless society. Younger generations have, therefore, always been the principal beneficiaries of gains in living standards made by organised labour, and the collective action of the labour movement has always sought to improve the lot of the next generation of workers, in the knowledge that sons would follow their fathers into the mines, and daughters would follow their mothers into the mills. This has nothing at all to do with selfishness.

On an emotional and intuitive level, then, the labour movement has always taken the future seriously; and in this sense it is well attuned to respond to the new threat posed by environmental degradation, which is in great measure a threat to the future. But there is also a further and more direct way in which 'environmental awareness' has long been embedded in socialist and labour movement campaigns to improve living and working conditions, through concern for the health of the working population.

It is important here to think about the related concepts of public and environmental health. In the international sphere, it is relatively easy to attract (Western) attention to problems such as deforestation and soil erosion, and their connection with issues of food security and climatic change. Environmental questions of this order are writ with an unmistakable capital E. However, in less developed countries the environmental issues which most immediately affect, and frequently cost, people's lives are very often to do with water supply and sewage disposal. These impinge upon the environment of many millions of poor people more directly and, to them, unignorably than the risk of future global warming.

It is easy to forget this from the perspective of a society with highly developed (albeit far from perfect) water supply and sanitation systems. Yet little more than a hundred years ago, when London was in the grip of cholera epidemics, the absence of such facilities was the most pressing issue of public, and therefore environmental, health. 'We ain't got no privez, no dustbins, no drains nor water splies and no drain or suer in the whole place' wrote 54 'poor and desperate residents of Soho' (with the alleged help of Charles Kingsley) in a letter to *The Times* in 1849. The environment for such people consisted wholly in crowded and filthy streets where, in Dickens' words, 'through the heart of the town a deadly sewer flowed, in place of a fine fresh river'; and a sewer, moreover, which provided untreated drinking water for the majority of the capital's population.

In aspiring and organising to overcome squalor, working class people in the early labour movement were making a perfectly clear statement about the kind of environment they wanted to live in; and if this doesn't seem much like a modern 'green' concern it should be set against the equally legitimate aspirations of the two-thirds of the world's present population who still don't have access to adequate water and sanitation facilities. This is not to say that modern green worries are the exclusive luxury of those who are no longer burdened by poverty. But it must be recognised that public health (and, indeed, poverty itself) is, and always has been, an environmental issue of foremost importance, precisely because it concerns the environment that people experience most intimately and immediately. The campaigns of the labour movement for medical provision, decent housing and services were, in this sense, all campaigns for a better environment.

On a different note it can be added that John Snow's discovery, during the London epidemic, of the waterborne transmission of cholera was a breakthrough in our understanding of how the spread and nature of illness is profoundly affected by the way that society is organised. This concept is now familiar to us. It is readily appreciated that international trading routes permitted the spread of not just cholera but, in an earlier epoch, bubonic plague; that non-communicable illnesses such as lead, mercury or asbestos poisoning result directly from environmental con-tamination; and that even diseases whose exact causes are not yet understood, such as cancer, might be correlated with particular kinds of individual and social lifestyle. Many contemporary virologists also believe that the emergence of viruses such as that responsible for AIDS may be the result of changes in human population structure and mobility, creating optimal conditions for viruses that have long existed at a low level.

No-one could claim that these developments are not relevant to an environmental perspective. But applying the new, 'environmental' label to health issues of this kind should not mislead us into thinking that the issues themselves are new. The nineteenth century cholera epidemics would now be considered a matter of environmental health, intimately connected with social conditions; and so too would the experience of the first generations of industrial workers, whose exposure to new industrial processes brought new, occupational health hazards. The early and enduring concern of the trade unions, and of organisations such as the Socialist Medical Association (established in 1930), with public health and with health and safety at work can therefore be seen as a forerunner of contemporary environmental concerns. Equally, the 1948 Factories Act and the 1974 Health and Safety at Work Act, both passed by Labour governments, have direct bearing on environmental health.

Health and safety in the workplace is a vital element of and in some ways a key to environmental protection for the simple reason that where industry pollutes, its workers will be the first to be exposed to risk. Clean, safe and healthy workplaces will, on the other hand, make for a cleaner, safer and healthier environment. Specific illnesses have always been associated with particular industries – pneumoconiosis in the mines, asbestosis among asbestos workers and, among textile workers, byssisnosis, which despite hundreds of deaths and maimings was not officially recognised as an occupational illness until the 1970s. These occupational hazards usually have their counterparts in public health risks, as is the case for example in pulmonary disorders resulting from the burning of coal, and even more pointedly in public exposure to asbestos used in construction.

Similarly, it is estimated that every year in the Third World 10,000 people die and 400,000 suffer acutely from pesticide poisoning (Repetto, 1985, quoted in Winpenny, 1991; Hay et al., 1991, quote even higher figures). Most of the casualties are farmworkers handling chemicals with inadequate training and precautions. The wider environmental damage caused by pesticides is well documented, as is their misuse; but the point to be made here is that environmentally hazardous substances often represent the most direct and serious threat to people who have to work with them.

Yet, of course, the risks from dangerous and polluting industries do not stop at the factory gates, as was demonstrated by the chemical explosions at Flixborough in 1974, and Seveso in 1977, where there are still no-go areas that were contaminated by highly toxic dioxins. A more recent leak of toxic gases from the Bhopal chemical works, in India, killed 2,000 people and injured 200,000 in 1983. Could such a calamity have happened if adequate health and safety standards were enforced? Or was the underlying truth that, as in so many cases of unclean and unsafe technologies, the absence of such standards itself acted as an incentive for Union Carbide to locate the factory in the Third World?

Even in highly developed countries, health and safety at work issues are still closely related to broader, public issues of environmental welfare. While the public at large is rightly concerned about emissions and spillages of toxic substances, the workers in those industries are the most likely to suffer the consequences of bad practice. (As can be seen from the record: the General, Municipal, Boilermakers and Allied Trades Union calculated in 1987 that 20,000 British people were dying each year from occupational diseases.) At the same time, it must be recognised that people are multidimensional: workers are also consumers, taxpayers and residents; they are also members of 'the public', and so ensuring a decent working environment is a crucial part of improving the total environment.

The historic campaigns of the labour movement for safer workplaces can thus be seen as providing the starting point for a more widely focused environmental perspective. But this is not to suggest that the labour movement, or the Labour Party, has concerned itself uniquely with the working environment, to the exclusion of other considerations. Two early examples show how our movement has long been enriched by a broader vision of the quality of life than is contained simply in the struggles for improved living standards and physical well-being.

The first is the interesting, and even odd, fact that from 1925 to 1931 no less than four annual Conferences of the Labour Party were presented with resolutions on animal welfare, calling for more humane conditions in slaughterhouses and for an end to poison gas experiments. It is surprising, and revealing, that party activists found room to consider such issues at a time of economic depression and great human privation, when the party was engaged in hammering out a practical programme of democratic socialism. Clearly this was not a party for whom only people mattered, whatever has been said since by non-socialist Greens about our supposed 'anthropocentrism' or human-centredness.

Secondly, the 1932 mass trespasses of Kinder Scout led by Benny Rothman and Ewan MacColl (who were imprisoned for their troubles) showed a clear appreciation of the importance of our natural heritage and surroundings, concerns which later led to a Labour government passing the 1949 National Parks and Access to the Countryside Act. The establishment of the National Parks not only served as a keystone of rural conservation, but represented a commitment to the environment as something whose value is not exclusively, or even primarily, economic. This, ever since, has been a rallying cry of the environmental lobby.

It is worth stressing that the trespass campaign was firmly rooted in considerations of equity and access, harking back to early radical traditions, such as the Diggers' demand that the land should be a 'common treasury for all'. A clear line can therefore be drawn from early, communitarian vision to modern environmentalism, with a unifying emphasis on collective rights and responsibilities. This, indeed, is tacitly acknowledged by almost all parties in the present environmental debate by their repeated recourse to the language of community – 'our common future'; 'our common heritage'; 'our common interest'; 'our shared destiny' – in the presentation of problems and advocacy of solutions alike.

The 1947 Town and Country Planning Act was also a landmark in protection of the rural landscape, both in its provisions for preservation of trees and woodland, and because for the first time it required permission to be obtained for development. The enforcement of planning control is absolutely fundamental for protecting the quality of our environment and, in a sense, sums up the Labour environmental philosophy: we cannot allow our environment to be destroyed by unchecked and disordered developments; if we value what we have, we must be very careful about allowing it to be altered.

In other, practical ways the post-war Labour Party intervened on important, crucial environmental issues. In 1955, the party conference passed a resolution calling for a ban on all air pollutants. The resolution was moved by the delegate from Sheffield Brightside and seconded by the Socialist Medical Association.

Speaking on behalf of the party's National Executive, James Griffiths talked about the way in which the nation's coal was being misused – not just in terms of atmospheric pollution but also in relation to the need for energy conservation.

During its periods in office, Labour introduced a wide range of environmental legislation, from the two 1951 Rivers (Prevention of Pollution) Acts, to the 1968 Clean Air Act, and the 1974 Dumping at Sea and Control of Pollution Acts. Birds, seals and endangered species have also been protected under specific Labour legislation in 1967, 1970 and 1976 respectively.

But this is not to present the greening of Labour as a *fait accompli*. Far from being hostile to an environmental perspective, many traditional labour movement concerns are directly relevant to such a perspective, and the environmental track record of Labour governments is creditable in many respects. However, it must be acknowledged that, on a more theoretical level, there are conflicting traditions within the labour and socialist movements, and these need untangling and evaluating if an environmental perspective is to be wholeheartedly embraced.

Firstly, the legacy of Marxism must be addressed. This is of particular importance and interest in the light of the ecological disasters in Eastern Europe that we are now learning about, following the break-up of the Soviet bloc. I do not share the view that the failure of the East European economies means we should abandon all attempts to find a democratic socialist model: it seems to me that communism in Eastern Europe was born out of totalitarianism, and that this had inevitable consequences for the kind of communism practised. But if the practice was flawed, we must accept that, in the environmental sphere at least, so too must have been the theory. For what was to stop the command economies, where goods are produced in accordance with a centrally planned notion of social needs, from taking full account of the environment? It would, after all, be very easy in states where all decisions are made centrally. But the fact is that, despite a considerable amount of (seldom enforced) environmental legislation, the Soviet Union and its satellites treated the environment every bit as recklessly as Western capitalism.

Part of the explanation undoubtedly lies in pressure to increase output, caused by the very failure of centrally planned economies to generate wealth. Where needs are acute, short term interests will nearly always be pursued, frequently at high environmental cost. There is an important lesson here for the 'deep green' anti-growth lobby: relieving poverty through economic growth can in itself be instrumental in reducing, rather than increasing, environmental degradation.

But in addition to this pressure, important aspects of Marxist theory leave environmental management out of account. First among these is the belief that the value of a resource or commodity is a function of the human labour which has been expended in extracting and manufacturing it. It should be remembered that this theory was developed in a critique of capitalism which, in Marx' lifetime, dramatically undervalued and exploited human labour. The rival, capitalist theory was, and remains, that value is determined by the laws of supply and demand in a competitive market. For capitalism, 'value' meant little more than the price at which commodities, and labour itself, could be bought and sold. As such, wages would always be held to a minimum so as to maximise profits arising from the difference between production costs and market price. In insisting that it was human labour that made a piece of furniture more valuable than a pile of wood, Marx meant to establish the entitlement of the labourer to the benefits of that added value, and so to set human effort, rather than market demand, at the centre of the concept of value.

But if it is labour that gives a piece of furniture its value, then the value of the original pile of wood will derive from the labour involved in felling the timber and sawing it. What, though, of the tree itself, in which no human labour was expended? Regarded simply as an asset of the state, and without an explicit commitment to sustainability, there is no constraint on indiscriminate depletion of stocks; just as there is no constraint on indiscriminate and rapid use of the environment's capacity to absorb waste and pollution.

In this, then, Marxism ignores environmental considerations just as much as the free market. In the capitalist economies, there is at least some leeway for demand to be affected by increasing scarcity of resources, since this will be reflected in commodity prices; and, in theory at least, demand can be responsive to environmental considerations, according to the level of public concern (although it should be said that in practice environmental awareness, and consequent drop in demand for goods such as tropical hardwoods, furs and whale oil products, has almost invariably followed very late upon the exhaustion or serious depletion of available stocks).

But if neither system has an internal mechanism for preventing environmental profligacy, government could in theory apply restraint to both. Yet, although this has happened increasingly in the capitalist economies (and it is worth noting the wide range and relatively long history of environmental regulation in the United States, bastion of the 'free' world), it did not happen in the Soviet bloc. Centralisation and the undemocratic structure of government was itself undoubtedly largely responsible for this: the concentration of power in few hands (and hands that are remote from the consequences of their actions) can favour obstinate adherence to failed policies, and the communist system was not open to the kind of popular pressure that got environmental issues on to the political agenda in Western Europe and North America. (It is with this kind of thought in mind that I examine the role of local and regional government in Chapter 3.)

But perhaps equally important in the East European experience was faith in the Marxist doctrine of historical materialism and inevitability. This regards productive activity as the essential, human characteristic which sets us apart from other animals, and the technology used in productive activity – the 'mode of production' – as determining 'the general character of the social, political and spiritual processes of life' (Preface to the *Critique of Political Economy* (1859), in Marx, 1974). Productive technology is seen not just as the determining factor in social life, but as an essentially liberating force. The technology of the hand mill gave rise to feudal society, the technology of the steam mill to capitalist society; and in due course these would be superseded by new technologies that would, inevitably, usher in socialist, and eventually classless, society.

The power and originality of this argument should not be underestimated; like much in Marx, aspects of this way of looking at things have in fact been widely incorporated into the world-view of most of us. Consider, for example, the contraceptive pill. It has been widely accepted that contraceptive technology affected not only the material conditions of many women's lives (by giving us new freedom and power over fertility), but also our social relations. It is even arguable that improved contraception has led to a re-evaluation of the ethics of personal relationships. Similarly, as I suggested in the Introduction, technological revolutions in the communications media have revolutionised our way of looking at the world, and this too has an ethical dimension.

At the same time there was, and remains, a strong case on compassionate grounds to seek in technology a release from poverty and grinding labour. But Marx, even if motivated by compassion, rejected the moral perspective in favour of something which seemed to him much more solid and reliable: historical necessity.

Thus, his conclusion of the argument about hand mills and steam mills would be that electric mills and any later developments would give us a socialist society. There is little doubt that this was what Marx hoped, and believed. He repeatedly argued that the 'historic role' of capitalism was to 'lay the material foundations' for socialist society, and that when this had been done the transition to socialism would be inevitable.

He was, of course, wildly wrong. Capitalism has proved adept at harnessing and surviving new modes of production, and the socialist case has, if anything, been hindered by spurious claims about its inevitability. This last is a crucial point. Belief in historical necessity relieved Marxists from the need to operate within an ethical framework, and allowed unimaginable horrors to be perpetrated unblinkingly in the service of 'history'. (Much as unimaginable horrors have been perpetrated by people, from a variety of faiths, in the name of God.)

There is a serious muddle at the heart of any approach which upholds both inevitability and a higher good. For if it is true that history sweeps us all along in an inevitable direction (towards socialism and fulfilment), what need is there for any individual to become involved in political or social action towards that end? Socialism will arrive on schedule whatever we do.

This, plainly, is nonsense; and it has proved a very dangerous nonsense. The richest seam in socialism has always been its moral content, and this is precisely what Marxism has encouraged socialists to leave out of account, as being some kind of namby-pamby bourgeois concern. In the history of the British labour movement it has fallen to other traditions, such as non-conformist Christianity or Owenite cooperation, to give the moral context for socialist debate.

Much the same can be said of technology. If technological advance, *per se*, is considered both good and irrevocable there is, again, no need for us to do anything but sit back and await a golden future. But this is absurd. Nothing has made its absurdity quite so clear as the invention, and use, of nuclear power. For here was a technology that no-one could unequivocally regard as a liberating force.

The invention of 'the bomb' and the subsequent nuclear arms race fundamentally, if not immediately, challenged our perception of the global environment. To the age-old human nightmares of famine, war and natural disaster was added the real fear of global catastrophe resulting from all-out nuclear war. The world, for the first time, was seen as breakable. This new idea, of the world's fragility, underpins environmental concern and may prove to be as significant a development in human understanding as was the idea that the world is round.

The issues of nuclear deterrence, unilateral and multilateral disarmament have, since their emergence, divided the labour movement. But the arguments have always been about the means for achieving a peaceful and stable world in the shadow of a new and frightening technology. No-one in the labour movement has seriously argued that nuclear weapons are in themselves a good thing, just as no-one has argued that abortion is, in itself, a good thing. Those who advocate abortion on demand, and those who advocate retaining a nuclear deterrent, both do so from the position that an intrinsically undesirable and unfortunate course of action is, in difficult circumstances, the lesser of many evils.

But for many socialists, and especially for those who became involved with the CND, the nuclear issue exposed the limitations of an orthodox Marxist view of technology. Technology could be a means of human liberation. But it could also be the means of our destruction. The subsequent development of other destructive technologies (both deliberately destructive, such as chemical and biological weaponry, and inadvertently destructive, such as CFCs) and growing evidence of the environmental damage done by existing industrial technology reinforced this new scepticism.

Quite clearly, we must have a critical and evaluative approach to technology. Technologies must be judged according to how well they fit human needs. Orthodox Marxism, however, always had the tail wagging the dog: technology not merely influencing, but completely – and benignly – determining the character of all human life. This view clearly pervaded Soviet attitudes to productive technology, lending an almost moral splendour to agroindustrialisation, and the nuclear and space programmes. As Chernobyl demonstrated, this technocratic vision was flawed.

It would be wrong to deny the influence of Marx on the development of West European socialist movements, but nor should his influence be overstated. The word 'socialist', after all, came not from Marxism but from Robert Owen or, to be more precise, from his followers, grouped in organisations such as the seminal Community Society of Rational Religionists, set up in 1835. Owen's influence was direct and practical as much as it was theoretical. From his earliest managerial experiments in the textile mills of New Lanark (in which he became a partner in 1800 at the age of 19, having accrued considerable earlier experience and capital entirely through his own industriousness), he showed that improvement of the social conditions of working people was perfectly possible, and even compatible with running a competitive business. Whereas leading public health reformers such as Edwin Chadwick believed that sanitary conditions, for instance, should be improved because they were a threat to the productivity of the working classes, Owen simply felt that it was not necessary for people to endure sickness and squalor. Sanitation was therefore one of the many social provisions in New Lanark and subsequent model communities. It was, however, only later in his life that he came to believe property must be held in common in order to overcome the worst aspects of competition between individual interests.

In contrast to the Chartists, who in the mid nineteenth century were campaigning for political rights of representation and universal male suffrage, Owen's main interest was with education, living and working conditions. The provision of schooling and better housing, the reduction in working hours, and the creation of more pleasant working and living environments (rather than smoke-filled cities, which he abhorred), were, for Owen, means by which misery and 'vice' could be eradicated. And what better way to make the point than by showing that these were feasible objectives; as, to a large extent, he did. If Owen was a 'Utopian', he certainly wasn't just a dreamer. All of his schemes were put into practice in the various communities he became involved with, in Britain and the United States.

Those communities were set up against the intellectual background of what J. K. Galbraith called 'the tradition of despair', established by the founding trinity of classical economics, Adam Smith, David Ricardo and Thomas Malthus. Galbraith quotes Carlyle's reference to these men as 'the Respectable Professors of the Dismal Science': dismal because in the work of each it was wholly accepted that the labouring classes would always live in poverty, with wages and living conditions held down to the minimum necessary for society to keep functioning. Misery was inevitable (Galbraith, 1979).

In place of despair, Owen not only focused attention on the distribution of wealth, rather than on its creation, but demonstrated in practice that a better life really was possible for working people. This, more than anything, encouraged the spread of his ideas. In 1840, 50,000 people were attending weekly lectures at the branches of his Rational Society, and his newspaper *New Moral World* had a circulation of 40,000: a truly remarkable figure in a society without any public education at all (Owen, 1991, Introduction). The rapid rise at that time of the cooperative movement was also certainly due in large part to the influence of Owenism.

The title of the newspaper is significant. Owen was an 'environmentalist' in the sense that he believed people are very much the products of their environment: that we are malleable, and so, given the right environment, improvable. This was an important contribution to educational theory (especially in an age when many people argued that educating the working classes would merely make them dissolute), but it is also relevant to the most fundamental discussion between socialism – or any political philosophy – and modern environmentalism. For environmental problems, on our understanding of them, are a result of the way that we use our environment, of what and who we use it for. If maximum prosperity, of one class or of all classes, is our ultimate objective, then this will result in maximum feasible exploitation of the environment; and, if we are not careful, exploitation which is not feasible.

Although he wanted to end poverty, Owen was not interested in prosperity for its own sake. What interested him was moral improvement: making individual people better, and society as a whole better and happier. His idea of a morally better society was one based on economic and social justice, community, cooperation and equality, to promote 'the well being and happiness of every man, woman and child, without regard to class, sect, sex, party, country or colour' (*The Revolution In The Mind And Practice Of the Human Race* (1849), in Owen, 1991).

The distribution of power and wealth is obviously important, as a matter of social justice. This answers the contemporary question of who the environment is to be used for. But what of the question about what the environment is to be used for? The Marxist idea – of human beings as essentially productive creatures – tends to suggest the answer that human advance will mean continual growth in productive capacity (and therefore consumption): the environment is a resource available for ever-more sophisticated exploitation. Owen's central concern with the moral welfare of people and society, on the other hand, suggests the possibility of a very different answer: the environment is to be used in such a way as to maximise human harmony and fulfilment – which need not, and probably cannot, be understood in terms of endlessly increasing prosperity.

The passage of Owen's I have quoted has a remarkably contemporary ring, particularly in embracing sexual and racial equality. In many respects it could easily form part of a 'mission statement' for the modern Labour Party. But the implicit values have not only retained their relevance throughout the last century and a half, they also hark back to, and derive from, a much older British radical tradition, spanning nearly five centuries from the Peasants' Revolt of 1381 to the sentencing of the Tolpuddle martyrs.

It was not political ideology as such that inspired these movements, but plain demands for certain fundamental rights based on a straightforward perception of what was fair and reasonable. In very many of these cases, justification, were it needed, was provided by the Bible. Wat Tyler appears to have been the strategist of the Peasants' Revolt, but the movement's thinker was a Catholic priest, John Ball. The Diggers' ill-fated 1649 experiment in non-violent communism was inspired and led by Gerald

Winstanley, a Baptist pamphleteer who blended Christianity with rationalist humanism. Foremost among the Tolpuddle martyrs was George Loveless, a Methodist.

Similarly, Tom Paine, one of Britain's most original political writers, was born into a Quaker family and, although he moved away from religion towards the end of his life, his work clearly drew on the concept of human equality in the sight of God. As an emigrant to America, this underlying value figured strongly in his campaigns against slavery and in favour of women's emancipation. 'The Rights of Man', published in 1792, advocated modern democratic government with a graduated income tax to support a 'welfare state' which would pay for public education, family and maternity allowances and retirement pensions. This effectively prefigured twentieth century British Labour Party policy and achievements.

Many other thinkers and actors would need to be included in a litany of influences upon modern Labour politics, starting from Hobbes' dictum that without some form of social organisation and regulation life would be 'nasty, brutish and short'. Of particular relevance to the environmental perspective, Rousseau, in his *Discourse on the Origin of Inequality Among Men*, addressed the specific problem of how to resolve the conflict between self-interest and collective interest in the use of commonly held goods. This has direct bearing on the question of environmental 'externalities' in modern industrial production – the environmental costs that are not included in production costs – where the rationally self-interested activity of individual producers and consumers conflicts with collective interest. Rousseau's answer, that a higher authority is needed to regulate social activity so as to protect collective welfare, is essentially socialist in spirit, and has been consistently echoed in the socialist case for more, rather than less, government intervention to secure a decent standard and quality of life for all.

But this directly raises questions about the structure and nature of democratic government: the way that collective will is to be expressed, and collective interest safeguarded. But if the answer lies in some kind of planning, it need not be in the kind of centralised structure adopted in Eastern Europe. William Morris, who was both interested in Owen's work and active in Marxist organisations, questioned in 1888 whether centralised planning was a correct or sufficient mechanism for ensuring either democracy or human fulfilment:

> there are some Socialists who do not think that the problem of the organisation of life and necessary labour can be dealt with by a huge national centralisation, working by a kind of magic for which no-one feels himself responsible; that on the contrary it will be necessary for the unit of administration to be small enough for every citizen to feel himself responsible for its details, and be interested in them; that individual men cannot shuffle off the business of life on to the shoulders of some abstraction called the State, but must deal with it in conscious association with each other; that variety of life is as much an aim of true Communism as equality of condition, and that nothing but a union of these two will bring about real freedom.
>
> (Quoted in Levitas, 1990.)

In rejecting the centralisation of control (the 'magic' of bureaucracy for which no-one is responsible) Morris identified an important, qualifying value for the idea of democracy and socialism: that it must be participative. A related idea underlies the claim that 'variety of life' is as important as 'equality of condition': work which is merely wage labour, divorced from personal creativity, is stultifying and degrading. Therefore in both work and social organisation, we must attend to the scale of human activity, so that individuals can be fully involved. (Again, this has direct bearing on what I have to say in Chapter 3.)

This concern with scale explains Morris' interest in Owen, and the Owenist communities, which reappear in highly idealised form in Morris' novel *News From Nowhere*. But if Morris deserves the attention of environmentally minded socialists (and he has, during the last 20 years, enjoyed something of a revival, through the work of left wing intellectuals like E. P. Thompson and Raymond Williams), it is not because of his presentation of these semi-rural havens as a practicable social model, but because of his implicit view of labour and fulfilment: that rather than trying to find ever greater rewards for labour (higher and higher pay and consumption) we should try to make labour itself more fulfilling or, in his words,' less painful'.

Where does this leave contemporary Labour politics? If there is a common strand woven through this rich backcloth, it is not one of strictly defined political ideology, or even of political economy. The connecting thread is, rather, one of shared values drawn equally from the Christian, rationalist and humanist traditions. These values broadly divide into three areas: firstly, a concern for social justice, freedom from economic oppression and equality of access to the means of livelihood; secondly, a concern for political justice, rights of representation in government and equal access to power, and for collective solutions to collective problems; thirdly, the belief that by concerted action the human lot can be improved, and that this imperative of hope is an imperative of action. We must at least try.

It is important to point out that such values are open to reinterpretation and enrichment by each generation. Equality and political representation, for example, for many centuries meant equality and representation for men; and only over the last century or so has the concept been recognised to encompass women too. A similar conceptual expansion took place somewhat earlier, in the recognition that slaves were human beings and should therefore enjoy the same fundamental rights as other men and women.

Because they are open to reinterpretation by new generations, these values are receptive to newly perceived problems and new ways of approaching them. I have already identified the invention of the atom bomb and creation of the nuclear arms race as a watershed in public opinion, because of the way it brought home to us the fragility of our environment (or, which is the same thing viewed differently, our enormous capacity for damaging it). Since that time, the labour movement has become rapidly and increasingly sensitive to environmental issues.

The legislation I have already mentioned, covering air and river pollution, National Parks and wildlife, are all cases in point. But, it could be said, these were on the edges of Labour's concern: they had not yet reached the centre. During the 1960s and 1970s, and even the 1980s, there was still a strong current of technocratic centralism (discussed in more detail in Chapter 5) which welcomed projects such as Concorde and domestic nuclear power, and the Party's public image was in part one of industrialisation and growth. But there was a growing caucus, within the Party and the broader labour movement, of people who accepted the need for a change of direction but saw this as a reason for reinterpreting, updating and widening rather than abandoning socialism.

In 1970, three years before the Ecology Party was formed, the Labour Women's Conference endorsed a document on environmental policy which contained a wide-ranging programme to control pollution of air, rivers, sea and land. It called for mandatory lead-free petrol; various pollution taxes embracing the polluter pays principle; strict controls on dumping at sea; and encouragement of a shift towards organic farming. Two years later, the Party issued a further document which among other things called for a more environmentally sensitive approach to the calculation of GNP. These earlier papers were taken up in a 1986 Conference statement which was widely praised in the environmental movement for its comprehensive, radical analysis and the far-reaching solutions it proposed, and which has served as the foundation for subsequent policy reviews.

The establishment in 1973 of the Socialist Environment and Resources Association was another milestone in the emergence of this 'red green' caucus. Writing in the Spring 1984 issue of the Association's journal *New Ground*, Robin Cook gave a detailed critique, from an environmental perspective, of the Labour opposition's then Alternative Economic Strategy, which was based on a target of full employment and 3 per cent annual growth of GNP. At a time when Labour, and much of the country, was reeling from the effects of mass unemployment, he bravely attacked the notion of economic growth as a universal remedy, anticipating Labour's 1990s concern with the quality of life by insisting that 'We ought at least to ask what quality of growth is desirable at least as often as we ask what quantity is necessary.'

This was a direct attack on the primacy of growth as the governing economic concept, made from an environmental perspective but also harking back to the socialist critique of capitalism as a system of endlessly expanding capital and endless need to exploit new resources, both human and social. Such a view can no longer be said to exist only on the distant fringes of socialist politics, as SERA's 1990 affiliation to the Labour Party and the Party's commitment to appoint a Cabinet level Minister of Environmental Protection equally attest.

During the last two decades green undercurrents have also

been felt in the trade unions, not only in the new understanding of health and safety as intimately related to environmental concerns, but also in specific issues, such as the National Union of Seamen's opposition to dumping radioactive waste at sea, the joint action of various unions on the control and use of pesticides, and the joint campaign against the privatisation of the water industry. The National Union of Railwaymen's support for the pressure group Transport 2000, which lobbies for an integrated and environmentally sensitive transport policy, and the National Union of Mineworkers' opposition to nuclear power are further cases in point. Of course, it can be said (and frequently has been) that this is mere pursuit of self-interest. But we should be careful about applying the word 'mere'. There is absolutely nothing wrong in discovering that poor environmental practice is against our best interests. Indeed, on what other basis are we to appeal to the public, if not by pointing out that improved environmental performance is, in the long term, in everyone's interests?

But this is not to suggest that the sectoral interests of trade unions need prevent them from taking the broader interests of society into account. A determination to do so clearly motivated the Lucas Aerospace Shop Stewards Combine Committee, who in 1975 drew up a plan to avert proposed redundancies by switching production from defence products to items such as artificial limb control systems, and radar systems for the blind. This not only anticipated more recent interest in the possibility of redirecting military technology in the post-Cold-War period, but also showed the willingness of trade unionists to think well beyond their own interests and about the social consequences of the production in which they are involved. Over the last few years, the TUC itself has taken a progressive stance on many environmental issues, adopting a General Council statement 'Towards a Charter for the Environment' in 1989, setting up an Environmental Action Group comprising leaders of some of the largest unions and, in 1991, passing a resolution in support of workplace environment funds to broaden the scope of work done by health and safety officers. Individual unions, notably the GMB and MSF, have been active in drawing up model workplace agreements between unions and management, to agree minimum environmental standards and performance.

It should be stressed that this new environmental awareness

did not just fall out of the sky or, for that matter, out of Ecology or Green Party pamphlets, but derives from the application of long-held values to new, environmental problems which have increasingly forced themselves upon our attention. There is no room for complacency: we must recognise that the scale and severity of global environmental problems do present a fundamental challenge to our past priorities and practice, because of the evidence that present levels of environmental consumption and degradation will result, if not in catastrophe, at least in severely curtailed opportunities for future generations. But in facing up to this challenge it is absolutely essential to have a framework of values with which to look for solutions to new problems. This, indeed, is the Labour Party's greatest environmental asset. It is reasonable to expect that, insofar as the problems really are new, meeting them will involve some changes in the framework itself, just as the framework was altered to accommodate racial and sexual equality. But, in the body of central, socialist values I have identified, we have an excellent starting point.

That does not mean there is no more thinking to be done. It is important, for example, that we reassess collectivism and be absolutely sure about what 'social welfare' is. Too often in the past we, along with very many non-socialists, have tended to identify social welfare with everyone in society having a high standard of individual – and primarily economic – welfare. This is wrong. We have always intuitively understood that wealth, however distributed, does not alone make for happiness; and environmental constraints now add an extra dimension to the argument, because of the newly perceived, real costs of creating wealth. Yet, properly understood, the welfare of society as a whole means much more than aggregated income, goods or services. We must, at the very least, enrich our idea of social welfare to embrace environmental benefits that are not only enjoyed collectively but can only be maintained through collective action.

A simple example illustrates the point: giving every adult a private car would, on one view, raise the level of social mobility, and thus well-being. But the consequences of accommodating so many millions of vehicles, in terms of congestion, noise, ugliness, loss of countryside, exhaustion of resources and atmospheric pollution, would certainly outweigh the benefits, so the total impact on social welfare would be negative. Yet this is exactly the direction in which we have been moving, and have been encouraged by government policy to move, for several decades. Obviously there is an alternative: the provision of an extensive and high quality public transport service. And, perhaps paradoxically, this also enhances choice.

This is not a new argument, and indeed it has recently come to be accepted in quite surprising circles. But the important point here is that it is an essentially socialist argument, containing a more far-sighted vision of social welfare than just a belief in raising the living standards of individuals, on an individual basis. Insofar as we seriously reconsider collective welfare, I believe we will move further away from reliance on increased consumption as the only means of human fulfilment.

At the same time we need to extend our idea of community. I have mentioned the historic, conceptual extension of political equality to include women and slaves. We now need to look further, to people beyond our frontiers, and address the global inequities in the distribution of power and resources that we have allowed to exist throughout modern history. Environmental issues are pushing us in this direction, both because, in our new, small world, the activities of one nation impinge directly on the quality of the environment in other nations, and because the pressure for development in the poor world will create new strains upon resources and upon the global environment's absorptive capacities. The historic concern of socialists with distributional equality and justice – and our long solidarity with anti-imperialist struggles – uniquely qualify us to play a new and responsible role in the international community.

Chapter 2

A global perspective

No serious review of global environmental problems can consider them in isolation from the economic activity and development which are their cause. Such indeed was the starting point of the United Nations Commission on Environment and Development, chaired by Norwegian Prime Minister and leader of the Norwegian Labour Party, Gro Harlem Brundtland. In a preface to the Commission's 1987 report she observed that 'the "environment" is where we all live; and "development" is what we all do in attempting to improve our lot within that abode. The two are inseparable.'

This is true on both micro and macro level, and in both industrialised and less developed countries. If a local authority in Britain decides that the economic development of a town centre or an industrial estate requires a new road scheme, then that scheme will have an environmental cost in terms of altering the landscape, forfeiting land previously put to other use and, quite probably, increasing the volume of traffic, noise and exhaust gases. If the national authorities in Brazil decide that the economic interests of the country are best served by cutting down another swathe of rain forest, there will be an environmental cost in terms of lost subsistence for forest peoples, lost habitats for wildlife, and lost biodiversity – the extinction of many species – for future generations.

Both of these are examples of microeconomic decisions and activities (which is not to imply that they are small in scale, but simply that they relate to a particular sphere of activity, rather than management of the economy as a whole). If we choose to view the world economy, and global economic activity, as a simple aggregate of microeconomic decisions, then the way towards environmentally benign decisions will be relatively straightforward. All we will have to do – as a new school of environmental economists are advocating – is to make sure that we add up environmental costs and take full account of them when making economic decisions. (Although whether all 'environmental costs' can be translated into financial costs is a very doubtful matter – one I shall discuss in detail in Chapter 7.)

However, microeconomic decisions, and even macroeconomic decisions at national level, are made within the framework of an existing global economic order. The main feature of this order is inequality in the distribution and consumption of resources, energy and environmental 'services' (such as the atmosphere's – limited – capacity to absorb carbon dioxide). This is an inescapable fact. And it is an inescapable fact that, insofar as the existing order has brought us to the brink of ecological catastrophe, withdrawing from the brink will involve fundamental changes in the distribution and consumption of resources and services. The world market will never effect such a transition by its own magical operations. Political will and concerted action are absolutely indispensable.

This can be seen by considering any of the global environmental issues that repeatedly appear on agendas for action. Population is a perfect example. Since the publication in 1970 of Paul Ehrlich's apocalyptic 'The Population Bomb', people in the North have felt anxious about the exponential growth of populations in poorer countries, and some highly unsavoury solutions have been proposed. Yet the link between poverty and rapid population growth has long been well established. Populations in the industrialised countries have stabilised, and in some cases are declining, while the populations of less developed countries continue to rise, increasing pressure on land and resources. This rise is not caused simply by ignorance of birth control methods (although this may be a factor in some cases, as may lack of access to contraception), nor, in any narrow sense, by 'culture'. The simple fact is that for the Third World poor, having large families is a rational mechanism, indeed the only practicable mechanism, for improving the chances of economic survival by broadening the available labour base. It has often been remarked that people in these circumstances know they will be dependent, in old age, upon their children, and that this is an incentive to have many; but the even harsher truth is that many poor families depend upon the labour of children long before they are adult, or their parents are old.

At the same time, it is clearly the case that where infant and child mortality rates are high, because of a combination of poor nutrition, inadequate medical provision and absence of basic services like water and sanitation, there will be even greater pressure to have large families because it is to be expected that one or more children will die. In Bangladesh, for example, one in eight infants die before they are 6 months old (compared with one in a hundred in Britain) and even that figure disguises much higher mortality in the poorest and worst served areas (World Water/WHO, 1987).

All this is well known. There is overwhelming evidence to support the view that populations will stabilise earlier, and at a lower level, if poverty can be alleviated, food security guaranteed, and basic services provided. Nor is there any technical difficulty in achieving such objectives. It is equally well known, for example, that the world already produces ample food to provide all its citizens with an adequate diet. The fact that half the world goes hungry, like the fact that Ethiopia continued to export food during the 1984–85 famine is a political fact, the result of policies, not the result of technical limitations.

Similarly, there is absolutely no technical difficulty in providing the world's population with clean water and proper sanitation. Nothing could be simpler from a technical point of view. We've played golf on the moon and created a multi-billion dollar industry in 'smart' weapons of mass destruction; it is clearly not beyond our native wit to sink wells for people to draw water from. The fact that we have not done so is a – sickening – reflection of the political values and priorities of the dominant powers in the world over the last few decades. And even when serious efforts have been made to address the most basic needs of poor people in the South, they have fallen short through undercommitment of resources. Such was the case, for example, with the International Drinking Water and Sanitation Decade, concluded in 1991. After ten years of unprecedented effort and intergovernmental cooperation, more people were without clean water and sanitation at the end of the decade than at its beginning

(*New Internationalist*, May 1990). Population growth had outstripped the advances made, graphically illustrating the fact that the longer such basic needs are ignored, the harder it will be eventually to meet them.

There are of course those – thankfully a small minority – who are unconcerned by population growth on the grounds that it is a 'Third World problem'. We are quite safe here in Britain, they believe, as long as we pull up the drawbridge of immigration controls. Nature will find her own way of dealing with excessive populations elsewhere, through famine and massive death if need be: they're 'only foreigners' who'll be dying anyway.

This view is not just morally repugnant, it is also incredibly stupid. It fails to grasp that population growth, far from being curtailed by disaster, is more likely to be curtailed by improvement of living conditions; and it fails even more fundamentally to recognise that our own welfare in Britain is intimately connected with the welfare of distant and poorer nations.

This is so in three, important ways. Firstly we have for more than a century relied on raw materials, including food, from colonies and former colonies to secure our manufacturing base and our own levels of consumption. Secondly, those countries have come to be important markets for goods and services that we produce. Thirdly, and most recently, having arrived in the last few decades at a global overview of environmental resources and services, we can see that our own share of these goods and services is disproportionately high; and insofar as greater rates of extraction and consumption will endanger the whole global environment, we have a vital interest in the way that poorer countries develop. It is, then, impossible to wash our hands of the developing world, not just for humanitarian reasons or out of historical responsibility, but because our environmental interests remain very much at stake.

To some extent, dependence on raw materials from less developed countries has diminished with technological advance. Cotton, for example, has been widely replaced in the modern textile industry by synthetic fibres, to the detriment of cotton producers in countries such as Egypt and the Sudan. Yet as recently as the late 1950s, and largely because of massive orders for cotton uniforms in the United States during the Korean War, substantial areas of Central America were turned over to cotton cultivation for the first time, in many cases replacing luxuriant orange groves (Black, 1981). By the 1980s, demand had fallen dramatically, and the crop had become an agricultural – and environmental – liability, occupying highly fertile land but needing evermore frequent dressings of pesticides. In Nicaragua in the 1980s, pesticide imports were several times the value of the cotton export crop (*Pensamiento Propio*, January 1989). For the government, beleaguered by war at the same time as trying to diversify the agricultural base, it was politically impossible to take the land out of private hands and let it go idle; so the revolutionary Sandinistas gave a massive subsidy to private cotton farmers, and some more of the Third World's resources were diverted northwards, to the pesticide manufacturers.

Sugar provides another striking example of the way that developing countries have danced a tune played in the North, with disastrous consequences for their own economies. Long before independence, countries such as Mauritius and many of the Caribbean islands were 'developed', initially with slave labour, as sugar producers, and in the post-independence era their economies remained geared to sugar as the primary export. But the development of sugar substitutes, both artificial and natural, and the wave of health consciousness in Europe and North America that led to a decline in sugar consumption, has resulted in a large drop in the world price for sugar and further undermined the frail economies of producer countries (Coote, 1987). Cuba too was caught in this sticky trap. With an economy geared totally to supplying sugar to the Soviet Union, what chance had Cuba of reducing dependence by finding new customers when, as well as the formal barriers, the bottom had fallen out of the market? Cuba became more dependent than ever on Soviet willingness to buy sugar above the world market price, at a time when that willingness was itself being eroded by the parlous state of the Soviet economy.

Some countries even diversified into sugar at precisely the wrong time. The Sudan contracted Lonhro subsidiaries to build a huge irrigation scheme and sugar mill at Kenana in the 1970s, just before the crash in world prices, with the unhelpful side effect of stimulating local demand for a raw energy but nutritionally inadequate food. It was useful and profitable work for Lonhro, but the Sudan, once viewed as a potential 'breadbasket of the

Arab world', is now suffering famine. It will never be known to what extent that famine might have been alleviated by policies directed at improving domestic food security.

A similar story can be told of nearly every cash crop, natural and mineral resource upon which Third World economies depend, from bananas to bauxite, from coffee to copper, from mahogany to McDonald's hamburger meat. Fluctuations in world prices invariably reflect changing demand in the First World where most consumption takes place; and price dips invariably wreak havoc on the economies of producer countries. Thus, decades after formal independence, many former colonies are as dependent as ever, if not more so, on the shifting requirements of neo-imperial powers. How, indeed, could it be otherwise when the original, colonial 'economic development' of these countries was explicitly aimed at supplying imperial need?

Perhaps the most abject example of cash crop dependency is that several Latin American and Caribbean countries have recently come, either directly or indirectly, to depend on income from growing plants for the drugs trade (Sage, 1989). This has nothing to do with the Latin psyche, despite the inherently racist portrayals, in much popular fiction and drama, of drug-dealing Generals. On the other hand it has everything to do with a European and North American taste for drugs, which itself can be seen as a form of escapism from material pressures. Bolivian or Peruvian farmers who grow coca, and Jamaican farmers who grow marijuana, are merely obeying the law of the international market – 'grow what you can sell' – and no amount of US drug enforcement officers or extradition orders will stop them until they have a sound economic alternative. The coca farmers are simply following the example of their forefathers who grew tobacco and coffee in response to an earlier acquired European taste for those drugs.

The other side of the dependency coin is the obvious need to import everything that is not locally produced. In many of the smaller, less developed countries such a category is breathtakingly broad, including almost anything made in a factory, from barbed wire to computers. Usually, energy must also be bought in, most commonly in the form of oil; and frequently so must expertise in fields as diverse as civil engineering and telecommunications. Military hardware is very often another major import: in 1977–78, the value of arms imports in both South Asia and Latin America exceeded the total of economic aid received (Sivard, 1991). Dependence on imports increases dependence on hard currency, and thus on cash crop or mineral exports; while foreign or transnational companies pick up useful contracts for infrastructural development and compete for internal markets through direct sales or through licensing arrangements for the manufacture of goods like soft drinks and cigarettes.

It is wrong to oversimplify. To an extent, the more unified conception of the world that has become available to us in recent years, through advances in information technology, may in itself be an inducement to generalisation. More than ever before we are able to take a 'global view', and this new position has, perhaps, ironically encouraged compartmentalisation and division of countries and regions into different leagues. But we should not be too taken with the descriptive power of phrases like 'the Third World'. For in fact, of course, there is a world of difference between Brazil and Bangladesh; grouping them together for almost any purpose will always be a rough and ready exercise. The Middle Eastern oil-producing countries don't fit a three-world model, and there are many other anomalies. Depending on what criterion is employed, the question of whether a country such as Argentina belongs to the Third World or not could give rise to endless, and futile, debate.

But even acknowledging this, it can be said without exaggeration that the circumstances and economic prospects of hundreds of millions of people in the Southern hemisphere are critically influenced by the historically fluctuating requirements of production and consumption in a small minority of wealthier countries. Now the question arises of whether this, and the global inequality of power and wealth it reflects, is itself an 'environmental' issue. Many would argue, even from a socialist perspective, that it is not; and that issues of global equity are, although important, conceptually distinct from issues of environmental sustainability (e.g. Jacobs, 1991).

Considered simply as a logical distinction this may be so. But, in practice, North/South inequity is central both to the likely aggravation of environmental problems, and to their possible solution. This can be seen firstly in the fact that Northern citizens, governments and policy makers tend to compile different agendas of 'global environmental problems' from those that most obviously occur to people in the South. From the North, global warming, overpopulation, tropical deforestation, and loss of habitats and wildlife are frequently seen as the most pressing issues. This is not so in the South, and so proposed solutions are often unpalatable to the Southern countries involved. It has, for example, recently been argued that macroeconomic structural adjustment programmes, as conditions of loans from the IMF and World Bank, can have an environmentally useful component; and that debt relief to poorer countries may have environmentally damaging consequences (Hansen, in Winpenny, 1991b). Such claims should be treated with caution. It needs to be shown that some greater insight is being offered than the thought that in multilateral aid we have a useful way of exerting green pressure on poorer countries, because such pressure may reflect our priorities, not theirs.

Even apart from the questions of sovereignty that are raised by the possibility of the North dictating environmental terms to the South (mirroring the way that economic development has been dictated by the needs of the North), there are sound, practical reasons for being attentive to a more South-oriented environmental agenda. It has, for example, been soberly predicted in commercial quarters that global energy demand will double within the next 50 years (Shell, BP; quoted by Anderson in Winpenny, 1991b). Demand from the OECD countries is expected to stabilise at roughly its present level, owing to new technologies and energy efficiency measures. The net increase in total demand, therefore, will come almost completely from less developed countries. They are expected to increase consumption from present levels of 45 million barrels of oil per day equivalent, to 200 million barrels of oil per day equivalent.

It must be stressed that even an increase of this magnitude would not bring less developed countries to anything like per capita equality of consumption with OECD countries. On the contrary, on this projection, per capita consumption in the USA would remain at five times the level of per capita consumption in developing countries.

These figures are not prescriptive, setting targets for ideal development. They are hard-headed, commercial estimates of what is likely to happen. And what they show is that developing countries will require a greater proportion of resources (although not enough to bring individual consumption up to OECD levels), and so will become more significant contributors to the environmental damage that results from consumption of those resources. On the specific issue, for example, of global warming, lesser developed countries can at present legitimately claim that it is a problem which has been caused almost entirely by the industrialised, polluting nations in the North. But in the coming years, in proportion to the nature and pace of development, we can fully expect a steady increase in greenhouse gases from the burning of coal and oil in the developing nations.

This fact underlines the vital importance of embarking on a new kind of North/South dialogue, especially at The Earth Summit in June of this year. It is essential, if only out of self-interest, that we secure the cooperation of the developing nations in controlling harmful emissions. But it is impossible to do that from the standpoint of preserving the status quo. We would certainly be rebuffed if we went to the negotiating table demanding a moratorium on economic growth, because that would be tantamount to saying that only we, in the developed nations, have the right to enjoy a reasonable level of consumption and material comfort.

Instead, we must be prepared to listen to what the developing nations have to say, and to take seriously their own environmental agendas. These, invariably, will emphasise not conservation – which, almost by definition, suggests preserving the status quo – but development, interpreted broadly as making the most of their available resources.

Obviously, all countries would prefer to use their resources in a sustainable way. But where immediate needs are great, and where capital investment is hard to secure, there are strong pressures to opt for short term 'solutions' that, in depleting the natural resource base, will only make the future more difficult. Debt repayments aggravate the situation. Impoverished countries, exactly like impoverished families, are thus perennially in the position of taking their only cow to market to sell for food – although the handful of beans they get will seldom produce a magic beanstalk.

The destruction of tropical rain forests is a good example of self-evidently unsustainable resource use that has, rightly, caused widespread public concern in Europe and North America; but that public concern has not yet been translated into government action. We must accept that our role in conservation of the forests must be more constructive than simply preaching restraint – which we ourselves have seldom practised.

There are many popular misconceptions surrounding the loss of rain forests. It is, for example, not true that stable forests are net providers of oxygen, or absorbers of carbon dioxide necessarily. However, it is clear that tropical forests do play an important role in climate regulation, through the cycle of evaporation and rainfall, and the dense vegetation protects soils from erosion. The burning of large areas also releases carbon to the atmosphere, and has been a significant factor in the greenhouse effect. But of perhaps greater, long term significance, tropical rain forests are important as genetic reservoirs, because they have such a rich variety of plant, insect and animal life, much of it still unknown to outside scientists, that may have applications for medicine and agriculture. In the province of Sarawak on the Malaysian island of Borneo alone, 2,500 tree species, 5,500 types of flowering plants and 20,000 kinds of animals and insects have so far been identified (*World Development*, UNDP, July 1991). A quarter of all prescribed drugs in the United States are based on tropical plants (Winpenny, 1991a), and new, disease-resistant strains of two dozen major world crops have already been developed using wild germplasm (Prescott Allen, 1988, quoted in Winpenny, 1991a).

The genetic diversity of the forests is therefore an invaluable resource for the future of the whole world, developed and developing. It is in all our interests to conserve the resource and arrest the present trend of rapid species extinction. But we can't do that simply by demanding a moratorium on further logging and forest clearance without the countries involved being compensated for immediate loss of much-needed income, and helped to find less damaging ways to make use of their existing resources, including standing forest. The province of Sarawak, which has autonomous control of its forests, will not simply forfeit the income generated by extracting two-thirds of world demand for tropical hardwood at the cost of 300,000 hectares of forest per annum (UNDP); it will require an alternative source of income to refrain from taking that wood to market.

So far, however, Britain and the other leading industrialised nations have refused to accept requests for compensation from the 27 countries that contain 97 per cent of the remaining tropical rain forests. At negotiations in Geneva in August, 1991, the Group of Seven rejected a submission from Malaysia asking for a reduction in the £373 billion debt burden (roughly half the Third World's total debt) borne by those 27 countries. This seriously undermines the likelihood of a global forestry agreement being signed during the 1992 UN Commission on Environment and Development conference in Rio de Janeiro.

As well as creating pressure for the rapid extraction of resources, debt, poverty, harsh living and working conditions and a shortage of decent work in the Third World inevitably encourage willingness to accept high levels of industrial pollution. A recent report on heavy metal pollution in Africa noted that dust from the streets of Lagos contains the highest levels of lead pollution in the world, reflecting the fact that Nigerian petrol has a lead content over four times greater than the European Community's upper limit. Smelters and metal processors in Algeria, Morocco, South Africa, Tunisia, Zaire and Zambia were found to have no effective pollution controls, to the extent that one official made the telling comment 'You can do pretty well anything you like provided it makes money.' The report also noted chronic contamination of the food chain from rock high in cadmium phosphate processed into fertilisers which are banned in Europe and North America. Similarly, widespread contamination of water courses was found to be caused by the uncontrolled use of medicated soap containing mercury. The soap is believed to be imported from the UK, where it would be considered a hazardous substance (Stevenson, 1991).

Why do Africans tolerate such grave levels of heavy metal pollution? Part of the answer is undoubtedly that medical authorities lack the resources fully to study the health implications. Many a case of acute lead poisoning may have been put down to a bout of malaria, which produces similar symptoms. But a more fundamental answer is surely that there are even more pressing risks to public health, such as inadequate water supply and sanitation, inadequate waste disposal and malnutrition. If your children are in danger of dying from diarrhoea, and if you don't have the wherewithal to feed them, you will be unlikely to spend much time worrying about the long term effects of air pollution or the ingestion of heavy metals, even if you are aware of the possible risks. Nairobi's 200,000 squatters and slum dwellers must have more immediate things on their minds. As, for that matter, must Calcutta's 5 million.

This kind of observation has led some to argue that concern with industrial (particularly air) pollution is a 'Western' pre-occupation (e.g. Hardoy and Satterthwaite, 1989). It is certainly true that the developing nations have yet to remedy basic public health problems (most notably, water provision and sanitation) which were virtually overcome in the nineteenth century in Europe and North America, and so have little attention to spare for health risks associated with industrialisation, of the kind that have concerned us for the last few decades. But this is not to say that industrial pollution is unimportant, particularly given the likely expansion of industry in the coming years. For if things are bad now, and if industrial development proceeds in a climate of non-regulation – a climate in which you can do what you like so long as it pays – then they are likely to become worse. That has ramifications for all of us. Acid rain and global warming have taught us that pollution is no respecter of national boundaries. Already, the ocean waters off West Africa are among the most highly contaminated from airborne lead pollution in the world, although the coastal region still has only a relatively small in-dustrial base. If heavy industry were to grow in Africa at the same rate as the projected figures for energy demand – a fourfold increase in 50 years – how contaminated would those coastal waters eventually be, and how large the area affected?

We have to accept that less developed countries wish to develop, to exploit their resources further, and that they will. The question is not whether, but how they do so: who will benefit from an intensification of economic activity, and who can contribute to make that development sustainable? So far, the richer nations have played an ignominious role in Third World development, not just because of the general constraints of the international economic system but through the particular actions of many private, often transnational, enterprises. In the first place it has become common practice to shift dirty technologies, that have been banned or superseded in Europe and North America, to the Third World, where environmental regulations are either lax or non-existent and where people are needy enough to tolerate primitive or dangerous working conditions. The Brundtland Commission reported that, in 1980, the total of Third World exports to the OECD countries would have cost over $14 billion more if their production had been subjected to American standards of pollution control. This indicates the kind of 'savings' to be made by locating industry in environmentally unregulated areas which are invariably eager to encourage foreign investment, to the extent of also placing few restraints on the export of profits.

Equally dishonourably, we have used the Third World as a dumping ground for goods that can no longer be marketed in the First World. To dangerous pesticides and dubious pharmaceutical products we can now add tobacco as a commodity whose declining popularity in the developed countries has led to a vigorous sales drive in the South. Not only is this appallingly cynical, in view of the health effects of smoking and the limited disposable income of the targeted people (for it is people who die of cancer, not 'markets'), but also it is a means of perpetuating an environmentally devastating crop. As well as using land that could be employed to grow food, tobacco is estimated to consume 12 per cent of the world's timber production, because of the large amount of woodfuel needed to cure the leaves (Ponting, 1991). Each year, trees covering an area the size of Switzerland are cut down for use in this way. But that has not stopped the tobacco giants, like Britain's own BAT (our fifth largest company, with annual profits in excess of £1 billion), embarking on an aggressive marketing strategy in Africa and Asia.

It has to be recognised that these are not neutral, economic facts, they are political facts about where power lies and about who benefits from productive activity. The principles of the free market have, in the last decade, been trumpeted throughout Europe and America with renewed confidence and complacency. The break-up of the Soviet bloc has been seen as a vindication not just of freedom and democracy but of capitalist economic theory and practice as well. But the intellectual respectability of such a view relies on the fact that the worst excesses of capitalism are being moved away from European eyes to the Third World which, in terms of human and environmental degradation, is paying an ever greater proportion of the cost of First World affluence. Moreover, the capitalist development models adopted by most developing countries over the last few decades have so far shown themselves incapable of meeting the aspirations of their citizens for an improved standard of life. This point has been made powerfully by Joe Slovo of the African National Congress:

> The opponents of socialism are very vocal about what they call the failures of socialism in Africa. But they say very little, if anything, about Africa's real failure; the failure of capitalism. Over 90% of our continent's people live out their wretched and repressed lives in stagnating and declining capitalist-oriented economies.
>
> (Quoted in *New Ground*, Summer 1990.)

Again, we must beware of oversimplification. Just as we can't really divide the globe into 'three worlds', we shouldn't either think in terms of an exhaustive dichotomy between un-trammelled capitalism and socialist Utopia. We cannot afford to sit on the high horse of socialist theory and refuse to get involved with the practical business of trying to make constructive changes where and when we can. To do so would be an abdication of responsibility. It is precisely this willingness to take responsibility that has always distinguished the Labour Party from those dreamers on the left who prefer a place on the sidelines of history, awaiting the socialist millennium.

But our commitment to getting involved and trying our serious best does not mean abandoning all radicalism. It is, for example, essential that the commercial activities of transnational companies operating in the Third World be subjected to greater controls, and we should not be afraid to say so. This is necessary not just because their record to date has been exploitative of both the human and physical environment of the developing world, but because it is increasingly important for all our sakes to meet the aspirations for growth of the poorer countries in a way that is compatible with safeguarding the environment for themselves and their descendants. The quest for greater profit, for a few individuals or companies, is no way to do this, and no substitute for coordinated development strategies.

Furthermore, if Third World development is to move towards sustainability, it will certainly need the benefits of the advanced, clean technologies of 'the West'. But this is something that governments themselves don't have complete power to bestow, since the most advanced technologies are frequently in the hands of transnational companies and industrial conglomerates, as a result of their own research and development programmes. There is a clear need to sponsor international research and development with non-commercial objectives and a specific commitment to technology transfer. In agricultural research, progress in this direction has already been made through institutions such as the International Rice Research Institute, in the Philippines, and the Centre for Wheat and Maize Improvement, in Mexico, although both of these have been criticised for actually destroying genetic diversity by ignoring the indigenous knowledge of local people and adopting a centralised strategy (Shiva, 1990). It is probable that research will be more fruitful and sensitive to local ecology if carried out by organisations that were set up as the result of local initiatives, such as the Madhya Pradesh Rice Research Institute. This Institute conserved 20,000 indigenous varieties of rice, *in situ*, in the Indian province of Chatisgarh, against the current trend towards use of only a few, high yield strains which require large agrochemical inputs and remove the natural disease barrier of diversity.

It may be noted in passing that the Conservative government throughout the 1980s encouraged a shift in research emphasis in exactly the opposite direction, bleeding our higher education establishments of the resources they need to function independently, and propelling them towards industrial sponsors. This was a devastating assault on the long-recognised excellence of British academic research in all fields. But, more than that, it was a clear expression of the ideological conviction that knowledge should be put at the service of profit. Against such a perverted view of human endeavour it must be affirmed that knowledge should serve people. The only way to achieve that is to direct research at problems people have, without the ulterior motive of making money by selling 'solutions'. Many academic institutions remain admirably determined to collaborate freely with Third World partners, but their ability to do so is hindered by the need to show a profit on the balance sheet. Similarly, dramatic increases in tuition fees for overseas students have threatened one of the most simple and important ways in which we can transfer knowledge and skills to the countries that most need them. Tory management of our higher education system has thus been wilfully parochial, and has slammed shut many small doors of opportunity for sharing the benefits of our expertise and research facilities.

But greater public funding of academic and applied research, nationally and internationally, will not in itself put clean technologies at the disposal of developing countries, for the reason already mentioned, namely that much of the most advanced technologies are in the hands of private conglomerates. This fact itself reinforces the need for greater controls on the operations of the transnationals. If they are to exploit the resources, labour and markets of the Third World they must be obliged to clean up their acts, rather than using developing countries to bypass proper environmental standards and as a dustbin for goods shunned by the industrialised nations.

One suggestion for putting the necessary pressure on the transnationals is to restrict their access to markets in industrialised countries if they fail to comply with adequate environmental standards in their Third World operations (Jacobs, 1991). Such measures would only be likely to succeed if adopted at an international level: the European Community, for example, would be in a powerful position to exert this kind of pressure if it were so minded. Under the auspices of the EC (or, for that matter, the UN Environment Programme) a commission could be set up to investigate complaints of environmental negligence on the part of transnationals (with the companies involved able to make representations to that commission). Even if it weren't empowered to impose any specific sanctions, the commission's findings would themselves publicise the activities of the worst culprits, stimulating consumer boycotts.

In the short term, this may seem an unlikely proposal: but it should at least be clear that international problems require international solutions and, particularly in the case of transnational corporations, international controls. The emergence of the European Community as a new forum for international policy is a highly constructive development, and we should not underestimate its potential as a catalyst for change. In many respects EC directives have already run ahead of British government environmental policy; it remains for a more outward-looking and truly international approach to be found.

The other way of improving the environmental performance of transnational, and indeed all, companies operating in Third World countries is to create a more regulatory economic climate in those countries themselves. Realistically, this can only be done through binding, international conventions and agreements. Only a far sighted government can be expected to take unilateral action to introduce adequate environmental controls, because of the fear that to do so would be to undermine the country's short term competitiveness and ability to attract investment from overseas (although, as the tide begins to turn towards cleaner technologies, there will be an economic advantage for those who have the foresight and capacity to remodel their industry and agriculture early on).

We are undoubtedly moving into an era of international conventions and agreements on resource use and pollution control. The 1987 Montreal Protocol on Substances that Deplete the Ozone Layer has set a useful precedent in relation to CFCs. Although it was criticised by some environmentalists as not going far or quickly enough, I believe that the fact that agreement was reached at all was a positive step, showing a new mood of realism among the 60 signatories, which included the major industrialised nations. But, in a sense, the whole question of international conventions brings us back full circle as the present difficulties in negotiating a forestry agreement have vividly illustrated Third World countries will not queue up to sign treaties that limit their freedom to exploit their resources without receiving in return either compensation for forfeited income or assistance in finding other development paths.

The point was put succinctly by Hans Alders, Dutch Environment Minister and President of the EC Council for Environmental Affairs, in a speech to a 1991 European Socialist Conference:

> We are asking [Third World countries] to cooperate in the success of international conferences, which *we* are organising because *we* are concerned about the environmental problems *we* have caused. And then *we* ask them to temper their growth, just when they are arriving at the stage when gradually they can be granted a measure of economic growth.

In nearly all cases where international conventions now seem appropriate the industrialised nations have been, and remain, responsible for most of the damage that such conventions would seek to limit. This was certainly so with CFCs and other ozone-layer-depleting substances; and it is equally so in the case of greenhouse gas emissions. Even on questions such as deforestation and species extinction it is worth pointing out that – admittedly a long time ago – Europe was once densely forested and home to many flora and fauna that have now been destroyed. Therefore, if we were strictly to apply the 'polluter pays' principle (in conjunction with a subsidiary, 'resource-depleter pays' principle), it would be perfectly clear that we in the industrialised nations should pay the consequences of our historical profligacy. Any appeal to natural justice will leave the bill firmly in our lap.

This has important ramifications for the kind of global agreements that can be negotiated fairly. Where conventions aim to agree on target reductions or to award pollution quotas, it will clearly make an enormous difference whether the targets are based on present contributions to total pollution or on the population of countries involved. For example, a commitment to reduce carbon dioxide emissions in every country by a flat rate of 20 per cent would seriously penalise non-industrialised Third World countries whose present level of emissions is relatively insignificant; whereas a country like the United States could make the adjustment and yet remain, on a per capita basis, by far the world's greatest contributor of carbon dioxide to the atmosphere. Such an agreement would, therefore, merely institutionalise and formalise the global inequalities which are already in place.

On the other hand, quotas and reduction targets for harmful emissions that were based on relative population size would almost certainly leave most Third World countries with a 'pollution surplus' to use up. If the quotas were fixed and non-transferable, then in order to be at all feasible they would have to be set at levels which the industrialised nations could reach through improved environmental performance. But even levels which required strenuous controls in the industrialised countries would – given the present disparities in carbon dioxide or CFC emissions, for example – allow many Third World countries considerable room to increase, in some cases very substantially, their net contribution to global atmospheric pollution.

This would have the virtue of redressing the present imbalance between North and South in the proportion of pollution caused: but it would obviously be disastrous for us all. The whole point of international agreements is, after all, to encourage restraint, and to bring about a net reduction in emissions rather than simply altering the proportions emanating from different countries. Morally, we must accept that people in, say, India have as much right as people in Britain to the benefits of, for example, refrigerators; but environmentally, we cannot overlook the potentially dire consequences if per capita ownership of fridges among India's 1 billion people rose to anything like British levels. This, in a nutshell, is the central dilemma of the environment and development issue.

A variation on the quota system would be to issue 'harmful emission permits', aimed at a net reduction, on the basis of population, and to allow those permits to be traded. Less developed countries could sell part of their quotas back to the industrialised nations who would need to buy quotas in order to maintain production at present levels. In this way, the Third World would stand to benefit very significantly from international pollution controls. Such a system would, in theory, contain a dual incentive to efficient and clean production, since countries with a quota surplus would, by minimising their own emissions, be left with a greater surplus to sell; whereas countries with a pollution quota deficit would also want to minimise emissions in order to reduce the proportion of quota they needed to buy.

But such a scheme begs various questions. What sanctions could be applied to those who exceeded the permitted quota? How would the total permitted level of emissions be arrived at? Would the permits have a fixed tradable price, or would the price be negotiable? If the price were fixed, this would imply putting a total, monetary value on maintaining the atmosphere, which is odd, to say the least; if prices were negotiable, a whole new realm of political intrigue and price fixing could be opened up. More fundamentally, what would the countries with quota surpluses do with the money they gained from selling them? Wouldn't there in fact be a disincentive for investing in their own development, because that would tend to diminish their current account income from permit sales? So wouldn't the money tend to be spent buying in goods from the developed nations, thus further formalising import dependency that would prove disastrous when income from licence sales declined, as Northern industries improved their environmental performance?

It seems likely, then, that the introduction of an internationally tradable permit scheme, even if it could be agreed in the first place, would have chaotic and unpredictable results. China, for example, would immediately acquire the tradable right to emit a quarter of all atmospheric pollution; and although it is hard to argue that the Chinese have no right to such a large share in the use of environmental resources, it is equally hard to see how present imbalances could be immediately redressed by treaty or fiat.

All the same, the logic of the case for per capita agreements deserves serious attention if only because it throws into relief the second major issue related to international conventions, which is that poorer countries must be provided with incentives to sign and abide by them. We in the industrialised nations, despite serious distributional inequalities within our countries, are in a position to consider at least trading off further economic growth against the longer term benefits of sustainability; most Third World countries simply cannot afford environmental regulation, unless there is a new breakthrough on technology transfer agreements, without sacrificing present income that is already insufficient to meet the most basic needs of large sectors of their population. Those countries cannot be expected to accept new economic constraints without receiving something in return.

There are thus overwhelming arguments for assisting Third World countries, financially and technologically, towards greater development at less environmental cost; and a willingness to do so is a necessary precondition of any serious global negotiations. Yet present trends are not promising. World trade, for example, is organised in a way that clearly favours the industrialised nations, and current negotiations in the General Agreement on Tariffs and Trade are set to consolidate rather than to challenge this pattern. The liberalisation of trade, the removal of barriers and the ideal of 'free trade', all of which are little less than sacred to the GATT, rely for justification on the implicit assumption of competition between free and equal partners. But the assumption is a nonsense. Frail Third World – or even East European – economies cannot possibly compete on an equal footing with

Japanese, American or European industries. Occasional bouts of protectionism among the industrialised nations themselves show how sensitive the issue can be even in highly developed and diverse economies. Developing countries which are struggling to establish a small manufacturing base will even more naturally look to mechanisms such as import and export controls to guarantee markets for their goods. Insisting that they compete openly on the world markets can thus be a powerful disincentive to diversify their economies; a means, in effect, of preserving the status quo and encouraging the Third World to stand by traditional products, even though these have failed to generate adequate or reliable income. Restructuring of world trade agreements, both in terms of paying a fair price for commodities and to allow weak markets to be protected, would therefore be an important element in any programme to ensure a better deal for the South. Indeed, many Third World governments would be more interested in obtaining this kind of concession, to allow them to build up their own economies, than in receiving transfers of cash or resources from North to South.

In some instances, apart from being a general straitjacket on Third World development, this system results in particular, environmental anomalies. Indonesia, for example, recently imposed a ban on the export of felled wood as a raw material, not only with a view to preserving its standing forest, but in the hope of stimulating local industry to manufacture and export articles such as hardwood furniture. Simply, the idea was that instead of exporting large quantities of wood, Indonesia should export small quantities of furniture, for the same or an improved return. And yet this was deemed to be in breach of the General Agreement, and against the spirit of free trade! Equally disturbing was the recent judgement that the US ban on the import of Mexican tuna (which is caught in nets that also trap dolphins) contravenes principles of free trade. This kind of anti-environmental intervention by GATT is something which must be resisted by international bodies like the EC and UNEP. In this regard it was encouraging to compare the GATT decision with the EC ruling that Denmark's strict policy on returnable drinks containers was not a breach of free trade within the EC. It is increasingly recognised that reform of GATT is essential to enhance Third World development. On the environment side, an environmental code should be formulated and adopted without delay.

As well as trade constraints, the debt burden continues critically to hinder development prospects throughout the Third World. Interest payments not only cut deeply into the level of public services that governments are able to provide, they also use up capital that could be invested in economic regeneration and diversification. The net results are political and economic instability, and enormous pressure to opt for economic activity that offers quick returns, in exports and hard currency, rather than attending to longer term needs through environmentally sensitive development. Inevitably, natural resources as capital assets are highly vulnerable to this kind of pressure. And indebted Third World countries are not unique in preferring rapid extraction and immediate income to long term security, as a moment's reflection on Britain's use of North Sea oil will demonstrate.

Nor should we allow ourselves to look on Third World debt as having arisen from the magnanimity of the richer nations. Anyone who has ever borrowed money from a bank or building society knows perfectly well that, despite the advertising hype, the transaction is strictly commercial, and that these institutions make their profits by lending money to us. And anyone who has been in the unfortunate position of having to borrow more money to honour previous debts will know something of what the words 'debt crisis' really mean: they have, in fact, very little to do with honour, and very much to do with ignominy, especially when the bank manager starts to tell us what economies we have to make in our domestic budgets. No holidays this year; no luxuries on the family table and eventually, as many have found, the horror of home repossession.

Debt relief, fairer trading terms, further untied aid, and compensation payments to countries asked to forfeit income from the further exploitation of natural resources would all be expressions of serious commitment to conservation and environmentally sustainable development. Willingness to consider these measures would also dramatically advance the prospects for achieving global agreements on pollution and resource depletion. But can we afford such measures?

Every year the 12 major military powers spend around

US$780,000 million dollars on defence (Sivard, 1991); and the arguments for turning swords into ploughshares have never been so strong. The progress in arms reduction talks and the end of the Cold War themselves provide an opportunity for reassessing military expenditure; and at the same time we should be more aware than ever of a community of interests in defending ourselves against poverty and environmental disaster. The transfer of funds from military protection to environmental protection is therefore a wholly logical step. If, for example, progressively over a ten year period, just a third of present military expenditure was put into a World Environment Fund, administered jointly by the UNEP and UNDP, by the end of the century the Fund would have a current account of $250 billion to invest in environmental regeneration in severely degraded areas (including countries in Eastern Europe), and to sponsor sustainable development in the Third World.

This may sound highly optimistic, even as an example of what could be done; and yet I believe that many individual governments are on the verge of recognising that environmental threats (including Saddam Hussein's use of environmental destruction as a weapon in the Gulf War) are as much a danger as anything else. So there is certainly real scope for a new agenda in foreign policy.

But having accepted the inevitability of greater economic development in Third World countries, and the need to play a positive role in encouraging that development, we must address a whole series of questions as to its nature, who it is to benefit, and how. For the third time, a cautionary note against oversimplification should be sounded. 'Development' is not a self-explanatory concept: it has perhaps meant something different to every politician and practitioner who has used the term; and when we talk about 'Third World countries' we are grouping together not only quite different economies and cultures, but also widely different governments with distinct political outlooks and ambitions. To call for Third World development, therefore, or even increased aid to the Third World, is not the end of an argument so much as the beginning. What is meant by such an appeal remains to be made clear.

It is not appropriate here to embark on a detailed essay on the subject, but some important considerations can be brought to bear. In the first place it should not be forgotten that the concept of development itself arose in a colonial context, where the main preoccupation was to develop colonies effectively as satellites of central powers; and the resulting relationships of economic subservience have survived the colonial era. At the simplest level, many people in both North and South now think of the process of development as one of becoming more like the industrialised, highly 'developed' countries of the OECD. But in fact it is plainly impossible for Third World countries merely to follow in the footsteps of the industrialised nations. Environmental constraints are themselves an important factor in this impossibility, as has been widely recognised in the last few decades; but even without considering environmental issues it can be seen that emulating European models is not possible for the great majority of developing countries, for the simple reason that the point from which they started life, as colonial entities, is radically different from the position of Europe or North America at the beginning of the industrial revolution. The conditions for parallel, if somewhat belated, development to occur in the Third World simply do not exist, because, if nothing else, there is a singular lack of new territories for Third World countries to colonise and exploit in order to bolster their own industrialisation.

The point is elementary enough: copying Europe, or the United States, or Japan is simply not an option for the Third World; and so those countries should not be looked upon as models. Yet precisely this attitude has persisted among Westerners of goodwill for more than a century, and in some quarters persists still. We Europeans, the reasoning goes, are more 'advanced', more 'developed'. Therefore we should share our privilege a bit by helping others become more like us. The problem with such a view is not any lack of authentic concern, but a lack of clearheadedness. It is simply not realistic to believe that Africa, for example, could or should develop in a way which is comparable with European experience, because the conditions for that kind of development do not exist.

And yet the former colonial powers have encouraged the kind of capitalist development in Africa which, to return to Joe Slovo's phrase, has left 90 per cent of Africans 'wretched and oppressed'. The creation of an African managerial and capitalist class, as the main instrument for pulling the continent into the modern age, has quite naturally failed to benefit the overwhelming majority of people, because that in itself has not been enough to break the fundamental dependency on the developed nations. National capital, public or private, has not been able to compete with international capital in the extraction of resources or the exploitation of markets, and so the natural wealth of the continent has drained steadily away northwards, increasing the gulf between Africa and the developed nations.

Large scale, multilaterally funded development projects have a lamentable record in nearly every respect, not least because they were in many cases prosecuted with complete disregard for environmental effects. The building of the Aswan High Dam, at enormous cost, is a good example of this. Although effective in regulating floods, the dam also retained the silt that for tens of thousands of years had been deposited at frequent intervals by those floods in the Nile delta, giving it some of the most fertile soils in the world, able to support up to three annual harvests quite naturally. As a result of this interference with the natural pattern of silt-bearing floods, Egypt experienced a 'forcible entry into the modern agricultural system of high input farming', with many peasant farmers unable to afford expensive fertilisers (Ponting, 1991). At the same time, evaporation losses from the dam and Egypt's increased share of the Nile waters created social, economic and political difficulties for upstream areas in the Sudan and beyond. Irrigation projects around the dam provided a new habitat for the snails which are vectors of schistosomiasis, doubling the incidence of the disease among Egyptians.

Nearly half of the World Bank's total spending has been in dam construction projects (Ponting, 1991), very many of which have had similarly high, social and environmental costs, in terms of flooded agricultural land, displaced populations, increased evaporation and rapid siltation. But even without so many technical failures, it is not clear that these projects could have had a favourable impact on the lives of the people in the countries involved. This is so because development of this kind tends to reinforce the export orientation of economies which are already far from self-sufficiency, and which thus become even more dependent on earning foreign currency. When commodity prices fall, such economies are left high and dry. Consider, for example, the case of Zambia, dependent on copper for 90 per cent of its export earnings, which has seen copper prices fall by two-thirds in the last 20 years (Ponting, 1991). 'Structural adjustment programmes' initiated as conditions for further loans from the IMF are also generally designed to safeguard debt repayments by maximising export earnings, at the invariable expense of domestic subsidies and social assistance programmes.

The assumption underlying prestige economic development projects has always been that generated wealth will 'trickle down' from government or from private capital to the poorest sections of society. But this flies in the face of human experience. We should by now recognise that wealth does not obey the laws of gravity, for it invariably trickles upwards from the labour of the poor to the pockets of the rich. Even in those Third World countries such as Mexico and Venezuela, which are blessed with highly marketable natural resources such as oil, the trickling down of revenue to the poor in the shanty towns has been conspicuous only by its absence.

From even such a brief sketch, in such broad outlines, certain basic principles begin to emerge. It is clearly either dishonest or stupid or both to suggest that the Third World can develop along the lines of the already industrialised nations. It is clear that grandiose development projects, conceived in the technocratic optimism of the 1950s and 1960s, have in the main failed: not just for technical reasons but, in large part, because the enticing vision of modern, capitalist development overlooked the little details of people's circumstances, livelihoods and real needs. And it is clear that development should focus not on how the South can serve the industrialised nations, but on how Third World countries can enhance their self-sufficiency and reduce dependency.

So in thinking about the question 'What kind of development?' I would argue that we must begin by shifting the emphasis to look not at national economies but at people and communities. This was the approach I began by adopting in the earlier discussion of population. We have now heard enough projections from demographers, be they pacifiers or doom-mongers. If we attended only to that kind of information, and worked out the future of the human race on pieces of paper covered with statistics, we would almost inevitably start to come up with conclusions that began 'In order for the population to stabilise, families must be limited to . . .'; and we would be only one step away from demanding legislation to that effect. Instead, of course, we need a more human approach in order even just to understand the problem. We must listen now not to demographers but to the mothers who have borne eight children in huts with mud floors, only to see two of them die within the first year of life. We should not be surprised to find that those women don't actually want to live that way, worn out with childbearing and poverty. And if we can, through listening to their needs, find ways to make their livelihoods more secure, their communities more prosperous and their children less vulnerable to sickness and death, then we should not be surprised to find them quite willing to forgo the principle of safety in numbers.

This approach, which is really no more than a human-centred attentiveness to people and communities, should inform all of our development thinking. In agriculture, for example, rather than being distracted by excitement at the technical wonders of Green Revolutions, we should look at the needs of small farmers and the communities who depend upon them for subsistence. From an environmental point of view this is particularly important. It is quite apparent that people with a stake in the management and use of their own, local resources make the best environmental custodians. Small farmers, who know that they will depend upon their plot throughout their lives (and that their children will in turn come to farm and depend upon it), have an overwhelming incentive towards sustainable farming: if they ruin the land, they and their family will have no future at all. The same cannot be said for large scale entrepreneurs like the Filipino rice barons who, after maximising their profits, can always take their capital elsewhere.

In terms of guaranteeing food security, there is always the temptation to look for technological fixes: hydroponics shows us the possibility of growing food without soil, and genetic engineering suggests many possibilities (as well as many dangers) for crop and pest management. Particularly in the case of genetically modified organisms we should proceed with extreme caution – since releasing new lifeforms into the environment could have unpredictable and possibly dramatic consequences on the existing ecological balance; and such organisms, once released, could not simply be recalled (in the way that we are able, albeit with difficulties, to decommission nuclear power stations). The dramatic spread of myxamatosis is one example of the way that deliberately introduced organisms had an impact far beyond the foresight of scientists involved in the project. This is why I argued strongly during the Committee stage of the recent Environmental Protection Act for a precautionary approach, as well as for setting up a commission, similar to the Warnock Committee, to investigate the ethical dimensions that this kind of technology opens up. And we must certainly resist the wholly reckless approach of Dan Quayle and others in the United States who advocate that genetically modified organisms should be controlled by no more than market mechanisms.

But while these technologies may well have an invaluable future role – and certainly shouldn't be dismissed out of hand – it must be appreciated that political solutions are more fundamental than technological solutions, and indeed that the prevailing distribution system will always determine the application of new technologies. We ought, for example, to have learned from the failure of the 'Green Revolution' of the 1960s to live up to its promise as the answer to the world's food problems, through the intensification of agricultural and land use methods. Part of that failure resulted from the fact that small scale producers were less able to afford necessary inputs, and to take the credit risks of relying on high yield but less disease-resistant varieties. Research also concentrated on grains such as wheat and rice, with relatively little attention given to maize, and almost none to crops like cassava and sorghum, although these provide subsistence for many millions of people. The net effect, therefore, was to favour large and medium scale producers as against peasant farmers; and while US grain exports increased tenfold, Latin American exports halted and Africa and Asia became much greater net importers (Redclift and Goodman, 1991). But surely, if the point was to eliminate hunger, it would have been better to develop technologies which had direct application to the people who were most likely to go hungry.

Inevitably, this raises questions of land tenure and distribution which are plainly political. We should not be afraid of this. We should not be afraid to support and to fund development initiatives which favour agrarian reform and redistribution, and which foster small scale agriculture, because this is clearly not only the fairest but the best way of enhancing food security and sustainable resource use. In the Amazon basin at present, the large scale cattle ranchers who are responsible for so much deforestation are actually subsidised by the Brazilian government, despite the environmental cost, and despite the extremely short lifespan (three or four years) of the pasture gained (Hecht and Cockburn, 1990). This has nothing to do with economic or environmental policy, and everything to do with the political power of the ranchers. We should not be afraid of taking sides against them, and with the forest peoples whose livelihoods are being destroyed.

This should not be taken as an encouragement to land nationalisation; if the 1960s taught us anything about development, it should be that the centralisation of land control, whether it be in the hands of the state or of large private enterprises, seldom works for the benefit of the poor. Nationalisation has a bad record in most Third World countries, because governments rarely have the resources necessary for effective management of large scale enterprises. Instead of centralising control, ways must be found of improving the prospects for rural people of meeting their own needs and producing a surplus for urban populations; and this can best be done by giving people at community level greater access to fertile land. This suggests the kind of far-reaching agrarian reform and cooperative programme attempted by the Sandinistas in Nicaragua (and targeted by the Contras during the war), where peasants were given titles to small parcels of land and encouraged through various kinds of state support to pool their local resources to increase output of basic grains. If the project foundered because of the various external pressures, the guiding philosophy was certainly right: food security is best improved by empowering communities at local level to meet their own needs, with external support where possible, but without external management or interference.

On a further, environmental note, we must realise that conservation measures which don't take full account of the needs of local people are not only unjust, but also will almost certainly fail

as conservation. We can't simply fence off areas of the Third
World and declare them protected habitats, or start reforestation,
soil and water conservation or catchment protection projects
without looking first at how such measures can be made to work
in the direct and immediate interest of local communities. Ideally,
conservation should go hand in hand with local development: in
the rain forests themselves there is great potential in this respect
for developing sustainable extraction and trade of forest products
such as resins, rattan, rubber, tannin, honey, beeswax, bamboo
and medicinal plants. Where the income of local communities is
lost through conservation, compensation must be provided. For
if those communities have no vested interest in conservation, and
are not compensated for forfeited income, we can only expect
prohibitions on certain kinds of resource use to be ignored.
National game parks are a case in point: if local people are not
provided with viable economic alternatives, can we expect them
to refrain from, for instance, poaching elephants for ivory.

Looking at development in this way, from the bottom
upwards rather than vice versa – from the needs of people and
communities to the structures of national and global policy – we
will indeed arrive at specific conclusions for national and global
economic policy. For example, if it is fair, reasonable and
environmentally wise to encourage small scale agriculture, and if
this will satisfy the needs of large numbers of Third World
citizens, then it is plainly not fair or reasonable to disallow
subsidies for such farmers. And if there is a need – as so
manifestly there is – for greater employment, then developing
economies must be enabled to diversify into manufacturing
industries, particularly to supply locally needed goods in import
substitution programmes, rather than simply exporting
commodities for value to be added elsewhere. Yet both of these
options, so obviously necessary, are at present directly undermined by global trading arrangements as regulated by the GATT.

It is impossible honestly to contemplate the problems of Third
World development without feeling overawed by their enormity.
And yet I believe that there are now real grounds for hope. To
begin with, we do have the ability to learn from our mistakes, and
if development projects have so far been ridden with catastrophic
errors of judgement it is at least arguable that lessons have been
learned.

British non-governmental organisations working overseas, such as OXFAM and Christian Aid, have long been advocating a more community-based approach, and a more far-reaching, sensitive analysis of the social and environmental impact of projects and technologies. On the basis of their extensive, direct experience, these organisations have come increasingly to argue the need for 'empowerment' of poor people and communities to overcome the constraints on development, many of which are fundamentally political in character. As David Bryer, Director of OXFAM's overseas unit, has put it, 'it is implicit in any form of intervention that, where people's lives are beginning to change, this is likely to lead to tension with those in power' (Nick Young, 1990, unpublished interview). This can be clearly seen in Eastern Europe at the present time. 'Those in power' is double edged in this context: it refers both to local powers, such as the Brazilian ranchers, and to international powers which may feel threatened by development initiatives that challenge the old relationships of dependency.

Inevitably, this kind of perspective has led to criticism from the right to the effect that OXFAM and others have overstepped their charitable status to start 'meddling in politics'. Such charges miss the point altogether. *The Concise Oxford Dictionary* defines 'politics' as 'public life and affairs as involving authority and government'. If development has nothing to do with public affairs then it has nothing to do with anything.

In fact, many voluntary aid organisations still devote most of their resources to emergency relief. In this they, like the donating public, are responding to the enormous human tragedies that television now so vividly brings into our homes. But after so much experience of tragedy, it is natural to look more deeply into the causes of famine and the suffering that is attendant upon natural disasters, and to seek remedies that will provide greater security for the victims. So perhaps the most important role of non-governmental aid organisations is to pinpoint issues, and to explore possible solutions through model and pilot projects that are attentive to the felt needs of the beneficiaries; and as such these organisations have many important insights to offer governments and multilateral agencies such as the World Bank.

The campaigning message that OXFAM got across in the early 1970s was expressed in the slogan 'Give a man a fish and you'll feed him for a day; teach him how to fish and you'll feed him for life.' The more recent message from the NGOs doesn't lend itself so well to slogans, but could awkwardly be summed up as 'Help a community to secure fishing rights for itself, and you'll feed that whole community for ever.' This (with the caveat that fishing stocks must be used sustainably) is an important advance in our understanding of development issues. It is not unreason- able to hope that the World Bank will take the message on board; and it would be patronising to believe that the message won't be understood by the general public of the industrialised nations, particularly given the new wave of concern about global environ- mental problems.

Furthermore, as I have argued, the emergence of those global problems itself underlines both the fundamental community of interest between North and South, and the differences in perspective that arise from the unequal division of resources and power. Clearly, a serious dialogue on development is needed, and the work done by the UN Commission on Environment and Development provides an excellent basis for that dialogue to proceed at the 1992 Conference in Brazil. The Third World will, I believe, find that as a result of concern over environmental degradation and global warming it has a new bargaining power, and that more respectful attention will have to be given to its difficulties and legitimate aspirations.

I also believe that we are beginning to see a new spirit of regional and international cooperation. Arms reduction negotiations and the Montreal Protocol on CFCs are not the only examples of this: 1991 also saw the signing of the Basle Con- vention limiting international transport of toxic wastes, and inter- national agreement to a 50 year moratorium on mining in Antarctica, which opens up the possibility of it eventually being declared a World Park. Important regional initiatives are being taken to clean up the Baltic and Mediterranean Seas, and a series of multinational conferences on the North Sea have agreed the need for joint management and protection policies. Equally significant is the 1982 Treaty on International Law of the Sea, which resulted from years of UN conferences considering issues such as the use of the seabed, contamination of the oceans and the distribution of any mineral resources that may in the future be extracted from the seabed. This staggeringly lengthy treaty has not yet been ratified, and there remain serious disputes about exploitation rights and zones of exclusive economic activity for maritime states. But, however long and complicated the negotiations, it is clear that negotiate we must, to resolve conflicts between national and global interest, recognising that economic or political might is neither a good arbiter of fair and sustainable environmental management, nor an adequate substitute for it.

International cooperation can only be mediated through international forums. We should therefore be looking progressively to increase the role and the resources of bodies such as UNEP and UNDP. The establishment of an Environment Fund to sponsor environmental repair and sustainable development projects is one practical way in which this could be done.

The European Community also has an important role to play, both in enhancing the European environment and in assisting countries beyond our borders – including those of Eastern Europe, to which we have a particular responsibility – to develop in a way that is compatible with environmental constraints. Again, I am hopeful about this. We have already had a positive influence on each other, with member states such as – to our shame – Britain having to improve environmental performance to meet more stringent requirements which will, of course, also be applied to new members.

Finally, it can be useful to stand back and take a broader and longer view. Some 5,000 years ago, the inhabitants of what are now the Philippine islands began, over many generations, to construct rice terraces to protect their agriculture against soil erosion. Many of those terraces are still under regular cultivation; as too are some of those built more recently by the Incas in the Andes. This commitment to sustainable development – which shows, in passing, that the concept is not so new as is commonly thought – stands in striking contrast to modern preoccupations with maximising short term gain, and what seems a psychological inability to consider a future beyond that which we personally will experience. We only have to consider, for example, the way that nuclear power stations, which have a lifespan of a mere 20–30 years, were built without any definite idea of how they would be rendered harmless at the end of that time. And even many of those most deeply involved in the environmental movement seem to have been seduced, from quite different considerations, into this same way of looking at the world, a way in which concern for the immediate future completely dominates the horizon. Hence, I would suggest, the propensity for issuing dire warnings about 'how long we've got left' – very seldom, seemingly, a period longer than our own life expectancy – before being engulfed by various kinds of apocalypse. On both sides of the green fence we seem to be locked into a culture of immediacy.

Against this, I find it reassuring that all human empires and economic systems have in fact proved very transient, and are becoming even more so. Thus, when we talk about the need for 'fundamental shifts in the balance of power', we may not be talking about something that can happen immediately, or even quickly, but neither are we talking about something that is impossible. Power has shifted fundamentally throughout history, over and over again (and often, as in Eastern Europe, much more suddenly than anyone foretold). Radicalism may therefore be visionary, but that doesn't make it wild; and it is a great deal more positive and productive than self-fulfilling despair.

This is not to understate the seriousness of the global environmental crisis, or the urgency of resolving it. But just as the situation is urgent and serious, so the opportunities for resolving it are unique, and considerable. The wave of environmental consciousness is still relatively new and it is still rising fast. I have little doubt that many environmental causes which now appear radical – and particularly in relation to equity and development – will in the next couple of decades be generally accepted as common sense, in exactly the same way that women's suffrage passed in a matter of decades from being dangerous subversion to an integral and unquestioned feature of democratic thinking.

Chapter 3

Making individuals count

Because ordinary people are excluded from much of the debate about environmental problems, the agenda tends to be dominated by 'specialists and experts'. Ordinary people lose both a voice in making their views known and a sense that they have a stake in improving things. Many people have neither the confidence about the issues, nor the sense of their own power, nor even a feeling that they share responsibility to do something about the degradation of the environment, to which we all contribute.

This must be changed. If individuals in all walks of life are not directly involved in measures to improve the balance between our activities and the environment around us then not only will it be very difficult to implement change, but any changes that policy makers do try and impose are unlikely to be really effective. Individuals and communities must be involved in deciding the best approach. Without the involvement and commitment of all of us, we have little chance of making real and lasting change.

While government has a clearly defined role – to give the right lead and set policy objectives – it must also focus on improving participation and empowering individuals and communities. The protection of the planet must be a common goal – it is only by working together that we can begin to achieve it.

It is often seen as part of the ideology of the right to stress the role which individuals have – but this is part of a very negative belief that fails to recognise the mutual dependence of individuals, on each other and on more organised groups and institutions. The right, especially under Thatcher, has followed the libertarian idea that the world is made up of many 'atomised' souls, and 'there is no such thing as society'.

A socialist approach is based on the belief that it is essential to give power to individuals, but we recognise that individuals do not operate in a vacuum, they are located within a complex structure of overlapping groups and interests – families, communities, workplace, social connections, etc. It is within these groupings that individual power is often most effectively exercised. We recognise the mutual dependence of individuals and believe that the actions of governments can help to build on the links between individuals, communities and governments.

Real protection of the environment must build on a strong relationship between individual and collective action. Degradation of the environment has clearly shown that the unguided actions of many individuals (the unfettered market) is unable to deliver the right outcome – that is, protection of the environment. It is now clear, even to those who have a simplistic belief in the benefits of free markets, that governments must take a lead, that governments must set standards and that governments must establish the right framework.

The power as much as the environmental awareness of individuals has been amply attested by the steady growth in the membership of campaigning organisations like Friends of the Earth and Greenpeace, by increased consumer demand for less environmentally damaging products, and by the huge leap in the vote for the Green Party in the 1989 elections to the European Parliament. This popular pressure has had a direct impact on politicians and decision makers. In Parliament, board rooms and council offices across the country the environment has suddenly arrived on the agenda, in many cases for the first time.

The surge in the Green vote during the European elections is of particular interest. It would be frivolous not to interpret it as in part a reflection of public concern with environmental issues, as well as a 'safe' way of making anti-Government protest. This was especially so because the European Parliament was commonly considered to be a talking shop with little power to enact policy that would affect people's daily lives. The Green Party's share of the vote in a general election will undoubtedly decline significantly, but politicians of every hue should have taken on board the message that much of the electorate now expects government policies to be fully informed by environmental considerations.

But this is not to fall into the politician's arrogance of believing that the impact of individual concern is confined to sending messages to government. If we look, for example, at the actions of early activists in organisations like Friends of the Earth, who 20 years ago were storing newspapers in garages for recycling, we can see that this kind of individual action fostered a broad shift in public attitudes, which was not passed down from council chambers or Parliament. Government, both local and national, has in fact only slowly responded to these shifting attitudes, whose prevalence has grown from the grass roots upwards. It took two decades for the government to adopt targets for recycling of domestic waste – and it will take a Labour government to meet, and exceed those targets – but the fact that policy was eventually adopted owes much to the tireless efforts of volunteer recyclers and the change in public, and eventually government, opinion they brought about.

Similarly, 'green consumerism' as yet owes nothing to government intervention. Preference for 'environmentally friendly' goods has been discovered, and effectively tapped, by the market system, and it would be foolish not to recognise the fact. Of course, that does not mean that the market place itself guarantees the truthfulness of manufacturers' claims, or that consumption of the green goods on offer is itself an environmental panacea. But demand from individuals has had considerable effect in changing the perceptions of some manufacturers and the range of products they make available, even if others have got no further than giving a green tint to their marketing strategies without any real improvement to products.

The other side of the coin is the power of the consumer boycott, now a well-tested and effective campaigning tool. Attacking companies directly through sales can bring more rapid changes in products than working indirectly through government. The CFC campaign is probably the best-known example. It had a direct effect on manufacturers of aerosols, who soon produced non-CFC alternatives (though not for refrigeration). The boycott also stimulated and then ran parallel with international governmental action in the form of the Montreal Protocol. This is closely comparable with the way that a long-standing boycott of

South African goods was used as the platform from which to lobby for the imposition of government sanctions.

An important development of the attempt to influence manufacturers through consumer preference and boycott is the pressure that can be brought to bear by organised groups of shareholders. This form of direct action is more advanced in the USA, where for instance shareholders in Exxon forced the company to adopt a strict environmental code of practice after the Valdez oil spill in Prince William Sound. Shareholders in the UK have used the same techniques, for example to put pressure on Fisons over the company's extraction of peat, and some environmental groups are now considering buying strategic share packages so as to gain access to shareholders' meetings, and argue the case for improvement to the company's environmental record. This is a perfectly legitimate and commendable campaigning innovation, which gives a novel and interesting twist to the notion of 'popular capitalism' as dreamt of by Thatcher and acolytes.

These are all ways in which the actions of individuals, both through the expressed preferences of 'market behaviour' and through the growth of campaigning organisations, have an important effect not just on government but on industry and on the general climate of public opinion – and the extent to which public opinion is won over clearly dictates the level of impact on government and industry.

At the same time, direct lobbying of government should not be underestimated. On the simplest and most individual level, many people probably underestimate the influence they personally can have as active citizens. If someone has a particular grievance, their elected representatives, at both local and national level, have a duty to take that concern on board. I have myself on many occasions, in common with my colleagues, taken up not only individual cases, but also broader issues of concern, because of a letter or surgery visit by one individual. Every letter to an MP, minister or government department has to be answered by someone. Even if the person writing the letter does not always get the reply they would like, they will know that their case has at least been made. And in fact, an MP's mailbag is not only an important yardstick of public opinion but can contain letters which put a genuinely new perspective on issues, setting out information or arguments in a way that challenges our pre-conceptions and obliges us to rethink our positions. Since taking on the environment portfolio I have received a great deal of correspondence drawing my attention to a broad spectrum of environmental issues, ranging from simple messages of support through expressions of frustration at the filth of city streets to detailed critiques of the British government's position on CFCs or carbon dioxide emissions. These letters display a real sense of what people care about and how they see the issues.

Ironically, organised letter-writing campaigns, where many people send the same letter or card about a particular issue, can in some senses dilute this individual power. While the sheer number of letters involved can have significant force, only one reply needs to be drafted, so the politician or government department only needs to think once about what to say. Separate letters making detailed points require a lot more thought.

Nonetheless, pressure brought to bear by individuals on the political process is often most effective when concerted and focused towards specific objectives. The individual efforts of conservationists to preserve wilderness areas and protect local flora and fauna, and the determination of individuals to retain access to the countryside through the monitoring of local footpaths and ancient rights of way, are best channelled through organisations such as the Royal Society for Protection of Birds, the Council for the Preservation of Rural England, and the Ramblers' Association. These groups can both sponsor local conservation campaigns directed towards public and council opinion and lobby national government directly for necessary changes in, for example, codes of practice governing agriculture and land use. Access to government and influence on policy through such organisations is an essential part of the democratic process, almost as much so as the casting of votes: indeed, it is an older established tradition, drawing on the rights established in Magna Charta to petition the crown. Moreover, whereas people only get the opportunity to use their vote once every few years, their voice can and should be heard throughout the lifetime of any elected body. This, in fact, is central to the kind of participative democracy we want to build on.

At local level, people joining together into single issue campaigns can also have a significant impact on the decisions of local authorities. Such groups often form to object to planning applications for new developments or to proposals for new roads. More recently we have seen the formation of significant local campaigns against planning applications to build incinerators in the North East and in East London. Developers can be forced to take the feeling of local people into account. Although the present system is too technocratic and not as responsive as it should be, and is too often bypassed by referral of decisions to the Secretary of State, it is clear that strong, organised local feeling can be very powerful, and could be more so.

There is a danger here: the NIMBY (Not In My Back Yard) syndrome. Most people would accept that we need, for instance, airports, but only the most avid plane spotters want to live next door to one. New developments will – understandably – always meet resistance from people who, even if they accept the need for the development to go ahead somewhere, would much rather it happened somewhere else. This certainly proved to be the case during the deliberations, spanning more than a decade, over the siting of London's third airport; and the same has been seen more recently over the routing of the high speed rail link to the Channel tunnel.

This illustrates the need for local environmental awareness to be underpinned and balanced by a broader perspective, but it also raises an important issue of equity. Generally speaking, the better off live in more pleasant surroundings, are quicker to spring to the defence of those surroundings, and are more vocal and influential in doing so. There is, of course, nothing at all wrong with people stating their case – indeed it is precisely this that we should encourage – but we must be very careful to make sure that all members of society have an equal opportunity to do so, and an equal opportunity to be heard. In this sense, the only way to prevent the NIMBY mentality from wielding undue influence is to make planning decisions strictly accountable, with greater consultative mechanisms and full involvement of all people whose surroundings will be affected. Of course, hard decisions will still have to be made, especially when choosing between rival sites for proposed developments. But we must be sure, if it is agreed in the first place that those developments really are necessary and desirable, that decisions are made on a 'level playing field', where individuals and communities have equal access to the decision-making process.

All of this is to acknowledge that individuals do, at least potentially, have an invaluable contribution to make to environmental protection, as campaigners, lobbyists, conservationists, environmental watchdogs or simply as concerned citizens who want to limit their impact on the environment through the use of less damaging products, from spraycans to motor cars with more efficient engines. The record of individual effort and involvement in all these areas is indeed impressive and heartening, especially considering the inbuilt disincentives to action.

For a perfectly understandable reaction to environmental issues, as presented in the media, would be a kind of despair that breeds apathy. On the one hand, the problems seem so daunting that it is hard to believe switching washing powders or installing a catalytic converter will make any difference. On the other hand, the debate is, inevitably, highly technical in nature, with many conflicting claims from different 'experts' and 'specialists', so it is hard to know what, or who, to believe. Do I, for instance, get rid of my old car and buy a new model with a catalytic converter – the environmental option urged by some – or is it more 'environmentally sound', as others claim, to keep my old car going for as long as I possibly can? And what about burning fuel to drive to the bottle bank, or taking old newspapers to be recycled when there is a glut in the market and they may end up in a landfill site anyway?

Despite such temptations to apathy, the evidence of public goodwill and environmental zeal is abundant. The challenge we as politicians face is to ensure that individuals and communities are able effectively to participate, both in the decision-making process and in the implementation of environmental policy. In other words, we must not merely acknowledge the role of individuals, but build on and enhance that role. And this can only happen if we ensure that individuals have a greater sense of their power, a greater sense of their ability to make changes. Individual empowerment is therefore the key to increasing participation, which will in turn feed back and enrich the democratic process.

Helping people to make informed decisions is in itself a crucial part of that concept of empowerment, for individual decision making is the central component of what we might call people's environmental behaviour.

My own instinct on environmental issues is invariably to think of my children. Like most women, I tried to do the 'right' things when pregnant. I read all the books and articles and, although blinded by over-information, did, I think, at least get the basics right: sensible eating, little alcohol, no smoking and some, if limited, exercise. I even changed to low-heeled shoes – which was quite an achievement for someone who had grown up longing for the day when she could have her first really high shoes.

I learnt how to breathe in labour, agonised over the temptation of an epidural, but had no qualms about the wisdom of breast feeding on demand. In other words I was a typical first-time mother in the 1980s and though I was an 'elderly prima gravida', I know that my contemporaries in labour were making their choices on the same basis – what is best for my baby?

The information about what is best in pregnancy, then as now, may have been conflicting, and may have moved in phases of what was fashionable, but at least it was sufficient to give women a basis upon which to make decisions. Yet although those decisions seemed big at the time, they are nothing like as difficult as some of the decisions to come later about what is safe for my child, and which often have to be made with virtually no information on which to base a judgement. What is in the drinking water? Is it safe to swim in the river or sea? How can I reduce the risks of my child developing asthma, which is aggravated by pollution? When is it safe to let my child travel alone? All mothers face these questions, yet we often feel we are having to make them in the dark.

Government must provide the framework to help people reach informed environmental decisions as individuals and consumers, and for making those decisions count in the way intended. The first step in this direction is to make information more freely available. In Chapter 5 I set out the full case for freedom of environmental information; here, one direct and practical way to provide this would be to introduce a statutory scheme of product labelling to give consumers a clear idea of the environmental impact of products they are buying, without having to rely on the competing, and often dubious, claims of rival companies who have recently begun to adopt 'greener than thou' marketing strategies.

Any such scheme would inevitably involve a complex process of balancing different considerations on the basis of the best possible scientific and technical advice, to give a 'cradle to grave' assessment of environmental impact: i.e. one that takes account of the whole life of the product, from extraction and use of any raw materials, through the expenditure of energy in manufacture and transport, the creation of any harmful byproducts, and finally to disposal. Of course, as in the case of advice to pregnant women, there will be conflicting theories about what is most ecologically desirable. This can already be seen, for example, in the debate between purveyors of steel and aluminium drinks cans, who argue, respectively, that much less energy is used to manufacture steel cans (although their economic value for recycling is very low) and that aluminium lends itself very well to recycling, because the price per ton is much higher (although producing it in the first place is both energy intensive and dependent upon often undesirable bauxite mining). But despite these difficulties, indeed, in a way, because of them – since individual consumers cannot all be expected to make their own investigations of the relative merits of, say, steel and aluminium – I do believe that government should take responsibility for guiding consumers in their choice, by requiring product packaging to carry some form of environmental assessment of the contents. Such an assessment would have to be made by a government-established but independent body, and the whole process should be transparent, operating in the context of full freedom of information so that the public can see for itself the basis on which assessments are made.

Product labelling highlights the sometimes contradictory need for information to be simple, clear and easily understood while at the same time being based on the most rigorous assessment of complex issues. Some might argue that a simple and reliable 'yes/no' – it is environmentally friendly or it isn't – would be the surest guide for consumers; but this would be the hardest for the experts to deliver without making very sweeping judgements. Recent experience in food labelling, with the requirement for full specification of contents and additives, does seem to suggest that the public is prepared to absorb quite sophisticated information:

many people, especially parents of children with allergic conditions, have become veritable dictionaries of what different 'E' numbers mean. Some food processors have responded to this trend positively, by giving more than the minimum required information. The Co-op, for example, has a 'consumer care' label on all its own-brand foodstuffs, giving a breakdown of the calorific value and nutritional content of the food.

A similar pattern can be expected if environmental information is made more widespread and specific. As consumers become increasingly familiar with environmental issues, they will feel better placed to make their own decisions about which products, materials or ingredients to avoid. In the same way that many mothers are now far more aware of specific additives in food to which their children might be allergic, environmentally aware shoppers will learn which are the damaging ingredients. Unfortunately, any comprehensive assessment of a product's total environmental impact would be considerably more complex than dietary information about foodstuffs. For this reason, a better approach might be to introduce an environmental 'seal of approval' (somewhat akin to the 'kite mark' for goods meeting certain design criteria) for products that can be recommended for their environmental virtues: composts that don't require peat, for example, and phosphate-free detergents. This would have the great advantage of simplicity, and ease of operation. Manufacturers who wanted to market their goods as 'green' would simply submit them for inspection; and consumers who wanted to buy less damaging goods would simply look out for the green seal. A more informative, but still simple method would be to give products a 'star rating' on a scale of one to five.

But whatever the details of the labelling scheme that is eventually adopted, this is a practical way in which government can take on the concerns of consumers, giving them the means to make effective choices which really do work in favour of environmental protection. Ideally, in this context, a labelling scheme should be taken on at EC level, but if progress is not rapid to improve existing proposals, our domestic government must give priority to establishing a national scheme.

There is, however, a more basic problem with green consumerism. Consumers can only choose from what is available to them, so they cannot force companies to go faster than they are pre-pared to, or ensure that absolute environmental standards are met. Companies will only go so far in trying to adopt green credentials. As soon as it looks as if there might be a cost attached, they will tend to lose interest – even if that cost could be recovered in other, reduced costs over a few years. And the responses of companies tend to be largely reactive: they will find out what their customers want and then try and supply it, but they do not in general like to act ahead of a trend, or take a principled stand.

Standard setting must therefore be a function of government. Were government to adopt strict environmental standards and targets, industry would move much faster in developing the technology to ensure that their products met those standards. As ICI complained to the Environment Select Committee in 1988, without clear guidance companies are left in a 'commercial vacuum'; and no company is prepared to take unilateral action which may put it at a commercial disadvantage.

In Chapters 6 and 7 I discuss the role of environmental standards for manufactured goods in redirecting industry and the economy towards sustainability. Here, I want to make the point that requiring manufacturers to meet certain, basic standards is actually a way of reflecting and reinforcing general public concern, and has direct relevance to consumer rights issues. We expect to be protected from goods that damage us personally (with the ignominious exception of tobacco). We expect additives to food and cosmetics to be monitored and controlled with an eye to our safety. We expect manufacturers of furniture and electrical goods to meet certain safety standards, so that the new kettle won't blow up in our faces or set light to the new sofa, suffocating us with poisonous fumes. We expect our children to be protected from dangerous toys. Are we not therefore entitled to expect that the goods we buy should meet environmental standards, so that they don't contribute to the impoverishment of our children's future?

Here too, then, government has an important and positive role to play in protecting the rights and enhancing the choices of individuals. This, indeed, is yet another inversion of Conservative free-market reasoning: for by intervening more, to guarantee that standards are met, we can, and should, improve the environmental quality of goods that are offered in the market, and improve the quality of choice that individuals have.

People, of course, are not just consumers, and it is not just as shoppers that we need more information! This need should be met by every local council having a shop-front office, situated in the middle of the high street, to advise and inform people about local environmental issues. People should be able to walk in and obtain information and advice or register complaints on a whole range of environmental questions. If the council's environmental health department was linked to regional and national networks they could tap into databases to obtain information about industrial emissions – what exactly is coming out of that factory pipe or chimney? Does it meet pollution standards and exactly how dangerous is it?

Ordinary people could readily find out what is in their drinking water and the river, what the local air quality is like, what materials are taken to local waste disposal sites and whether landfills are leaching toxic materials into groundwater or producing methane which might cause a local hazard. In nearly all cases access to such knowledge would help put fears at rest and help people to understand how their local environment is managed and regulated. But if there was real cause for concern, imagine how much more powerful and effective the voice of local residents would be if they had facts and figures literally at their fingertips via a simple-to-use computer system.

This is not a pipedream. Already, in parts of the United States and Europe, pollution control and monitoring data collected by industry is transmitted by computer links to regulatory agencies on an hourly or daily basis. In some cases, corporations involved in hazardous waste disposal even arrange for computer links to local community centres, such as colleges and schools, so that the safe operation of incinerators can be checked at any time of the day or night.

Clearly, increased access to information would markedly improve environmental management and accountability. And although I am not claiming that this would solve every problem overnight, I do believe that increasing the amount of meaningful information which is available to the public is one of the most effective ways of truly empowering ordinary people and increasing pressure for environmental improvements where these are needed.

The provision of information also enables individuals to become directly involved in questions of local environmental management and, just as importantly, makes them feel that their involvement is valuable. Involvement of local people is a powerful means of enhancing the monitoring of environmental quality. Pollution enforcement officers – however many we have – will never be able to catch every fly-tipper, every water polluter and every individual who breaks smoke control regulations. So the inclusion of ordinary people in towns and villages up and down the country in the day to day activity of protecting and improving the state of their own environment could make a vast difference to the effectiveness of regulatory bodies.

Shop-front environmental offices would, then, be a simple and very valuable way to start informing and involving people directly in the management of their local environment. But when it comes to action by the community and the expression of the will of the community, it is to local government that we must turn. For this is really what local government must be – the institutional expression of the community, literally the community acting for itself. Of course local government is not perfect, and no doubt often fails to live up to this ideal, especially in the climate of reduced democracy, centralised control and financial strangulation with which local authorities have had to contend throughout the 1980s.

It is at local level that the majority of environmental problems which affect us on a daily basis are tackled. Local government is responsible for a range of activities which impact directly on the environment: housing, land use planning, transport (including light urban rail and bus systems, road repairs, traffic and even airports), and economic development. Councils also look after collection, disposal and management of domestic and commercial wastes, open spaces, parks, recreation, conservation, street cleaning, environmental health and food safety, trading standards and education (including adult education).

So, much of the environment we experience is managed by local government. This has long been the case. Indeed, when local and municipal government first started to assume real powers in the mid-late nineteenth century, problems of environmental and public health were of major and immediate importance – in particular the need to introduce functional infrastructures of water supply, sewerage and public housing. Even today, in the absence of any real coherence in environmental decision making at a national level, local authorities are already providing a multipurpose function in environmental management at local and sub-regional (county council) levels. But to what extent is this management amenable to local participation and how do local authorities ensure that the best decisions are taken, not just for the environment, but also in the interests of the whole local community?

I have already described the beneficial impact which more accessible local environmental advice centres could have in providing and receiving information. But whilst there is obviously a need to collect far more information than we do now, and present it in an understandable form, there is considerable scope for local authorities to take immediate steps to make the information they do have more readily available.

Some authorities are already moving in this direction – many, including my own local authority, Kirklees, have appointed environmental advisers and units in addition to their more conventional environmental health and planning departments in order to increase the flow of environmental information to the community. Some, for example Watford, have also taken steps to make their environmental health department more accessible to the public. But because of budgetary constraints, these authorities are very much in the minority, and most still depend on highly motivated officers in conventional departments to deal with the new wave of environmental (especially pollution control) issues.

As a result, few local authorities are able to make sufficient information available on questions like street cleaning, waste recycling and other issues of direct relevance to the quality of the locality. But there are opportunities which could be seized. Some authorities, such as York, now publish 'customer contracts' and these could be extended to cover a range of environmental issues – with information about levels of provision and service targets. Authorities could make more information available at various stages of decision making – on planning applications for instance. Where 'environmental impact statements' are required for new developments, authorities could ensure much greater community involvement. Councils will only retain public support for difficult decisions if the public are closely involved from the early stages.

Once informed, the next step is for individuals to be involved. This will usually require the introduction of systems which enable ordinary people to adopt good environmental behaviour in a convenient and not too costly manner. Household waste reduction and recycling is the most obvious example.

Although waste separation and recycling via kerbside collection is in its infancy in this country (unlike 'drop-off' schemes such as bottle and paper banks which have been in place for some years), in areas where pilot schemes have been set up, for example in Leeds, the effort put in by the local council has been rewarded by a high rate of public participation. This cooperative effort, involving the council, the community and waste recycling businesses, is a perfect example of different forces coming together to achieve a mutually desired and environmentally beneficial end.

Inevitably, such schemes are far more likely to achieve early success in neighbourhoods where residents already have a high level of civic interest and already feel involved to some extent in community objectives. People in leafy suburbs who are asked to put out their recyclable paper, aluminium, glass and plastics in a brightly coloured bin once per week may be relatively easy to motivate. They already have a 'nice' environment, and so will perhaps be more receptive to appeals to protect it than less privileged people in inner cities. But I believe that in all local authority areas (and not just the well-to-do ones) there is scope to harness people's natural instinct not to waste, provided there is a concerted commitment from the local authority.

It is more difficult to organise household sorting and separate collections of refuse in densely populated areas like high rise housing estates because of the more complex logistics of organising and collecting the waste. But I have no doubt that with a little creativity, for example the placing of well-designed bank systems in convenient roadside locations, most reluctance to participate on the part of local people can be overcome. This may be supplemented by public education initiatives, and indeed by schools themselves.

Many types of local environmental initiative can be enhanced by the application of a little 'lateral thinking'. For instance, tree planting projects in Islington were found to be far more effective when local children actually planted and named their own tree. Once local children had a stake in their survival, they made sure 'their' trees were protected and tended properly.

Despite the logistic and social difficulties, it is vital that 'problem areas' are not omitted from involvement in local authority environmental schemes. This would merely serve to heighten the alienation many people already feel about their environment and about 'white middle class environmentalism'. Local authority mechanisms for environmental improvement must embrace the whole community. This may require the use of informal networks, a decision to operate environmental awareness-raising schemes in several languages and, of course, a sensitivity to any cultural differences which might affect the success of the scheme.

Given the opportunity, pressure for environmental improvement will come from the community. This pressure will be reinforced and made more effective by maximising public participation. But it is important that local officers and elected representatives do not wait for this to occur spontaneously. It is vital that pressure from the grass roots is matched by leadership from the top. Councillors and officers of an authority have a responsibility to inform themselves about environmental initiatives elsewhere, to share expertise gained through links with other authorities and outside organisations and experts, and to introduce new and innovative methods of solving problems. Recent initiatives by the local authority associations have shown what is possible, given commitment at the local level (ACC/ADC/AMC, 1990; Barwise, 1991). There is now a wealth of experience to be shared and learned from. In the end, authorities must have the will and the means to put new ideas into practice. They should also set themselves ambitious targets for recycling which maximise local business opportunities. In parts of the USA, counties and municipalities have adopted targets above 50 per cent for domestic waste recycling and maintain active information clearing houses to match waste recycling streams with potential business users. Public participation rates in kerbside recycling schemes exceed all expectations.

In the same way that an effective and innovative local

authority needs a general power of competence to take action in the interests of the community, perhaps local government should also have a general duty to protect and enhance the environment. Such a duty could be interpreted very broadly and might need to be linked to a strict list of functions, but it would leave considerable leeway for local discretion and enable local authorities to act more effectively on behalf of the community to protect and enhance the local environment. If such a duty were, for example, applied to planning decisions, it would tilt the argument in favour of appropriate conservation and increase the power of the local community in relation to developers.

Much of what I have said about the contribution that individuals can make relies on the development of links and on working together. This can perhaps be understood as part of a general need to build a sense of community so that people feel that they are empowered to take responsibilities as well as to exercise rights. A 'sense of community' sounds, like motherhood and apple pie, the kind of ideal which all politicians, regardless of persuasion, would endorse. But paying lip service to the ideal is meaningless without a commitment to build and motivate the community. Individuals must feel respected before they will respect either those in authority or their neighbours. This will only happen if government takes action to end the serious inequalities and disparities which are so glaringly obvious in many of our communities – both urban and rural.

I have focused on the need for greater participation from ordinary people in the decisions that are taken at local level. However, it has to be recognised that despite the apparent readiness of local communities to respond to environmental initiatives, enhancing participation and improving the efficiency of environmental decision making is not always easy – problems remain, both of a social and a structural nature.

In the social dimension, the experience of the equal opportunities movement provides valuable lessons. Many efforts failed in the past because of apathy. People felt they were too busy or that these matters were not their responsibility – the politicians are there to make the decisions. This is a symptom of a more general malaise. Many people have simply lost faith in democracy. As the activities of government locally and nationally become more sophisticated and technocratic, so they seem more distant to ordinary people. The old communities have been lost and new ways of living tend to be more dispersed and reliant on the use of independent communication systems which have in turn discouraged the development of new forms of community. Certainly this is reflected in the very poor level of voting in local elections.

I believe that this may change again in time, but it is a fact that in areas where turnout was 50–60 per cent in elections for the old, small urban district councils, turnout in polls for the replacement authorities is now around 30–40 per cent. There is an increasing sense of loss – people are beginning to miss what they have lost in family and community terms and are rediscovering the importance of maintaining strong links with local networks. With the increased emphasis on care in the community, this is especially true for older and vulnerable people living alone and increasingly dependent on these networks for support.

The need for a coherent social community is particularly pressing in matters concerning the local environment. For when it comes to improvement of the quality of the local environment, positive action must be community based – it cannot simply be imposed by governmental authorities seeking to delegate standards from above. From action on waste reduction and recycling to local transport schemes; from conservation projects and the creation of litter-free green spaces to making streets safer for children – all these depend on positive participation and support from the community.

The environmental agenda therefore gives us a real opportunity to begin rebuilding a sense of community. For on almost no other issue is public concern so apparent and so in tune with what politicians in local and national government want to achieve. We have the chance to create positive action out of the enthusiasm and commitment which is undoubtedly there, if latent in many cases, in the community.

This opportunity has been squandered by successive Conservative administrations. There are many examples which may be cited to illustrate their lack of interest and even hostility towards local government and the social and environmental services it provides. The abolition of the very community-oriented and green-inclined Greater London Council was perhaps the most vindictive.

Of the structural obstacles to effective and democratically

accountable environmental management, perhaps the most obvious is the lack of a strategic tier of decision making which can balance the needs of local communities with regional and national priorities. I shall return to the question of planning inquiries and environmental impact assessments later in the book, but it is worth pointing out here that there are some questions which simply cannot be resolved satisfactorily (still less democratically) by the present planning system.

In my view, there is now an irrefutable case for regional government in the United Kingdom; and such a system could greatly improve the way in which planning decisions are reached. Regional government would be better equipped to make decisions about, for example, the siting of sewage works or hazardous waste incinerators, which are always likely to stimulate local objections but where a decision must nonetheless be made. Moreover, I would like to see regional government responsible for a wide range of strategic resources and services which are best managed on a sub-national level but which are not amenable to control by local and municipal authorities.

The arguments for regionalisation go beyond the management issues – there is a wider question of principle concerning the need to devolve powers to the most appropriate level for democratic control. This principle ('subsidiarity' in modern Euro-parlance) enshrines the common sense idea that, in decision making as in all else, you don't use a sledgehammer to crack a nut: decisions should, in the interests of effectiveness and democracy, be taken at a level which is as close as possible to the people who will be affected, and at a level which is most appropriate to the issue. It is fine for a parish council to decide on where to site a bench and to advise on building materials to be used locally, but district councils are the appropriate bodies to set up and run environmental information centres. At a higher level, European directives should apply to large combustion plants, as the pollution caused by them knows no national boundaries.

There is no doubt that strategic industries such as water, waste disposal and transport are best planned at a regional level. This applies whether the industries concerned are in the public or the private sector. In addition, there are key land resources, such as forests and national parks, which are best safeguarded within regional plans for tourism and economic development. When regional government comes to Britain it is logical, therefore, that it should control planning and be responsible for other matters, such as a regional waste strategy with impact on the quality of life and the regional environment. From this will flow a number of sensible outcomes. It is worthwhile considering a specific example to illustrate the concept as it applies to environmental management.

A region which wished to promote heavy industry, chemical manufacturing and so on would have to ensure that all wastes arising from such industries were treated and disposed of safely within the region (thereby observing the principle that everyone should be responsible for their own wastes and deal with them as close to the point of their production as possible). If required, a region would propose a new site (or sites) for particular wastes and then be responsible for piloting the development through the inquiry system. At this point, regulatory agencies at national, regional and local level could decide their position based on the environmental case which was being made, and if necessary oppose the development if it was likely to contravene environmental quality objectives or principles of integrated pollution control, defined on a national basis.

Even if the regulatory agencies chose not to oppose the development because there was no threat to human health and it was the best environmental option for a region, they could nevertheless provide local communities who feared the development on environmental grounds with expert assistance and grants for representation at inquiries. This is precisely the approach adopted by the US Environmental Protection Agency in cases where it has an interest but where an objection is best carried forward by the community or an environmental organisation. Where new amenities, such as sewage works, have to be built and cannot be sited away from residential areas, affected people should be entitled to direct compensation or a rebate on locally levied taxes.

By these means communities would be assured of support and fair treatment, and the region would have a mechanism of obtaining the best environmental decision without having to override local objections by relying on the less than democratic stroke of the Secretary of State's pen.

An intriguing question remains about what might be the shape of regional government in Britain. Scotland and Wales form natural social and geographic regions. But what about England; where should the boundaries be drawn? Most importantly, what are the natural social and geographic affiliations which would enable the economic and ecological responsibilities of the regions to be discharged most effectively?

Undoubtedly, major responsibilities of UK regions would be economic development, planning, and the management of natural resources and wastes. Hence, they would be central to any effective move towards sustainable development in Britain. They should not be regulatory, in the sense of implementing and enforcing standards for, say, the quality of water or air; this must be done by a national agency (albeit with a decentralised administrative structure). I shall return to the question of regulation later in the book, but we cannot have different regions setting different standards in order to lure industry to their area.

From an environmental perspective, land and water would be the most important basic resources managed by the regions. These generate natural boundaries in the form of mountains, hills and river systems – which are sometimes referred to as 'catchments' in geographic terms. Interestingly, since the beginning of time, communities have developed along river basins and have been drawn together within the natural physical barriers which surround river systems. So there is often, but not invariably, a social coherence between towns and communities united by natural geographic regions, which could form the basis of the boundaries for a regional tier of government.

There is another, practical aspect to consider. Industrialised societies produce a lot of waste: domestic refuse, industrial wastes (solid, liquid and airborne), construction wastes and agricultural wastes. Whether these wastes are disposed of on land or whether they are discharged directly into water courses, the most sensitive receiving environment for leachates from landfill sites, for industrial effluents and for farm run-off is the water environment: groundwater, lakes, rivers and streams. We have a good deal of rainfall in this country, and if we are not careful, all wastes (however carefully stored) may leach and eventually affect our water resources. Thus, since regional governments should also plan waste policy, it makes sense for them to take into account the principal environmental impact these wastes are likely to create.

Hence a case can be made, on both social and environmental grounds, for the future boundaries of regional government to take into account geographical, or what I would prefer to call the 'ecological', factors. An ecological basis for regional government makes a lot of sense from a resource management perspective, and I firmly believe this would actually work out in practice. One could start out with the present boundaries of the ten regional water companies, which are based on river basins. These boundaries should not be viewed as sacrosanct, as there are a few anomalies and obvious difficulties, but let us see if local and national governments and their agencies could work with structures of this size and shape.

I have little doubt that ecologically defined regional government will be adopted at some time in the future, as an invaluable step to enhance environmental management and protection. But to achieve rapid and lasting change at local level, we will also need to promote change in individual behaviour. For older generations this may require a fundamental shift in how people relate to the world around them. Changing attitudes on this scale depends on a good deal of promotional activity and creativity on the part of local authorities, to make it convenient and simple for individuals to take more personal responsibility for their local (and indeed global) environment. But for the younger generation, it is a simpler task – most children are usually very receptive to a culture of waste avoidance and care for the planet.

In my experience, the enthusiasm and interest of young children for learning about the environment and then taking practical steps to do their bit is quite remarkable. My own children are both of primary school age and I, in common with many other mothers, never cease to be amazed by the knowledge they have about the world's environment – from what causes depletion of the ozone layer to how we might save the rain forests. I was quite serious when I recently warned Labour's prospective parliamentary candidates about doing their home-work before going into schools to talk about the environment and simply to admit it if they did not know an answer, because the chances are that the children will know more about some of these issues than the candidates! I am not saying that all youngsters are perfectly informed, but it is often the case that the young set the pace for awareness, so that when a family goes shopping it may well be the children who take a lead in demanding recycled paper and so forth.

We now take for granted that when an appeal is launched by a television programme like *Blue Peter*, the number of bottle tops, stamps or old coins which children send in will invariably exceed the target. Yet if this early enthusiasm is not focused and maintained by putting specific environmental issues into a wider context (ideally at school), there is a great danger that by the time these children arrive at their early teens, it will be lost.

Young children are open minded – keen to adopt new ideas and ways of doing things. And the nature of learning at primary level makes it fairly easy for teachers to include environmental themes in broad-based projects. Indeed, from the many good projects which I have seen in schools, teachers have been very quick to adopt environmental themes – perhaps partly as a result of the availability of attractive teaching materials from environmental organisations and from industry.

We must ensure that this early enthusiasm is not dampened when children move on to secondary school, simply because learning is then constrained within subject-based examination syllabuses. Unfortunately, the environment is not an issue which fits easily into strict curricula. Indeed, trying to break it down into subjects can easily detract from the most important concept of all, which is that environmental concerns touch every area of life and so are relevant to all subjects. Environmental studies can appear as a branch of geography. But when secondary school pupils learn about atomic physics, about economics, about biological systems and about the industrial synthesis of organic chemicals, they should also be taught about nuclear waste, about environmental cost–benefit analysis, about population dynamics and about techniques of clean production.

Yet the immense pressures on teachers and children to meet examination-based criteria may well mean that the environmental components, which should be incorporated in all subjects, become add-on extras which are considered after everything else. With the new trend towards more prescriptive curricula in the UK (where standard assessment targets are laid down on a mandatory basis for all subjects), this tendency may be exacerbated.

This presents us with a dilemma. Within the present secondary school system, it might be counter-productive to try and allocate specific time periods for environmental education. This could imply that the environment is a subject which pupils could think about for one or two hours once a week but which otherwise bears no relation to the subjects they spend the rest of their time learning. With a prescriptive system, if a subject is not specifically identified it may well not be covered; but if it is prescribed, it has to be separated out.

To resolve this problem may mean that we have to modify further the examination system, though not in the way prescribed by Conservative Ministers who have attacked the whole concept of coursework assessment and integrated studies in favour of a narrow and rigid examination approach. By narrowing education down we would fail to recognise the maturity of the children we are trying to educate and effectively prevent them from using their own judgement about the impact of their actions and decisions on the society and world they live in.

Many of the skills and attitudes which are so important for a positive approach to environmental problems relate to other areas of life as well. They are to do with citizenship, democracy and participation – about having a stake in society and the environment in which we live. To enable pupils to learn and think about these issues demands a broader approach to education. It requires that due emphasis is also placed by the school qualification system on extra-curricular environmental activities, for example helping with insulating the homes of pensioners, conserving local habitats or setting up recycling schemes. The values and skills which these activities generate cannot be gained through narrow examination-driven learning – they are part of a wider 'education for life', elements of which help to create an active, responsible and participative citizenry.

It is also important to recognise social factors which come into play as children turn into young adults. Early enthusiasm for environmental projects and an environment friendly lifestyle can give way to other influences. Adolescence brings new pressures, and things that seemed important at 8, 9 or 10 can be quickly forgotten. Suddenly other things take priority – the right pair of trainers, the latest record, keeping up with friends on the latest trend. The pressures to consume and to conform are considerable. Young and enthusiastic recyclers can be transformed into adolescent cynics who, even if they still think there are problems, don't see what they can do or even that it is that relevant to their lives.

Clearly there are psychological barriers to be overcome. We need to create a system of environmental education in which issues remain relevant and interesting, and which influences the way people behave. The purpose of environmental education must be to help change behaviour – to prepare the next generation for the changes they will have to make to accommodate the need for environmental sustainability in all aspects of their lives. We should perhaps talk of education for, rather than about, the environment.

To be meaningful, education for the environment must be relevant to pupils' own experiences, and therefore to their own environment. Many children in urban areas suffer from a degraded quality of life as a result of factors which we would not necessarily categorise as environmental in the strictly 'green' sense. Apart from pollution, dirt and litter, for many people the problems of a poor environment stem from poverty, poor housing, bad planning and unemployment – all the recognised causes of deprivation. Environmental education should recognise these links, otherwise those children are likely to grow into adults who do not see the relevance of the conventional 'green agenda' to their own lives.

The local environment provides the richest teaching material and it also creates the possibility of the children themselves taking positive action towards improvement. The 70,000 hectares of school grounds in Britain are an excellent starting point in which ecological studies can be made, experiments conducted and environmental enhancement projects set up. One recent publication (Young, 1991) notes a variety of such initiatives, including landscaping, the planting of broadleaved copses, and the creation, in a South Wales comprehensive, of ponds, meadows and an area of bog. School buildings themselves can also be used as case studies in a variety of cross-curricular exercises. What are the school's heating requirements and how are these met; what energy source is used; how could efficiency be improved?

The environment surrounding the school – whether rural or urban, leafy or covered in tarmac – also lends itself to exploration and study. The 'nature walk' need not be confined to village primary schools: what lies outside the school gate is the environment for the pupils, and the more they are encouraged to investigate and think about it, the more environmentally aware they will become. In urban areas, traffic flow can be monitored from a variety of different criteria: what is the proportion of cars to buses; how many cars are carrying only one person; are vehicles observing the speed limit? As well as transport, schools could study local industry, rivers, population, retail distribution: all aspects, indeed, of their own environment and local environmental impact. This kind of practical study is not only worthwhile in its own right, to build up a critical appreciation of the local environment and ways it could be improved, but would unquestionably be the most effective way of putting into context issues such as acid rain and climatic change. Many teachers have discovered their own ways of tapping these potential learning opportunities to good effect.

Too often the impression of environmental issues seems to be of lots of different problems each requiring its own expensive solution – that environmental protection is about stopping people doing things. Environmental protection can become terribly negative. Rather than simply teaching children and young adults about the global problems, we must show them that something can be done at a local level and that they as individuals can make a difference. This is the great value of focusing attention on the immediate environment. Everyone will be able to think of improvements they would like to see, and study of particular issues such as transport or water pollution will bring greater understanding of the practical problems and realistic possibilities.

It is, of course, not just children who need to be educated. Given a general increase in environmental monitoring, regulation, audits and impact assessments, there will be a growing need for professional skills that are at present drawn somewhat haphazardly from people of widely differing backgrounds. We need therefore to look at tertiary education and vocational training. But designing and improving courses for environmental health officers, pollution inspectors or environmental auditors, for instance, is only a part of the answer: in fact, concentrating on that alone would run against the spirit of much that I have said, for it would suggest reliance on a new breed of 'experts'. Although there will indeed be a need for people with particular, environmental expertise, an even more fundamental need is for environmental understanding to be built into the vocational training of all occupations so that people in all sectors of the workforce develop a sensitivity to the environmental impact of their actions in both their working and private lives. The logic of this is perfectly simple: all of us are implicated in 'environmental problems'; so only if we all become aware of the environmental dimension of our lives can we all become part of the solution.

Vocational training should therefore have an environmental component irrespective of occupation, from degrees in business or farm management to City and Guilds certificates in construction skills or catering. Public and private sector employers should be encouraged to give staff day or block release for in-service training to heighten awareness of environmental issues, in tandem with measures to improve the company's environmental performance.

Local councils themselves can give a lead here, by ensuring that education for the environment is extended throughout their own workforce and by improving involvement so that council workers share the council's overall objectives and participate actively in reaching them. From street cleaners to social workers, from copy typists to canteen workers, every member of staff makes a contribution to the environmental impact of a local authority and every member of staff should feel they have a stake in reducing that impact. The pioneering work of Labour local authorities like Kirklees (at metropolitan level), Lancashire (at county level) and Basildon (at district level) in initiating formal environmental audits provides an excellent indication of how a commitment to environmental excellence can be formalised and extended throughout a local authority's operations.

At the heart of all the proposals laid out in this chapter lies a concern not just for the environment but for democracy too. Environmental problems are, by their very nature, social problems, because they are experienced not just by individuals but by communities and, in the broadest cases, by the whole of society. But in addressing the problems, we must also address the issue of who is to decide what must be done. If we believe in democracy, we must see that the burden, and opportunity, of decision should lie with each and every one of us. The case for making individuals count, by providing more information, education and the means for participation, is, therefore, wholly irrefutable.

Chapter 4

Public perception and setting the agenda

It seems rather obvious that human well-being depends on the quality of the immediate environment. If individuals are housed properly; if they have access to reliable transport; if they have adequate heat and lighting; if people have a plentiful supply of safe and wholesome food and water; if their immediate surroundings are pleasant, with open spaces free of litter, noise and fumes; if all of those factors which go to make up a decent local environment are guaranteed, then on a physical and material level, people can claim a reasonable quality of life.

However, our well-being is not solely dependent on physical and material factors. There are also a number of very important psychological, social and spiritual issues to consider in defining how humans relate to their environment. This is recognised in the World Health Organization's *European Charter on Environment and Health* (1989), which states that:

> Good health and well being require a clean and harmonious environment in which physical, psychological, social and aesthetic factors are all given their due importance. The environment should be regarded as a resource for improving living conditions and increasing well being.

The second of these two statements would make some environmentalists wince, implying as it does a somewhat human-centred philosophy. But, there are many socialists who would endorse the validity of a perspective which has a pedigree stretching back to Hippocrates. There is certainly enough suffering in the world today to justify dealing with immediate humanitarian priorities with at least as much urgency as those of the environment. In fact,

one of the principal distinctions between socialist environmentalism and the 'deep green' or 'ecocentric' perspective is that
socialists see human freedom and well-being as equal moral imperatives to those of protecting the environment and preserving
natural resources. The deep greens are inclined to play the ecological card as a 'trump', whereas socialists see humankind and
the environment as being mutually interdependent – different
sides of the same ethical ace, to continue the card-playing
metaphor.

The socialist argument applies as much to the subsistence
farmer of sub-Saharan Africa as it does to the urban slum-dweller
of Lima or Liverpool. People who lack security for themselves
and their families and who have no expectation of a decent
quality of life do not make the best stewards of their local
environment. Nor do they become excessively concerned about
more remote problems (in time or space) such as global warming,
the depletion of the ozone layer or reductions in biodiversity in
the tropics.

But we must of course recognise that human well-being is not
guaranteed only by material conditions and physical safety. It is
important therefore to consider what people actually think about
their environment. What most worries them, and to what do they
attach most importance? These questions are also important in
drawing up a democratic programme of environmental protection, because we must take full account of public perception, the
way this affects confidence in official bodies and the extent to
which it determines participation (or lack of participation) in the
choice of environmental strategies.

There are now a wide variety of information sources available
to the interested reader in the developed world which catalogue
the multitude of environmental problems which we face. (See
Bibliography.) In addition to these specific sources (most of
which, although accessible and well written, will not be
assimilated by the population at large) there is a constant stream
of television and radio programmes and newspaper articles for
the general public to digest. The question may be posed as to how
much this deluge of information is increasing the level of real
understanding of environmental issues within British society; or,
conversely, to what extent people may now be approaching a
state of complete overload and confusion. This issue is important

because public support for radical environmental policies will only be forthcoming if both awareness and concern can be sustained at relatively high levels.

Internationally, how far and how deep does an appreciation of the dangers of environmental degradation really extend? A radical 'Third World' perspective on environment and development is being forged by politicians, professionals and specialists from less developed countries. But what is the level of understanding and capacity for action in those who cannot read a newspaper, receive a radio or television broadcast or even vote for a change in government policy? In this last category we may place the majority of the inhabitants of the planet.

There is evidence to suggest that despite the plethora of information sources available to ordinary people in developed countries like the UK, the depth of genuine understanding which permeates society remains rather low. Much of this evidence derives from opinion polling and psychological surveys of the general public. However, it is important to recognise that as a single, simple entity, 'the general public' does not actually exist. Moreover, some polls may be distorted by the way that questions are put, and so may mislead, or disguise as much as they reveal. Nevertheless, it is worth examining in some detail what we do know about people's environmental awareness and concern, starting with a brief clarification of who actually constitutes 'the public'.

Individual members of society belong to families, social and community groups, occupational groups, trade unions, political parties, environmental organisations, amenity societies and so on. Each of these groups has its own set of allegiances, shared values and communications networks. Individuals and groups may overlap in their memberships and affiliations, and these in turn may be permanent or temporary. Thus, when discussing the relationship of 'the public' or 'society' to 'the environment' or indeed individual 'environmental issues' (a different concept), it is important to bear in mind the complexity of the structures which are being considered.

Opinion polls certainly reflect a cross-section of public attitudes, but they are necessarily limited in their analysis, and seldom provide any detail of underlying factors which inform ethical judgements. For example, in a 1990 MORI poll for the

Worldwide Fund for Nature (WWF), it was found that 65 per cent of Conservative voters and 55 per cent of Labour voters wanted to see government action to restrict timber imports from countries which did not manage their rain forests in a sustainable manner. In contrast, 43 per cent of Labour voters and only 38 per cent of Conservative voters wanted to see government money going to help the countries concerned. How should this be interpreted? Which set of voters exhibited the greatest concern for rain forests? It could be said that Labour voters were less inclined to restrict timber imports because of the likely social and economic costs to the exporting countries. Alternatively (or additionally) Conservatives may be generally less sympathetic to the concept of development aid being used for protecting rain forests.

In research conducted by the University of Essex, respondents were asked to consider two statements beginning with the proposition 'No more nuclear plants should be built . . .'. One statement concluded 'even if this means shortages of energy with possible effects on industry and employment', the other ended 'until the problem of the storage of nuclear waste is solved'. Only 23 per cent of respondents agreed with the first version compared with 66 per cent who concurred with the second (Brown and White, 1987). Does this mean that nearly one-quarter, or nearly two-thirds of the population wished to see the government phase out nuclear energy? Clearly the answer depends completely on the context and perceived outcome of such a policy.

Social attitudes surveys conducted for the Department of the Environment (1989) showed an increase in apparent level of public concern between 1986 and 1989 on nearly every one of the issues covered. The principal exception to this was a decline in the percentage of people who claimed to be 'very worried' about radioactive waste, following the peak of concern immediately post-Chernobyl. Polling of this sort does little to shed light on public priorities which in turn may bear no relationship to the magnitude of the environmental threats being considered.

There is no strictly logical reason why concern about oil spills should have almost doubled from 27 to 53 per cent between 1986 and 1989 whilst concern about radioactive waste declined from 62 to 58 per cent. The mathematically measured risks of pollution by oil and radioactive waste transport and disposal remained largely unchanged over the period in question. It may be relevant to note that the pictures used by the DoE's polling organisation to depict oil pollution were different in the 1986 and 1989 surveys. But probably of much greater significance is that, in March 1989, the tanker *Exxon Valdez* deposited 10 million barrels of crude oil in Prince William Sound, Alaska. Images from this disaster featured in news media for weeks and undoubtedly contributed to heightened perception of the dangers of oil pollution which were in turn reflected in the results of the 1989 survey.

Similarly, there is no obvious explanation for the fact that sewage contamination of bathing beaches should be considered very worrying by 59 per cent compared with only 44 per cent of respondents who were very worried about the greenhouse effect in 1989. The increased risks of gastro-enteritis and minor infections from bathing in sewage-polluted seawater are certainly important, and they are immediate risks, but in scientific or environmental terms they hardly compare with the potentially cataclysmic effects of global warming.

According to the BMA (1990) there are three main psychological factors which influence how people assess environmental risks. One is personal experience. This includes vicarious experience: what people read, see or hear from the news media. People who have a direct or indirect experience of environmental hazards are likely to be more cautious and aware of possible risks. The second determinant is the 'dread factor' whereby the fear of large, catastrophic incidents impinges on individual beliefs and behaviour. Third, and possibly most important, is the ability or inability of individuals and communities to influence events and minimise their exposure to hazards. It is worth examining a few examples of how each of these factors may affect public perception of environmental problems.

In the case of direct or indirect personal experience, the proverb 'once bitten, twice shy' seems to apply fairly generally. Some of the most salient examples involve water. It is a medium to which everyone is exposed on a daily basis for drinking, cooking and washing. Water also provides an important leisure amenity, be it at the seaside or in a local canal or gravel pit. It enters the realm of daily personal experience for people at home, at work and at play.

There are few parents who have never visited the seaside with their children. Swimming and paddling in the sea are recreational activities which are strongly associated with many people's idea of a traditional British summer holiday. However, although they and their families may never have experienced illness directly as a result, there has been sufficient discussion of the problem of sewage pollution of bathing resorts in the British media to make this seem a significant and immediate environmental hazard to many holiday-makers. Parents interviewed on the beach by television reporters now readily volunteer that they would not allow their children to swim in the sea. Doubtless their concerns are exacerbated by aesthetic and cultural factors which evoke disgust at the very prospect of bathing in dilute sewage effluent; but there is also a clear and heightened sense of personal or family risk.

Another example of the effects of personal experience is the number of people who now prefer to consume only bottled drinking water. In Britain, consumption of bottled waters rose from just a few million litres per annum in the mid 1970s to more than 100 million ten years later. The number and diversity of bottled waters on the shelves of every supermarket in the country bear striking witness to this phenomenon. Interestingly, it is often asserted that whereas the French have always drunk bottled water for what it contains, the British have only recently started drinking it for what it doesn't contain! Sales of simple household water filters have soared in similar fashion. Research by the Robens Institute found that, in 1988, 44 per cent of people expressed fears for their health and 27 per cent of respondents claimed never to drink water direct from their domestic taps.

Again, widespread publicity based on the revelation that 11 million people in Britain lived in water supply areas which failed to meet European quality standards coincided with the personal experience of many individuals who found the water from their tap unpalatable in any case. One recent correspondent of mine was advised by her water company to add a drop or two of lemon juice to her tap water to improve its taste!

Unpalatability in fact has almost nothing to do with risks to health or failures to meet chemical and microbiological quality standards. Moreover there is obviously a need for caution with regard to the claims of bottled water companies as the *Which? Report* of April 1991 pointed out. Yet the bottled water companies have been quick to coin slogans which emphasise the naturalness and safety of their products: 'The Water That Cares' and 'You Are What You Drink' being among the most obvious examples.

For many people, direct experience of drinking water quality problems is more than a matter of not liking the taste. In recent years, major incidents of drinking water contamination have involved industrial contamination of the River Dee by phenol in January 1984, the accidental addition of 20 tonnes of aluminium sulphate to the water supply of Camelford in July 1988, and the waterborne outbreaks of *Cryptosporidium* (a parasite) in Oxford and Swindon (1988–9) and Hull (1989–90). In 1990, no fewer than 79 incidents of chemical or microbiological contamination were notified to the UK Drinking Water Inspectorate (DoE, 1991). Over the last ten years, incidents of contamination of public drinking water supplies have involved millions of consumers. In many cases customers have been advised either not to drink the water, or to boil it before consumption. People tend not to forget such incidents, however short lived they may be. The combination of direct experience and unfavourable publicity goes a long way in explaining the current disenchantment of the British public with domestic tap water.

Direct experience of pollution and environmental degradation is commonplace in the decaying urban environments of many of Britain's inner cities. There can be few more miserable human experiences than growing up in overcrowded, noisy, cold, insanitary and damp housing, subject to constant airborne pollution from smoke and fumes and with no access to open, unlittered green spaces. Such conditions are prevalent in the sprawling urban squalor of many cities in less developed countries and the effect of this type of environment on human health and well-being is well known (Harpham *et al.*, 1988). Indeed the World Health Organization's 'Healthy Cities' initiative and the United Nation's 'Habitat' programme recognise that these effects are not limited to less developed countries and make explicit the universal linkage between the quality of urban environments and human health and well-being.

However, far from being banished in the nineteenth century, these conditions persist as daily reality for millions of people living in late twentieth century Britain. Ailments such as gastro-enteritis, asthma and even tuberculosis increased in the

1980s as a direct result of increases in poverty and decreases in environmental quality. Outbreaks of dysentery in Bradford and Hull in the early 1980s were linked with breakdowns in the sanitary infrastructure in Yorkshire at the time (Johnson, 1985). In Grangetown, Cleveland, a community of 4,000 lives in the shadow of an ICI petrochemical complex and a British Steel works. The community has twice the national average of asthma sufferers, up to three times the rates of death from lung cancer and life expectancy ten years less than normal (Ghazi, 1990).

Increased incidence of asthma and tuberculosis has been directly linked to damp housing conditions, but these are not the only hazards associated with our built environment. It is now known that many materials and systems incorporated into modern buildings also create adverse impacts on human health due to a variety of physical, chemical, microbiological and psychological effects. Furnishings, lighting, ventilation and wall-coverings have been implicated in a number of office-related disorders sometimes described collectively as 'sick building syndrome'.

In such a complex area, where so many physical, social and psychological factors interact, it is not easy to quantify the extent to which direct personal experience of environmental quality affects individual beliefs and behaviour. However, the results of the surveys undertaken for the Department of the Environment showed that the percentage of people who were 'very worried' about fumes and smoke from factories increased from 26 to 34 per cent between 1986 and 1989; there was an even greater increase in concern about traffic fumes (from 23 to 33 per cent). The number of people who were very worried about litter and rubbish increased from 30 to 33 per cent, and noise from 10 to 13 per cent. According to statistics collected by the Institution of Environmental Health Officers, the number of incidents of rat sightings and complaints increased by about 20 per cent between 1988 and 1989. Complaints about noise increased from 24,472 in 1979 to 59,132 in 1987–88.

Interestingly, in the 1989 DoE survey, 61 per cent of people thought that the primary responsibility for the decay of inner cities rested with central government, compared with only 33 per cent who thought local councils should be held responsible. On such issues as the fouling of streets by dogs and litter, people clearly assigned more of the blame to local councils. But on traffic exhaust fumes nearly ten times more people blamed government than blamed local councils (58 versus 6 per cent).

Clearly there are few environmental impacts as direct and unpleasant as litter-strewn and dog-fouled streets, unhealthy, uninhabitable housing, and industrial complexes belching grit and smoke. There is no doubt that when people are given the choice, they prefer to live in houses with gardens rather than in high rise flats with noisy corridors and non-functional lift systems. Given the choice, people prefer to walk clean streets and breathe clean air. Sadly, for many people there are no choices. For the many hundreds of millions of people who live in urban squalor around the globe, lack of an alternative is the single consistent theme in their relationship with the environment.

This reality, and this real experience of environmental degradation, is inevitably reflected in people's perceptions of environmental problems and priorities. But what of environmental threats that are unrelated to personal experience? For we do not have to experience environmental deterioration personally for the possibility of disaster to impinge directly on our beliefs. As I mentioned in Chapter 1, the potential social and environmental impacts of nuclear war significantly influenced the attitudes of an entire generation towards military technology and its political control. Yet the direct impacts of nuclear warfare have only been experienced by a very small number of people alive today (and no-one of my age or younger).

Several films have attempted to portray what the run-up and aftermath of full scale nuclear war might feel like. Indeed, the most memorable have devoted particular attention to the feelings and behaviour of ordinary people; *On the Beach, Threads,* and the cartoon *When the Wind Blows* come to mind. The reality of a full scale nuclear holocaust remains (thankfully) outside the realm of human experience. Nevertheless, as a source of fear and dread it retains its potency, partly because of the unpredictability of the outcome. Also, graphic representations of disasters tend to remain in people's minds, leading to an overestimation of the frequency or likelihood of a disaster occurring. It does not matter that newsreel from Hiroshima and Nagasaki is now very old, nor that films like *Threads* are fictional. The images remain powerful.

The 'dread factor' that arises here can also be provoked by the prospects of such potentially devastating incidents as the explosion of chemical plants and accidents associated with the generation of nuclear power. Throughout the second half of the twentieth century people have been coming to terms with the fact that technology, and especially the application of new industrial technologies, can sometimes go catastrophically wrong. The disasters of Seveso (Italy, 1976) and Bhopal (India, 1984) resulted in environmental and human health impacts of enormous magnitude. In the case of Seveso, the Icmesa chemical plant released a cloud of trichlorophenol (TCP) and dioxin which put at risk the health of a population of 30,000. Ninety women had pregnancies terminated in order to avoid the risk of malformations. In Bhopal, the release of 40 tonnes of methyl isocyanate gas, possibly contaminated with phosgene, resulted in at least 2,000 deaths, and tens of thousands suffered physical and emotional distress in the aftermath of the incident.

Although not on the same scale, Britain has experienced significant incidents involving chemical plants in Bolsover (1968) and Flixborough (1974). The net effect of these incidents, and many more like them around the world, has been to heighten general public awareness and increase suspicions concerning the reliability and safety of systems operated by the chemical industry. And for those living in the immediate vicinity of existing or planned plants, the fear of disaster can become quite oppressive.

The dread of nuclear accidents can be equally powerful. It can now be seen that the idea of 'atoms for peace' was a myth. Civil nuclear power was developed for entirely the wrong reasons in the 1940s and early 1950s: specifically, for the production of weapons-grade plutonium. It was sustained by a combination of vested interest and official deception between the mid 1950s and mid 1970s; and it was not until the 1980s that it was accepted as an economic liability. But it is the accident record of the industry and the resulting threats to human and environmental health which is leading to the demise of nuclear power. Fears which could be dismissed as groundless in the 1960s and 1970s could hardly be denied following the near disaster of Three Mile Island in March 1979 and the subsequent catastrophe of Chernobyl in April 1986.

The problem of nuclear waste management has long been

recognised by the industry and its critics. But throughout the 1980s, the arguments against nuclear power focused increasingly on the real fear of disaster. Anti-nuclear campaigners used cartoons and photomontages which drew obvious associations: gravestones or skeletal sheep against a nuclear industry backdrop, a reactor with nuclear warheads protruding from the side. A poster and leaflet produced by the Socialist Environment and Resources Association depicted a reactor next to Nelson's column and posed the question: 'If nuclear reactors are so safe, why don't you see any in central London?' The industry responded with a multi-million pound advertising campaign including videos, leaflets and posters featuring (among other things) idyllic farm scenes with nuclear reactors in the background. Meanwhile, British Nuclear Fuels opened a £5.7 million visitors' centre at Sellafield.

According to *British Social Attitudes* reports (Jowell *et al.*, 1987), in the two years immediately preceding Chernobyl, the number of people who thought nuclear power posed 'very serious' risks actually declined (from 56 to 44 per cent for Conservative voters, from 70 to 61 per cent for Alliance voters, and from 79 to 75 per cent for Labour voters). However, since 1986 public opinion polls have suggested a sustained lack of public enthusiasm for nuclear power. Post-Chernobyl, support for the construction of more nuclear power stations declined for all voter groups: from 39 to 18 per cent for Conservatives, from 25 to 11 per cent for Alliance supporters, and from 10 to only 4 per cent for Labour supporters. The percentage of people who agreed with the proposition that nuclear power creates 'very' or 'quite serious' risks for the future increased from 75 per cent before Chernobyl to 77 per cent in the immediate aftermath and 79 per cent in the following weeks.

These observations undoubtedly reflect the widespread mistrust that technologies like nuclear power now inspire. They also show that fear can be a powerful determinant in how people relate to specific environmental threats, regardless of the protestations of governments and the industries concerned.

The third major influence on the public perception of environmental risk is the degree of control which individuals and their social groupings can exert over developments which affect their environment. In an ideal world, people would trust the integrity of institutions of local and national government to ensure the effective regulation and protection of the environment. In this ideal world private corporations would also behave in an honourable way, respecting the rights of people and the planet and avoiding the imposition of risks on the community simply to make money.

However, the level of trust placed in public figures to tell the truth about the impacts of science and technology is remarkably low. In a 1985 MORI poll, only 28 per cent of respondents said that they trusted scientists working for major private companies and 12 per cent trusted civil servants. Government ministers scored lowest with a mere 11 per cent. In contrast, 31 per cent trusted environmental groups and 67 per cent trusted doctors. In a society which vests so much responsibility in private and state institutions, these figures do not bode well for the effectiveness of environmental decision making.

Psychological tests have shown that risk acceptability decreases by at least a thousandfold when exposure to the hazard is outside the control of the individual or the community. An individual may be quite content to accept the annual risk of death of one in 8,000 for the self-imposed hazard of using the roads. Yet the same individual may be less inclined to accept the one in 10 million risk associated with radiation releases from power stations or pesticide contamination of drinking water.

These last are exactly the kind of risk levels which are determined as 'acceptable' by government committees adjudicating on behalf of the rest of society. They may be calculated for exposures to radiation or toxic chemicals in foods, air, soil and drinking water. Such committees are invariably serviced by civil servants, and often include representatives of commercial and industrial interests. Sometimes, government does not even bother to convene a committee. In setting out guidance for the water industry and the Drinking Water Inspectorate on pesticide levels in drinking water, the Department of the Environment literally invented 'advisory values' for 35 compounds at levels ranging between two times (for hexachlorobenzene) and 10,000 times (for DDT and heptachlor), the maximum acceptable concentration of the EC drinking water directive.

When it came to selecting a site for dumping low level nuclear waste in the mid 1980s, it was the process of political expediency and behind-the-scenes dealing which caused greatest anger. The perceived unfairness in the site selection process exacerbated local fears and prompted storms of protest. Thus, the government company NIREX experienced considerable difficulty in establishing any public support whatsoever in the four candidate locations: Elstow, Killinghome, Bradwell and Fulbeck. All were in the constituencies of Conservative MPs. And perhaps the greatest admission of the political nature of the selection process came when, just six weeks before the 1987 general election, all plans were abandoned.

If the process by which risks are calculated and standards set is not transparent and accountable, there is a real danger that the public will not find them acceptable, even though those risks may be extremely small for the individual. If a risk is perceived as being imposed from outside, by agencies which do not command public trust, and for reasons which are not necessarily clear, there is a strong likelihood that people will object. This sense of mistrust is as applicable to proposals to build a nuclear waste repository as it is for the setting of standards for drinking water quality, and is a major feature of what has become known as the NIMBY (Not In My Back Yard) syndrome, already discussed in Chapter 3, where individuals and communities reject any new development out of hand.

This phenomenon is now so pronounced that those industries and developers who are forced to do battle in public inquiries and impact assessments have expressed their frustration by coining an alternative, more perjorative acronym to describe public resistance: BANANA – 'build absolutely nothing anywhere near anyone'. An American variation on the theme is NOPE – 'not on planet earth'.

If we accept that public perceptions and beliefs are influenced by a number of factors – personal experience, dread and degree of control – it is relatively easy to see how priorities (as defined by opinion polls) may be influenced by circumstances. Similarly, it is very simple to imagine how opinions may be subject to bias by the deployment of techniques of education, awareness raising or unashamed propaganda for or against a particular aspect of environmental concern. There are some powerful psychological forces at play, and they may be manipulated by all sides of the argument in order to sustain essentially value-laden positions.

Some environmental organisations are especially adept at

raising issues based on an overriding belief in the justice and urgency of their cause. They pressurise and embarrass governments (and indeed individual ministers) as well as those who are directly responsible for the creation or management of environmental problems. There is no doubt that their tactics, partly driven by the demands of television and the press, have the effect of constantly setting and changing the environmental agenda, sometimes to the chagrin of those who have to react and respond to the issues once they are raised. In the UK, two of the most effective organisations in this respect are Greenpeace and Friends of the Earth (FoE). Largely as a result of constant appearances in the media, both organisations saw massive increases in their memberships throughout the 1980s.

In that period Greenpeace specialised in peaceful but confrontational tactics, meeting polluters head on both nationally and internationally. Daring and illegal stunts were commonplace: climbing up chimney stacks to protest against acid rain, blocking nuclear and industrial effluent pipelines, steering small inflatable craft alongside nuclear waste dumping vessels, and intervening physically to protect whales, dolphins and seals. This approach resulted in tragedy on one occasion when the French secret service destroyed the Greenpeace flagship *Rainbow Warrior* in a crude and cynical operation to protect the French nuclear weapons testing programme. A Greenpeace photographer was killed in the incident.

In this country at least, Friends of the Earth have tended to avoid methods involving personal risk. However, they have never been averse to exposing problems in a confrontational manner. They have exhorted members to bring pressure on the European Commission to initiate court action over failures to meet EC standards for bathing water quality. FoE also initiated a very costly legal challenge to the British government's interpretation of the EC drinking water directive. At local level FoE groups have often been in the forefront of campaigns against pollution problems and regularly participate in pickets and protests that attract the attention of local news media.

Apart from a few smaller organisations and locally based protest groups with particular battles to fight (such as Sons of Neptune, who fought a high profile campaign against Yorkshire Water in the Scarborough area), the rest of the environmental and conservation movement has tended to eschew the headline-grabbing techniques of Greenpeace and Friends of the Earth. Bodies like the Council for the Protection of Rural England, the Worldwide Fund for Nature and the Royal Society for the Protection of Birds believe that there is merit in working with existing structures and procedures of government and, in the case of WWF, make a virtue of collaboration with industry.

These organisations are not usually afraid to challenge government in public when they think it appropriate (indeed, WWF joined Greenpeace and Friends of the Earth in throwing down a 'green gauntlet' to the government in 1988), but they do try to maintain good relations with all parties (political, environmental and industrial). Like Greenpeace and FoE, they produce coherent, well-argued briefs, they lobby and they educate; they do not, on the whole, confront. The only real exception to this is in the formalised adversarial context of public inquiries and legal interactions. Otherwise, they tend to operate with a philosophy of cooperation rather than confrontation, trying not to put government on the defensive and to get results by building up relationships. Nevertheless, the more headline-grabbing tactics of Greenpeace and FoE tend, by definition, to command more public attention and so can lead to rapid changes in the political and environmental agenda.

But whichever their chosen tactics, there is no doubt that both the established organisations and the more campaigning, confrontational environmental groups have been increasingly successful in raising the issues in recent years, forcing government ministers into a reactive but accommodating stance. Governments in Europe and North America can no longer afford to dismiss environmentalists; they must make all the right noises in order to appear reasonable and concerned even if no action is then forthcoming. In Britain, early evidence of this was provided in Mrs Thatcher's 1988 Royal Society speech. The fact that she believed she must make an 'environmental speech' was a sign of the new profile environmental issues had; but having made the speech she then dumped the issues. The British government's 1990 publication This Common Inheritance was a tangible manifestation of this: lots of words and pictures, beautifully produced, and almost completely devoid of political commitment. The net result has been no significant improvement on the environmental front.

Accommodation and soothing words have not been restricted to governments. Throughout the 1980s, agriculture and industry, having been cast as the principal villains, exhibited a very defensive response to the rise of environmentalism. This reaction is now giving way to a more sophisticated approach: sponsorship deals, awards for environmental improvements; a little more time spent on green claims and self-promotion and less time spent on the megaphone.

The problem all of this creates for modern socialists is that we are left with a distinct feeling of unease that although the debates are valid and exciting, there is still a considerable lack of real popular involvement. Battles are being fought out between powerful lobby groups with only brief and occasional interventions from government. Sadly, at least in Britain, the political interventions which really count seem to come exclusively from the European Community, with all the problems of democratic accountability which this involves. EC directives on bathing and drinking water quality are a case in point. The British government has dragged its feet in the enforcement of European standards to the extent that, for instance, six years after the deadline for complying with the drinking water directive, the UK had failed to meet requirements in no fewer than 4,536 separate cases. Writing to the Conservative government in October 1991, EC Commission member Carlos Ripa de Meana complained of 'a disturbing pattern of lack of stringency in enforcing compliance with the Directive'. Translated into non-bureaucratic English, this means that the British government has been ignoring its responsibilities: worse, it has been actively undermining the EC directive by granting water companies exemptions from meeting required standards, without any evidence that those standards could not be met using known purification techniques.

Yet although they are invariably welcome, EC environmental directives do not appear to be initiated and developed by any transparently democratic process so much as a system of lobbying and counter-lobbying of the Commission. Even the European Parliament appears to be played off against the member states by an increasingly influential and technocratic secretariat. This is not meant to denigrate the commitment and foresightedness of the individuals concerned, it is just to sound a note of caution that my constituents (like every other EC citizen) are not actually involved in the process.

Meanwhile, in Britain there is a burgeoning 'environmental industry' which in the absence of a lead from government has produced rather more commentary than action. Also (especially galling for an opposition politician), the Great British Media remain far more intrigued by the content of a public disagreement between lobby groups and the government than they are about the announcement of a policy which would actually solve the problem. Even some of the environmental correspondents seem more interested in a good scandal than in a proper analysis of how things could be put right by greater emphasis on values of equity, freedom and concern for future generations (in fairness to them, this is probably because their editors would see this as boring or 'political').

In short, many of the current environmental debates are not particularly democratic. And unless we are careful, they may become less democratic and less participatory in the future. Basic, political principles should determine much, and people don't need to be environmental experts to participate in debates on these; but, inevitably, at least some of the issues will become more technical, more complex, less tangible and therefore less accessible to the great majority of people who do not happen to be scientists or active members of environmental organisations. This tendency is also reflected in the changing nature of the main campaigning groups.

In recent years, there has been a significant increase in the level of professionalism of all environmental organisations. The early passion and naivety of organisations like Greenpeace has been replaced by a more sober and less cavalier approach, with specialist staff who are not just well meaning but well qualified too. In the UK, Friends of the Earth have restructured with a view to improving management systems and communications with the grass roots. Token salaries and sleeping bags on the floor have been replaced by company pension schemes, committee meetings and merchandising. For both organisations, mass membership has provided the resources for ensuring detailed background research, higher quality office accommodation, sophisticated communications systems, links with the European Commission, in fact all of the trappings of modern multinational operations. The passion and the hard work remain, but the content and the packaging have changed significantly.

None of this is said by way of criticism or nostalgia for the days of innocence; there is no doubt that Greenpeace and Friends of the Earth were very effective throughout the 1980s and they are now reaping the rewards of the public support this generated. But, it is in the nature of organisational development that at some point creative anarchy must defer to the need for efficiency and the introduction of systems. This is precisely the point which has now been reached by our two main campaigning groups. It will be interesting to see how they develop and whether all their present supporters stay the course. This may depend on the way in which they respond to those political developments which they have helped to precipitate.

The more established groups have also become increasingly professional in their approach, adopting conventional political lobbying strategies when previously the 'old boys' network and a quick telephone call would have sufficed. In their own way, issues of planning, conservation and environmental law are becoming every bit as technical as nuclear waste disposal, global warming and water pollution. Thus, the individuals who work on matters of public policy for bodies such as CPRE, WWF and the RSPB are invariably both articulate and expert in their field. However, most of their members (including the retired colonels) probably have absolutely no concept of the complexity of the matters which are now discussed by their full time officers in environmental conferences and in the cafeteria and Committee rooms of the House of Commons.

There is indeed a real danger that in a field of intensifying technical debate, the public will become increasingly sidelined. Public inquiries provide the perfect demonstration of this. These events are no longer public interactions at all; they comprise series of expert depositions by well-organised interest groups, with the developer invariably mobilising resources several orders of magnitude greater than the objectors. Experts may provide assistance to local communities, but because there is never enough money, their input is usually very limited (Clark, 1991). And in any case the really heavy guns are signed up well in advance by the principal protagonists. Sometimes the local community is fortunate and will find its case bolstered by a local authority or an environmental organisation prepared to commission the required advocacy and expertise. Sometimes they are on their own, armed only with their fears, beliefs and a desire to exert some control over their immediate environment.

Another example of this sidelining effect is the process of environmental impact assessment. Environmental statements are now required under EC law for a number of types of development. In this country there is a plethora of commercial companies able to undertake the analyses on behalf of developers. It is usual for these companies to incorporate consideration of a wide range of potential impacts, for example those which might affect local land use, air and water quality, noise levels, ecology and economy. All of these may be predicted (usually with some degree of certainty) and subsequently measured after the development has been concluded for the purpose of validating the predictions. However, other factors which impinge on the psychological and social effects on the local population, e.g. aesthetics, are almost impossible to quantify and therefore rarely figure very prominently in environmental statements. Yet these are precisely the areas where local people could actually contribute to an otherwise arcane and complex exercise in technical juggling.

It is also noteworthy that the government has in fact failed in its duties to carry out proper environmental impact assessments of large building projects. This came to light in October 1991, when it was discovered that the European Commission had called for new assessments of several British developments because of the lack of seriousness and rigour in those which had been carried out. This is not just further evidence of the government's half-heartedness in environmental matters (and the problems of accountability this presents, when there is a conflict between EC directives and the approach of domestic government), it is an indictment of any method of impact assessment which neglects to involve local people. In one case – the East London River Crossing – the existing assessment had failed to mention that there were five schools, including special schools, for children with learning difficulties and respiratory disease within the corridor of the proposed crossing. Information of this kind could only have been left out as a result of a wilful failure to consult the community to be affected: the original assessments, in other words, were shoddy in part because they were undemocratic in nature.

The evidence of public opinion polling cited earlier also seems to indicate that there is a good deal of scope for better public understanding and involvement in environmental issues. The present situation is confused to say the least. How otherwise could the British people be more concerned about sewage on bathing beaches than global warming or ozone depletion? How else could 7 per cent of respondents in one opinion poll state their belief that nuclear power stations are fuelled by Radox (a brand of bubble bath)?

There is no suggestion that environmental organisations, the media and the planning process are contributing directly to public confusion, but one can only wonder what the effect is of a constant diet of environmental scandal, public disagreement between experts, predictions of disaster and counter-assertions that 'all is well' being taken as justification for inertia by government departments. At the very least, it is a recipe for mistrust and disillusion.

There is a theory – the 'worry beads theory' – which argues that the public only has a limited capacity for exercising personal concern on issues as diverse as fear of unemployment or ill health, mortgage repayments, heating bills, what to feed the children for dinner, and so on. Thus, for many people, and especially those who are concerned but confused about the issues, it is a very logical move to subcontract the need to worry about the environment to an environmental organisation. People who would otherwise feel oppressed by the need to do something tangible are thus relieved of their responsibility by sending an annual subscription to a professional organisation which will act on their behalf.

It is a little like buying organic vegetables in the supermarket; they may be wizened and expensive, but the minor sacrifice involved in the purchase is more than compensated by the feeling of well-being which is induced in those who would otherwise worry about the amount of pesticides entering the environment.

Thus we arrive at the ultimate paradox. The more inactive and procrastinating the government, the more scandals emerge in the media. The greater the level of background media noise on the environment, the greater the apparent need for individuals to respond. However, because of the increasing number and complexity of issues, there is less likelihood that individuals will feel able to cope and a greater probability that they will simply rely on environmental organisations to think and act on their behalf. Hence there is a danger that the environmental organisations (as organisations, not as people) may even develop a curious dependency on governments which have an appalling environmental record. (In other fields, the symbiosis between 'disaster professionals' and disasters and between development workers and underdevelopment is a well recognised phenomenon.)

And the scope for strange symbioses does not end there. There are obvious conflicts of interest which arise with commercial sponsorship of environmental causes by oil and chemical companies. This trend will increase as the message of corporate social responsibility permeates British board rooms. There is something bizarre about a car company sponsoring international conferences on environment and development. It is almost as incredible as a chemical company which seeks to imply in television advertisements that it is solving problems of environmental degradation and world hunger by selling fertilisers and pesticides.

It is also worth examining some of the more oblique connections and potential symbioses which may emerge. Take, for example, the privatisation of monopoly public utilities. There were some environmentalists who welcomed electricity privatisation because they believed it would spell the end of nuclear power generation (because private capital would not underwrite the risks involved). Of course, this ignored the politics behind privatisation – the Government was not going to risk any such failure. In reality environmental considerations went to the wall and we now have an electricity industry which advertises consumption not conservation and thus actively promotes waste. Meanwhile, the nuclear industry has been kept in public ownership.

Similar quirks of environmentalism may emerge in the gas and water industries of the future. During the process of water privatisation (1985–89), opposition politicians, trade unions and environmental organisations were as one in drawing attention to the environmental dangers inherent in the British government's policy on water. Underinvestment was putting at risk the environment, public health and the jobs of water workers; selling the industry to private enterprise was not the answer. Eventually we secured considerable concessions: the creation of the National Rivers Authority as a separate regulatory agency, certain 'guarantees' on standards (subsequently eroded in regulations) and the imposition of a number of duties on water companies – which may eventually be tested in the courts – to care for habitats and wildlife.

In the 12 months prior to sell-off, the coalition of anti-privatisation forces launched a series of campaigns on bathing water quality, drinking water quality, ownership of catchment areas and freedom of access to land. Problems of drinking water quality came to the fore: nitrates, lead, aluminium, pesticides, polycyclic aromatic hydrocarbons – all received coverage and left their mark on the increasingly tattered reputation of the water industry. The effect of this broad-based and democratic campaign (it united 60–70 per cent public antagonism to water privatisation with conventional parliamentary and extra-parliamentary opposition) was to wring from the government and the water industry long overdue spending commitments totalling £28 billion.

But what now? We have a profit-led industry whose main prospects for growth lie in diversification and the installation of plants which they can justify to the financial regulator as being essential for meeting new environmental standards. The 'cost pass through' provisions of the 1989 UK Water Act permit the water industry to lay the bill for any new standards directly on the doormats of consumers, almost regardless of cost or benefit. I have called this the 'consumer pays principle'. Thus it is entirely conceivable that the water industry of the 1990s will view the demands of the environmental lobby with rather less anxiety than it did in the 1980s. Those demands may themselves be good for business. The private water companies' attitude may well become one of 'if you want it, you can have it – it increases profits and the consumer has no alternative but to pay'.

These examples are not intended to impugn the motives of all those in the industry nor indeed those environmental organisations who occasionally find themselves in bed with profit-led, commercial interests. Both are legitimate groups with valid points of view. However, it should be crystal clear by now that just as market-led economies adapted and evolved to a certain, but insufficient extent, to embrace social and humanitarian demands in the twentieth century, so they will evolve and adapt to embrace environmentalism in the next few decades. The explosion of green consumerism illustrates that this process is already well underway. Moreover, when the interests of business and environmental organisations coincide, there may be substantial scope for distortion of priorities for public and private investment.

From all this, it is apparent that at the present time, the vast majority of people are insufficiently in touch with the issues to participate effectively in the agenda-setting process. Ordinary citizens relate to their environment in a confused, semi-detached way. A number rely on environmental organisations to set the pace, but these groups would themselves accept that they are unable to balance priorities and achieve the kind of dramatic progress which is now required at a political level. They are not impartial, have no democratic mandate, and despite the growth in their memberships, few have truly participatory mechanisms for policy making.

Unless another force intervenes to protect the quality of life of present and future generations there will be no progress. Governments of the right may be forced into reacting to the latest scandal but they will never show leadership on environmental matters; they are not interested in equity and have no ideological basis for ensuring reductions in the present rates of resource depletion. This is why modern, democratic socialist intervention is so necessary to guarantee genuine participation, to untangle the increasingly impenetrable debates between lobby groups, and to bring fresh values to decisions concerning the protection and enhancement of life on earth.

We must begin with measures to draw public perception closer to reality. We can only really tackle issues such as global warming if the public fully appreciates the need for decisive action, and rates the problem as being of grave concern. This calls for a major and sustained programme of awareness raising; and this is something that must not be left to the pressure groups but that government must take on, through public service announcements in the media and through information delivered to the workplace and to every household in the country. We need, in short, to talk honestly and directly to people from all communities and walks of life about the problems; because people from all communities and walks of life must participate in the solutions. If we adopt measures radical enough to make any impact on greenhouse gas emissions, through energy taxes or a more public-oriented transport strategy, for instance, then the effects will be felt by everyone; so clearly we must explain the need for what we propose, and obtain a mandate for doing it.

In the same spirit of open and decisive action, we must eliminate all unacceptable risks by strict regulation. If government is seen to be setting and enforcing standards – based on a precautionary approach rather than snatching figures out of the air or selecting 'acceptable levels' of contaminants that won't interfere too much with present practice – then public confidence will be restored and much will be done to reduce the worry and fear that many people experience when thinking about environmental issues.

Chapter 5

Knowledge, information and freedom

It is now crystal clear that the present system of government in Britain is ill-equipped to meet the current range of environmental challenges, let alone any future (as yet unknown) crises which may emerge. Through lack of scientific knowledge, lack of effective systems for education and information exchange, and lack of appropriate institutional arrangements we risk a major break-down in our capacity to protect future generations from environmental catastrophe.

Because, as we have seen, the majority of environmental issues and their solutions are becoming increasingly technically complex, many individuals (including politicians) are reluctant to address them. This is a grave mistake. While accepting the complexities, politicians have a responsibility to educate both themselves and the public, and then put in place the mechanisms and systems which will allow society to break through the inertia and uncertainty which paralyses current environmental decision making.

Three key elements of effective environmental management for which governments and politicians have a special responsibility are: scientific research (acquisition of knowledge), freedom of information (dissemination of knowledge), and the promotion of improvements (application of knowledge). In the latter case, government has to get its own house in order and reform or re-invigorate those institutions which are presently failing to respond to environmental imperatives. This chapter is particularly concerned with these three aspects of policy. All need urgent reform in order to establish both the social and environmental accountability of government.

Government also has a number of other, more general responsibilities. Perhaps the most important of these involve creating the right educational and economic frameworks for promoting environmental improvements, as discussed in detail in Chapters 3 and 7. But here I shall examine the key areas of knowledge acquisition, dissemination and application, starting with the vexed question of science and technology.

There are few people who would deny the importance of science and technology in shaping the nature and quality of their existence. Recent generations have seen scientific advances and their application in everyday life as almost invariably beneficial. The introduction of machines and new technologies may have displaced a number of jobs in certain (often unhealthy) industries, e.g. milling, mining and chemical manufacturing. But on the whole, Western civilisation has adopted scientific innovation in a largely uncritical way. Labour-saving gadgets in the home, the availability of rapid systems of communication and transportation, and plentiful supplies of heat and light are features of modern, affluent society which few would wish to see curtailed. Life-saving drugs and relatively inexpensive supplies of good quality food and water are available to the majority of people in Europe and North America – something which would have been unthinkable just four or five generations ago.

Despite the well-understood connection between warfare and technological advance, socialists have traditionally perceived science and technology as liberating and progressive forces. There have always been concerns about the impact of new technologies on jobs, especially where they lead to de-skilling or redundancy. But on the whole, advances have been welcomed. As noted in Chapter 1, this attitude was particularly fundamental to Marxism, but in recent times not many in British politics embraced the concept quite so wholeheartedly and enthusiastically as Harold Wilson. The Atlee government had been responsible for setting up the Scientific Civil Service as a means of enhancing the effectiveness of British science, but Wilson was to place science and technology at the very centre of his personal electoral appeal.

Wilson's election manifesto of 1964 laid the foundations for a real burst of 'technocentrism' in British government, providing a springboard for projects as diverse as supersonic aircraft (the Concorde project) and the acceleration of nuclear power. The opening paragraphs of the manifesto promised 'A New Britain – mobilising the resources of technology under a national plan; harnessing our national wealth in brains, our genius for scientific invention and medical discovery'. This phenomenon was common to social democratic governments throughout Europe. In West Germany, systems analysts and planners were responsible for decisions on housing and transport which had far more to do with technocratic values than democratic ones (Stretton, 1976).

In Britain, the technocentric approach was symbolised by the massive expansion of science and technology in the higher education sector (including the inception of The Open University), and the creation of a new Ministry of Technology. Under Tony Benn (1966–70) Mintech became a 'super ministry . . . incarnating Wilson's faith in the white heat of science-based industries as the motor of expansion' (Hennessy, 1990).

The wider labour movement was happy to share Wilson's vision. One of the most successful and flourishing trade unions of the late 1960s and 1970s was the Association of Scientific, Technical and Managerial Staffs (now merged with TASS to form the Manufacturing, Science and Finance Union). Formed in 1968 following the merger of smaller bodies – the Association of Supervisory Staffs, Executives and Technicians (ASSET) and the Association of Scientific Workers – ASTMS grew from 70,000 members at its inception to 400,000 ten years later. This was due in large part to its image as a high tech union with modern leadership, as well as its vigorous policy of recruitment in newer industries.

Although a relatively small union, ASSET had ridden the crest of the technological wave in the early 1960s, being especially successful in the civil aviation sector and maintaining an influential parliamentary committee under the chairmanship of Ian Mikardo MP. According to Jenkins (1990), it was in this committee that ideas such as The Open University were first proposed (by Harold Wilson himself) and from which flowed the original impetus for governmental controls on some technological developments, including the inception of the Genetic Manipulation Advisory Group.

Under Wilson's sponsorship Benn and Jenkins represented the apotheosis of Labour's technocentrism during its period of government in 1964–70. Benn was enthusiastic about nuclear power. In a speech in January 1968 he claimed 'we shall soon have a reorganised Nuclear Power Industry to convert our un-rivalled lead in atomic technology into a powerful export effort' (Benn, 1974). And in a meeting with Soviet Premier Kosygin in May 1969, Benn raised the subject of fast reactors:

> I told him how very advanced we were in this field and how we had generated more nuclear power than the rest of the world put together, including the USA: our fast reactor would be on-stream in 1970/71. He was evidently impressed.
>
> (Benn, 1986.)

Even as late as February 1970, in a speech to the Manchester Technology Association Benn asserted 'the generation of electricity by nuclear or hydro power is immensely cleaner than any other method of providing light and heat'.

It is interesting to note that both Benn and Jenkins have since embraced environmentalism in a very real sense – the former publicly disavowing his previous support for nuclear power. These changes in attitude on the part of two significant players coincided with much wider scale changes in attitudes throughout the labour movement in Britain during the 1970s and 1980s, as described in Chapter 1.

In contrast to this traditional, almost unquestioning socialist commitment to science in the service of humanity, politicians of the right have maintained a more ambivalent attitude, tending to support primarily those aspects of basic and applied research which serve strategic or military purposes or enhance short term profits.

Applied science and advanced technology in the form of new processes, better machinery and new plant can certainly improve efficiency, reduce labour costs and thereby enhance profits. In Conservative terms therefore, technology is invariably perceived as 'a good thing' and any industry which wishes to compete and succeed would be wise to invest in it. Emergent technologies involving chemical manufacture, electricity and mechanical innovation were the real motive force in the expansion of the British Empire during the nineteenth century and were adopted with alacrity by the industrialists of the time (Hobsbawm, 1990).

However, applying conventional, liberal free-market principles, governments of the right have never interfered very much in the process, and for the first half of the twentieth century they didn't intervene at all. Science was not formally incorporated into such key areas as education and the Civil Service until the middle of the twentieth century (and then by the 1945–50 Labour Government). In a radio broadcast in January 1957, the Conservative Prime Minister Harold Macmillan bemoaned the low level of technological education and claimed it as one of the four problems of greatest concern to his government; the others were defence, the development of nuclear power, and Anglo–American relations (Payne, 1960). But this concern was exceptional and short lived. The *laissez-faire* Conservative governments of Margaret Thatcher were frequently accused by the scientific community of complete lack of interest in applied science and technology, the result of which will doubtless have long term implications for British manufacturing industry.

The two major (and related) exceptions to this general Conservative disinterest in industrial technology are of course defence and nuclear power. Out of a total government commitment to research and development of £4,600 million in 1987–88, the Ministry of Defence received no less than £2,200 million – 48 per cent (COI, 1990).

Basic science, on the other hand, is knowledge, knowledge is power and even governments of the right recognise the importance of looking after certain aspects of this intellectual endeavour. Science can provide excellent cover for safeguarding strategic interests. Under the guise of respectable 'scientific research', the United Kingdom has maintained bases in the South Atlantic and Antarctica for many years. Unlike all other bodies under the wing of the Natural Environment Research Council, the British Antarctic Survey (BAS) also has special funding arrangements and logistic support courtesy of the Foreign and Commonwealth Office and the Ministry of Defence. This support was increased and consolidated after the Falklands conflict. In 1990–91, BAS received £43 million from NERC's total Science Budget allocation of £136 million. This compared with around £30 million for all environmental research in the universities and polytechnics.

Right-wing arguments can also be made for basic or fundamental scientific research which underpins nuclear fusion, space travel and the 'star wars' initiative. This type of science is all about political control. If socialists' identification with science can be traced to the Marxist view of liberation through new modes of production, then the interest of the right in certain types of science finds its roots in the endeavours of the early botanists, taxonomists and explorers who paved the way for the rape and domination of Latin America, Africa and large parts of the Far East.

Thus, in recent years the left in Britain and Europe has had a fairly consistent, if increasingly critical, ideological commitment to science and technology as agencies of political progress. In contrast, the right has exhibited a more lukewarm attitude, only providing unquestioned support to those aspects of scientific and technical endeavour which have strategic political or economic influence, leaving the rest (especially since 1979) to survive as best they might in the jungle of the free market.

The conclusion which must be drawn from this brief analysis is that like most human constructs, science and technology are tools; they are available for governments to ignore, use (or abuse) as they see fit. However, as tools scientific activities are certainly not politically neutral. In 1982, the developed world was spending 45 per cent of its total energy research budget on nuclear power generation and only 15 per cent on research into renewable energy sources and conservation. And governments like the UK's, which regularly spend six or seven times more on military research and development than on social, environmental and health research combined, are demonstrating clear political preferences (BSSRS, 1983; Turney, 1984).

Fortunately, at least for politicians on the left, our analysis of science and technology is now considerably more sophisticated than it was 20 or 30 years ago. We now recognise both the successes and the failures of technological advance, and we have learned some hard lessons about the need to intervene when things are getting out of democratic (or scientific) control. We have learned that there is nothing quite as dangerous as the certainty of the technocrat – whether in the upper echelons of the Civil Service or on the board of a public corporation.

The principal influence on this shift in socialist attitudes towards science and technology has been the emergence of environmentalism. The lone voices of caution in the 1960s (most notably Carson and Ehrlich in the USA) built into a crescendo of global concern which by the mid 1970s had started permeating almost every wing of the West European labour movement. By the 1980s, few on the left had any misconceptions about the danger of an uncritical approach to science and technology. The realisation that technology could destroy as easily as it creates grew inexorably during the three decades following the publication of *Silent Spring* (Carson, 1962). And with the disasters of Seveso, Three Mile Island, Bhopal and Chernobyl, socialists and non-socialists alike could no longer ignore the conclusion that our capacity to inflict catastrophic damage both on ourselves (as citizens and workers) and the environment is now enormous.

Throughout the 1980s the dilemmas continued to multiply. New challenges were posed by biotechnology and the availability of techniques for modifying the genetic characteristics of living organisms. Genetic enhancement of plants and micro-organisms could bring immense benefits to agriculture and health. The application of a species of the bacterium *Pseudomonas syringae* to crops has been shown to improve markedly their resistance to frost damage by preventing the formation of ice crystals in cold weather. Baculoviruses can be engineered to attack insect pests, thereby eliminating the need for some chemical pesticides altogether. Bacteria can now be 'custom designed' to break down chemical wastes and even toxic contaminants in the environment. 'Live vaccines' can be produced which could help reduce the massive death toll from preventable diseases like cholera and dysentery in developing countries.

But genetically manipulated micro-organisms may also be used for military purposes, to attack enemy populations directly or to harm their agriculture, thereby weakening their capacity to defend themselves. Some biotechnological techniques could result in reductions in the market for agricultural products from developing countries (UN, 1990). As with all emergent technologies, ethical and scientific choices have to be made if they are to be harnessed for good rather than hijacked for less benevolent objectives.

Other choices have to be made at an even more fundamental level. Do we really wish to continue with technologies which have few, if any, real benefits for human well-being if their environmental consequences are so severe? Fast cars, nuclear power and high technology weapons systems spring to mind.

However, whether technologies are familiar or not, established or nascent, society needs a set of criteria for judging their value, the advantages and the disadvantages of their application and the costs and benefits of their adoption. Whether we like it or not we need scientific understanding to judge the value and validity of scientific innovation. Breakthroughs in science and technology can provide vital solutions to real problems, improving conditions both for humankind and the planet. They can also unleash destructive and life-threatening forces which need to be controlled or eliminated altogether.

We need mechanisms for ensuring that governments and ordinary people can make informed choices on technical issues so that real human needs can be met without compromising the quality and safety of the environment. This requires the ability to measure environmental factors accurately, to assess the impact of technical innovations, to predict the outcome of environmental changes that are presently underway and to make the necessary adjustments to ensure that all human activities are ultimately sustainable. In short we need an attitude to science and technology which promotes excellence and creativity but demands caution and openness to criticism by or on behalf of society.

Britain must develop a socially and environmentally accountable science and technology policy – one which places as much emphasis on human well-being and environmental sustainability as it does on economic, industrial and commercial success. Present-day socialists firmly reject the antipathy of some 'deep green' environmentalists towards science and technological progress. But they do not overlook the reasons (described in Chapter 4) for the increasing disenchantment of ordinary people with some of the side effects of this progress. It is up to socialists to forge a value-based science in the service of people and the planet.

Although much of their work is shrouded in mystery, the majority of scientists are very ordinary people. Their communications with the outside world may be prone to overuse of jargon but they bring to their activities a system of aspirations, values and attitudes just like everyone else. They have beliefs and personal views which may differ markedly from those of their closest colleagues. A few work with dogged and selfless determination, and achieve little of note during their careers, others may make international reputations on the strength of a string of brilliant ideas throughout their working lives. The overwhelming majority are somewhere in between.

In fact, there is little which is really mysterious or glamorous in the lives of scientists. Very few indeed are 'ivory tower' boffins who require no external stimuli in order to produce good work. In fact, collaboration and cooperation with a free exchange of ideas and information invariably produces the best science. Nobel prizes are won on the strength of teamwork in the service of humanity, not on the basis of overweening personal ambition on the part of individuals. In science, as in life, overly competitive attitudes and isolation are usually the enemies of progress.

Fortunately, the majority of working scientists, particularly those involved in health and environmental research, do wish to collaborate in a spirit of free inquiry to help improve social and environmental conditions. Like most members of society, these individuals respond to encouragement and the provision of incentives. Few are motivated solely by personal reward and aggrandisement. But sadly, Britain's scientific community has been badly mistreated in recent years. Underfunding has caused divisiveness and inefficiency as scientists have been forced to compete with each other for ever-scarcer research grants. This has been especially noticeable in the field of environmental science. Scientists in academic and research institutes have suffered from poor career prospects (often exacerbated by the insecurity of fixed term contracts), a chronic lack of facilities and a steady erosion of core funding for basic research.

Even in industry, where some competition is inevitable, the enforced short-termism due to UK government policies throughout the 1980s has resulted in a dramatic reduction of innovative output. Understandably, when industries are dragged from one recession to another and subjected to crippling interest rates for several years in between, training and research are the first budgets to be cut. The consequences of this will be felt by UK manufacturing industry for many years to come.

Meanwhile, Britain has failed hopelessly to support properly scientific and engineering innovation in areas where major new opportunities are arising – most crucially in the field of pollution abatement technology. Instead, companies in Germany, Switzerland, Scandinavia and the USA have been left with an almost 'free run' in developing plant and processes which British industry will need to meet ever-tighter constraints imposed by European environmental regulations. And where British scientists have made breakthroughs, the consequent development of products has very often taken place abroad.

Against this background of government neglect for both fundamental and applied research, British scientists involved in environmental science and technology have been marginalised. It must therefore be the duty of a future Labour government, committed to radical and rational environmental policies, to provide both leadership and resources for environmental scientists and technologists. Good scientific understanding of the problems and the availability of technologies for their amelioration are central to effective environmental management. Government must harness the creativity and commitment of the environmental science community if the appropriate technical and engineering solutions are to be researched, developed and adopted. Labour governments should therefore bring scientists into the centre stage of environmental policy making. Different ideas and approaches should be debated and scrutinised in an open way between scientists, environmentalists, industrialists, the business community and ordinary people (as consumers and employees).

To demystify the issues and allow the public to participate fully in these discussions it will also be necessary to engineer a dramatic improvement in public understanding of the scientific issues underlying environmental questions. As I have repeatedly stressed, failure to educate ordinary people results in the debate simply becoming a battle of ever-noisier 'experts' with the public left uninvolved and powerless on the sidelines. This can lead to errors in decision making and risks considerable distortion of priorities.

In Chapter 3 I also emphasised the importance of increasing the quality and availability of environmental education. However, it should not be overlooked that an environmentally aware society will also participate far more effectively in debates and decisions about the nature of science and the direction of technological change. This must be an essential component of any socialist environment policy. Participation is also heavily dependent on freedom of environmental information and access to mechanisms and institutions which allow environmental rights to be exercised. I will return to this issue later; but first we must examine the practical means of ensuring good science and the development of environmentally sustainable technologies in Britain.

British environmental research is not inefficient, nor is it second rate – quite the opposite. Britain has some of the best-respected environmental scientists and technologists and some of the best-run environmental research institutes in the world. However, there are two very real problems. First, these institutes have had a very poor deal and suffered real cuts in core funding in recent years. Moreover, despite the magnitude of environmental problems we face as a country, the outlook remains bleak. The Natural Environment Research Council predicted that if government policy did not change, there would be an additional 10 per cent cut in real terms in the period 1991–96 (NERC, 1991). Second, and probably connected, nearly all Britain's expertise in strategic environmental research is completely dislocated from the policy-making machinery of the Department of the Environment (in this context, 'strategic' means medium–long term research which is required for effective governmental policy making).

For decades, much environmental science was perceived as passive, filled with ecologists and natural scientists capable of describing the way natural systems work but contributing little of direct relevance to mainstream economic activity. It has always been considered valuable to map the earth's resources, to describe and, as far as possible, predict the weather and to maintain a presence in Antarctica and the South Atlantic. Apart from anything else, these activities were helpful in planning the long term exploitation of natural resources by British industrial and agricultural interests. But understanding the behaviour of aquatic and terrestrial ecosystems, cataloguing species and researching longer term trends in climatic and oceanic features never, until recently, attracted much political interest.

Recently, however, it has become abundantly clear that a proper understanding of natural systems and their biological and physical components is essential for the future well-being of the planet. Natural resources, whether they are aquatic, mineral, petrochemical or organic, must be managed in a sustainable manner. We need to know where the resources are, how extensive they are, and what steps must be taken to preserve those in danger of overexploitation. We also need a better understanding of the dynamic interactions between climate, oceans and land masses. Environmental changes are underway, and it is no longer an academic matter if the earth's natural systems are so disturbed that they begin to threaten entire civilisations with famine, flooding or poisoning.

Long term monitoring is vital to the process of understanding environmental change. Only because air and water quality has been measured for a number of years can increases in persistent pollutants be detected and reversed. Only because the abundance and diversity of freshwater fauna and flora were catalogued over decades could the effects of acidification be measured in a quantitative way and ameliorative action adopted in Europe. And only because there has been painstaking collection of real data (literally over centuries) can predictive models of global climate change now be calibrated and fulfil their potential as aids to political decision making.

In the future it will be increasingly important to draw together the output of many diverse sources of long term ecological and environmental research if governments are to attempt to prioritise areas for action and investment. In Britain, the responsibility for this currently rests with the Department of the Environment (DoE), but the Department's own research capability, and its ability to keep abreast of developments in relevant fields, are both woefully inadequate.

Most government departments faced with the need to develop policy to avert such potentially cataclysmic events as global warming and ozone depletion might be expected to maintain a vigorous strategic science capability. After all, the costs of getting things wrong are very great indeed.

Other government departments in the UK which have to deal with rather more routine technical issues maintain strategic research facilities and have done for many years. The Department of Trade and Industry (DTI) sponsors the National Physical Laboratory, the National Engineering Laboratory, the Laboratory of the Government Chemist, the National Weights and Measures Laboratory and the Warren Spring Laboratory. The Department of Transport has the Transport and Road Research Laboratory. The Ministry of Agriculture, Fisheries and Food (MAFF) has laboratories and research stations concerned with every aspect of food and fisheries production, including food quality and veterinary matters. The Ministry of Defence has a number of defence research establishments which together receive funding of more than £1 billion per annum. The Overseas Development

Administration, through ODA, sponsors the Natural Resources Institute. The Department of Health has access to a powerful array of research institutes and units at national and regional levels, funds the Public Health Laboratory Service and has effective links with the medical charities and the Medical Research Council units.

In contrast, the DoE maintains just one major strategic research facility, and that relates solely to the built environment – the Building Research Establishment. Scientific expertise in nature conservation is kept at arm's length within the now fragmented conservancy councils for England, Wales and Scotland. Otherwise, the majority of strategic environmental research is performed in the Department of Education and Science (via the Advisory Board for Research Councils which supports the Natural Environment Research Council and its research institutes), in the laboratories of the DTI (most notably Warren Spring), and in the Water Research Centre. Universities and polytechnics are also involved in some strategic environmental research, but are mostly engaged in research of a more 'blue skies' or basic nature plus a certain amount of applied work for industry.

Perhaps this state of affairs was understandable during the 1960s and 1970s when the full magnitude of global environmental threats was not appreciated. But Britain has now blundered through the 1980s and beyond with no formal linkage between environmental policy making and the country's most important centres of excellence in such globally crucial areas as climatology, pollution control and conservation. This means that on such issues as global warming, ozone depletion, acidification, marine eutrophication, rain forest protection and biodiversity, Britain has no really coherent way of forming policy. This approach is now becoming something of a major liability.

Naturally, civil servants in the DoE do attend conferences (sometimes even speaking at them); they sit on advisory boards for environmental research institutes; they commission research from universities and polytechnics; and they play a role in the Natural Environment Research Council and its committees. But these activities fall far short of ensuring an intimate and effective linkage between high quality environmental science and high quality national environmental policy making. Little wonder that so many of Britain's important environmental decisions devolve by default to the Departments of Transport, Energy, Trade and Industry, MAFF and of course the Treasury. The DoE simply does not have the scientific and technical competence to carry through the arguments.

A Labour government would ensure that Britain's environmental scientists and technologists are mobilised as they have never been mobilised before. They would be given the responsibility for coming up with reliable systems for mapping, measuring, modelling and managing environmental resources at home and abroad. But they would also be given the freedom and encouragement to be creative and productive in helping to solve the immense problems we face at local, national and international levels. Only if our environmental management systems are both comprehensive and reliable will government be reasonably sure of making the right decisions to protect existing resources and achieve long term environmental sustainability and equity. And only if our environmental scientists and technologists are given the freedom and encouragement to innovate will the solutions to current problems be found.

The directors of key environmental research institutes should have a 'direct line' to government (as some of the predecessors of the British Geological Survey did decades ago). Those bodies presently buried in the Department of Education and Science should be taken out, dusted off and brought centre stage. Their scientists should be rewarded properly and encouraged to follow their own paths of inquiry as well as working on systems for solving urgent environmental problems. Government should agree programmes of long term research with institutes and research groups which promote stability and career security (especially important for young scientists) while setting fair targets for academic and strategic research output. Government should also agree a long term framework with the key institutions for establishing and maintaining a creative and dynamic balance between curiosity-led, basic environmental science and the strategic work which is so vital for immediate policy formulation.

By continuing the present trend in expenditure on defence research and development (from 0.8 per cent of GDP in 1964 to 0.42 per cent in 1989), there is no reason whatsoever why investment in both basic and strategic environmental research should not double within the lifetime of a parliament. Adding to this the potential for increased investments in applied research and development (especially clean technology) there is now a real opportunity to give 'green science and technology' the boost it needs to enable us to understand and solve the problems we face.

However, increasing the pool of knowledge needed for effective environmental management is not, in itself, sufficient to ensure better practice. If governments are to achieve improvements in environmental quality at local, national and international levels, and if incipient disasters are to be averted, systems must be put in place which ensure that knowledge is disseminated and acted upon.

As outlined in Chapter 3, this may be achieved through improved access to environmental education, involving primary schools, secondary schools, colleges of further education, polytechnics and universities (including The Open University). There must be greatly increased opportunities for formal (academic) and non-formal environmental education (via environmental and conservation bodies, trade unions and other organisations). And there must be a massive increase in the availability of professional training to meet the rapidly growing needs of organisations involved in environmental management and regulation. Short courses, daily and weekly release schemes and block release courses will be needed to maximise opportunities for environmental professionals at all levels.

Government must ensure that information is available to all who seek it, in a form they will be able to understand – whether it is the Commission of the European Communities, or an individual worried about a local issue. Only when knowledge is collected and disseminated effectively will citizens and their representatives be properly empowered to participate in environmental decision making. When complex issues arise, people must also be given access to sympathetic, impartial sources of technical advice to help them understand the implications for themselves and their families.

Thus, having acquired the best available scientific knowledge, the second 'key' to the implementation of radical socialist environmental policies is the establishment of real freedom of environmental information. Governments must place trust in people if people are to place trust in governments.

The 1990s will be characterised by an explosion of technical data concerning every aspect of life: work, leisure, lifestyle, services and products. This surge in the amount of recorded data which will be collected coincides with revolutions in information technology which enable data to be transmitted, catalogued and analysed at extraordinary speed. Provided, therefore, that the results of strategic research and environmental monitoring are published efficiently, it will be possible for those with access to new information technologies to form opinions and make decisions on environmental issues every bit as quickly as departments of local and national government. In theory information should become more readily accessible as the decade progresses. This should enhance the effectiveness of environmental and consumer organisations and, ultimately, the quality of environmental decision making. However, the question remains as to whether the benefits of this improved accessibility will extend to all members of society, and whether the information will be in a form that can be assimilated through conventional democratic processes.

It is one thing for industrial and other lobby groups to have access to the latest sources of intelligence on environmental research, on new UK and European legislation, on statistics describing air and water quality and on the progress of planning applications. It is quite another for this data to be presented in an understandable form to ordinary people.

For many years, it was even difficult for holiday-makers to discover whether the beach they were visiting was polluted by sewage or not. In the early 1980s, the British government designated only 27 beaches to comply with the microbiological provisions of the EC bathing water directive. In contrast, Luxembourg (which has no coastline) designated 39 and Italy designated 3,500. The effect of the British policy was to limit testing of UK bathing waters to a handful of resorts. Holiday-makers had no means of assessing the likely quality of the bathing water at their chosen resort unless they took the exceptional step of researching the matter with the local authority or buying a special booklet 'The Golden List' produced by the Coastal Anti-Pollution League.

Many campaigns and several years later, the government conceded the need for more testing and eventually identified more than 400 bathing waters. A voluntary poster scheme was also introduced, whereby local authorities could post the results of bathing water quality at beaches. However, it is by no means certain that ordinary members of the public understand the relevance of the information contained on these posters. Even information which is technically correct is not necessarily informative.

Labelling of foods and other products is subject to considerable misunderstanding because of the technical impenetrability of the information provided. The terminology of food additives is especially notorious for its obscurity. Labelling which describes the energy and water consumption characteristics of machines used in the home is exceptional, and poorly understood by the public. Thus, provision of technical information (especially jargon-loaded information) is not enough; it must be presented in a form which people are able to assimilate and act on.

In some areas, information has not just been obscure or inaccessible, it has remained secret. For example, until recently it was not possible to discover the composition of industrial discharges into public sewers unless the industry concerned chose to make such information available. And yet it is industrial contamination of sewage sludge which causes difficulty in reusing the material as a fertiliser and soil conditioner. And it is the water charge payer who meets the expense of dumping or incinerating industrially contaminated sludge.

Secrecy invariably surrounds the activities of the atomic energy industry. The decisions which lead to the selection of potential nuclear waste disposal sites by NIREX are far from transparent. And when something goes wrong, it is not the automatic response of government ministers or civil servants to press for a public inquiry. Details of the 1957 fire at the nuclear waste processing facility at Windscale did not emerge for decades. Only now are the full facts about post-Chernobyl contamination in Britain becoming available.

Similarly, despite mounting evidence of real illness resulting from the contamination of Camelford's water supply in 1988, the Conservative government has still (in 1992) to concede the need for an inquiry into the secretive way in which the water authority and government departments dealt with the incident and its aftermath. In my own dealings with the water industry I have experienced the same peculiar predilection for restricting access to information. One water company refused to send me a copy of a press release, despite the fact that it had already been sent to the newspapers! Another refused to tell me the names of its major shareholders – common knowledge in the City of London, available at Company's House, but not available to an MP on request.

In this context, it was highly revealing that in his much-heralded 51 page document on citizen's rights published in July 1991, Prime Minister Major did not mention freedom of environmental information once. Perhaps this is not surprising since the right to live and work in a decent environment was not mentioned either. In contrast, the Labour Party has, since 1986, been formally committed to reversing the assumptions on confidentiality of environmental information.

Labour is also committed to a Freedom of Information Act and a European Environmental Charter, and in its charter on citizen's rights makes explicit how this will apply to environmental matters. We believe in the right to a clean environment; the right to safe water, air and food; the right to information; the right to take citizen's action against polluters; the right to seek independent advice on environmental issues at work; the right to refuse to undertake work which creates pollution; the right to initiate audits at the place of work; and the right to participate in decisions which affect the environment.

In the USA it is acceptable for government to demand that industry maintains public registers of its toxic releases, and it should be equally acceptable in the UK. If computer software is available to establish 'audit trails' of toxic waste movements, there is no reason why such wastes should not be tracked by waste regulatory bodies from the time and place of their creation to the time and place of their treatment or ultimate disposal. There is no reason why water suppliers should not provide their customers with an independently audited statement of the quality of their tap water when they send out their annual bills. Bathing waters could easily be given simple pollution classifications, for example a 'star rating' which would be readily understood by holiday-makers. Products and processes could be given an independently assessed 'green label' as proposed by the European Commission.

At a local level, parents should be able to find out about the implications of local pollutants on the health of their children. If there is a problem with smoke from the local factory, if neighbourhood play areas suffer from excessive traffic fumes or if there are plans for a new waste disposal facility, parents should be able to get honest and independent technical advice from their local environmental health department. Schoolteachers who wish to involve children in environmental projects should be able to obtain readily understandable information including computer-generated colour maps on 'geographical information systems' which show the quality of the local environment. Interested individuals and organisations should be able to obtain historical data on local environmental quality so that changes can be monitored over time, and with respect to changes in land use and demographic factors.

Two instruments which can be employed to enhance greatly the accessibility of environmental information to ordinary people are environmental audits and environmental impact assessments.

Audits are undertaken by local authorities, public institutions, commerce and industry in order to assess the overall impact of an organisation and its activities on the environment. Typically, audits are undertaken on a regular cycle, usually annually or biannually, and include consideration of such factors as procurement policy, impacts on local air, water and land quality, land use policy, energy and transport policies, risks and emergencies and waste policy (minimisation, reuse, recycling and disposal).

For industrial concerns, it is also very important to include 'life cycle analysis' of raw materials, products and wastes: where do they come from, is the source renewable, and if not is it managed in a sustainable fashion? At the present time audits are voluntary, do not need to be published and reach no recognised standards. Consequently, although public authorities and institutions do tend to publish audits and 'state of the environment' reports, industrial and commercial bodies rarely do so.

Environmental impact assessments are undertaken under EC legislation and (in the UK) under Town and Country Planning Act regulations, when developers are proposing schemes involving major industrial or civil engineering activities, e.g. the construction of refineries, thermal power stations, waste disposal and treatment facilities, nuclear waste repositories, smelting and chemical plants, motorways and ports. Environmental impact statements should include consideration of all potential impacts, not just those selected by potential developers.

Both audits and impact assessments provide an excellent opportunity for involving ordinary people in an exchange of views with those who manage or seek to intervene in the management of the environment. Indeed there is a growing body of literature which explains how this may be done most effectively (Wathern, 1988; Barwise, 1991). For example, it is typical in local authority audits to set up an advisory forum comprising local interest groups and key individuals who can help steer the audit towards issues of greatest local concern.

However, in commercial and industrial audits, the opinions of local people (and even the workforce) are not always taken into account. Similarly, in some environmental impact assessments (especially those undertaken 'in-house' by the developers rather than commissioned from independent consultants), there is a tendency to treat the views of ordinary people as a hindrance rather than an opportunity to improve the proposed scheme. There is, besides, no guarantee that a so-called 'independent assessment' is complete: as was demonstrated by the assessment carried out on the East London River Crossing in 1991, when local residents were obliged to complain to Brussels. The European Commission found that the assessment contained no information on soil, flora, fauna, mammal, reptile and amphibian populations, and that no mention had been made of five special schools in the Crossing's corridor.

It is abundantly clear, therefore, that there must be a much higher and more uniform standard of environmental impact analysis in the future. This should involve a formal vetting procedure by the Environment Protection Executive that Labour is committed to setting up, possibly based on a formal quality assurance scheme or British Standard.

Failure to involve people properly in issues of environmental management can prove very damaging in the long term. Priorities may be distorted and expensive errors made. For this reason, and because we believe that people should be able to exert control over their local environment, a Labour government should seek to establish formal rights of public involvement in auditing and environmental impact assessment.

Moreover, the process of auditing should itself become mandatory rather than voluntary, and the results should be made publicly available. Nowhere is this more important than in industrial situations where the workforce is often best placed to detect threats to its own well-being and that of the environment. Workers must therefore be given rights to initiate environmental audits, to be involved in corporate environmental policy, to have automatic access to information on environmental performance and to receive protection against victimisation for expressing environmental concerns.

In Britain, all these requirements could be met by establishing rights to environmental information within a Freedom of Information Act, by formalising public and employee involvement in environmental auditing and impact assessment, and by devoting resources to the development of information systems which provide for maximum scrutiny by public and employees.

Socialists are committed to fairness and transparency in all environmental decision making whether at local or national level. It is logical therefore that a Labour government should give maximum priority to the dissemination of knowledge in a readily understandable form using advanced but 'user-friendly' information technologies. There must be provision for a universal 'right to know' and a 'right to be involved' on all matters concerning the environment. The way in which data are collected and delivered to the community and to employees is thus of paramount importance.

But even if knowledge is disseminated effectively, and people are empowered in their relations with government and industry on matters of environmental policy, there remains a requirement to ensure both the accountability and efficiency of decision-making processes. There is no value in the public having all the facts and winning all of the arguments in a planning inquiry if the Secretary of State then simply overrides the decision for reasons of 'the national interest'.

Thus, to complete the circle of knowledge acquisition, dissemination and application by government, it is necessary to consider the way in which government and government institutions function at present, particularly with respect to environmental assessment, regulation and protection.

There is no doubt that public confidence in government and its institutions to safeguard and improve quality of life will be a factor of increasing importance in years to come. However, in Britain, successive Conservative governments have perpetuated mistrust by deliberately maintaining a fragmented system of environmental regulation and enforcement and by subjecting the system to both under-resourcing and political interference. Thus, ordinary citizens, environmental organisations and local government have been trapped in a policy vacuum, subject to conflicting messages from different government departments and having to deal with a range of separate agencies both inside and outside government.

Meanwhile industry, far from being protected by this wall of confusion, was left struggling – always trying to catch up with the latest European Community legislation or international convention that had been fudged and delayed until the last possible moment by British civil servants. An excellent example of this was the UK government's volte-face on the sea dumping of sewage sludge.

Throughout the 1980s, Britain insisted that putting 5 million tonnes of sewage sludge every year into the North Sea was not contributing to marine pollution. However, other members of the North Sea Conference were becoming increasingly concerned about algal blooms and other evidence of too many nutrients (e.g. sewage) entering the North Sea. They let it be known that Britain would come in for a very hard time at the March 1990 meeting of the Conference.

The last thing the British government needed at that moment was to be isolated in yet another European forum (this was at the height of Mrs Thatcher's period of Euro-chauvinism). So Chris Patten, the UK environment minister, announced a ban on sludge dumping immediately before the start of the Conference. This stunned the UK water industry; they had no warning, no contingency plans, and no time to research alternative, environmentally beneficial uses of sewage sludge. Within the year Thames Water, the largest North Sea sludge dumper, opted to incinerate the lot, passing on considerable financial costs to their customers and switching the environmental costs from the marine environment to air pollution and landfill. This policy was decided with virtually no public involvement.

The 1980s were characterised by this sort of foot-dragging and incoherence in government departments. On some issues this was compounded by sheer dishonesty on the part of ministers. For example, while publicly claiming to observe the provisions of EC directives on bathing and drinking water, government was preventing the water industry from investing in the treatment plants and new technologies needed to meet the standards. Wealthier water authorities like Thames Water were obliged to pay back loans quicker than made sound business sense, and the industry was forced into such a corner that the only way out for a Conservative government refusing to invest was privatisation and passing the bill to the consumer. This process resulted in a complete collapse of public confidence in the water industry and a post-dated commitment for the customers of privatised water companies in the 1990s of tens of billions of pounds.

During the Thatcher years the increasingly untenable assertion of 'no evidence of damage to the environment' was never far from the lips of environment ministers. It was used to justify continued dumping of waste and sewage sludge into the oceans, lethargy on controls to limit acid emissions from large combustion plants, and total inertia on toxic waste imports (which increased from 4,000 tonnes in 1981–82 to 52,000 tonnes in 1988–89). The only guiding principle appeared to be 'the solution to pollution is dilution', or that profit matters above all else.

Ministers had no desire to exert real controls, and no mechanism for elevating environmental concerns within government departments. Meanwhile, the situation outside government was becoming farcical. The National Rivers Authority was set up as a semi-independent agency, but regulatory responsibilities for drinking water and the discharge of dangerous substances into water remained firmly within the Department of the Environment. The water industry was shunted off into the private sector.

Elsewhere, responsibility for monitoring air pollution (principally ozone, nitrogen dioxide, sulphur dioxide and volatile organic compounds) was placed with the Warren Spring Laboratory (now an executive agency of the Department of Trade and Industry), while regulation was split between Her Majesty's Inspectorate of Pollution (part of the Department of the Environment) and the local authorities.

To this day, the National Radiological Protection Board

remains a misnomer (it does not protect, it merely advises government). The Nuclear Installations Inspectorate (NII) is in the Health and Safety Executive (sponsored by the Department of Employment), British Nuclear Fuels Ltd and NIREX (the treatment and disposal agencies) are private companies, and because of the failure to privatise nuclear power, 'Nuclear Electric' is now run by the Department of Energy. Along with NII, Her Majesty's Inspectorate of Pollution (part of the Department of the Environment) is also involved in regulation of the nuclear industry, being responsible for implementation of the Radioactive Substances Act (1960).

Domestic waste regulation, collection and disposal are dealt with in a variety of ways depending on what part of the country one happens to be in; it is divided between district councils, metropolitan boroughs, waste regulatory authorities, county councils, new local authority waste disposal companies and, of course, the private sector.

In its 1990 White Paper *This Common Inheritance*, the government specifically rejected calls for a major overhaul of Britain's incoherent system of environmental management and regulation, despite the fact that nearly every organisation in the country concerned with environmental protection was pressing for it. Then in the summer of 1991, in another volte-face, John Major announced that an Environment Agency was on the agenda – only for it to be rapidly shelved again following disagreements between the Department of the Environment and the Ministry of Agriculture, Fisheries and Food.

In contrast, the Labour Party has been committed to a unified system for pollution control and regulation since 1986 and has published two detailed discussion papers on the subject. Labour's main commitments are to appoint a cabinet rank Minister for Environment Protection, and to create an independent Environment Protection Commission and Executive which would ensure full separation of environmental regulation and management functions, thereby eliminating the 'poacher and gamekeeper' syndrome once and for all. The structure is also designed to integrate control functions for every aspect of pollution, whichever medium it affects (air, water or land), to ensure freedom of environmental information, and to ensure impartiality and integrity in all aspects of environmental management.

The idea of an independent agency responsible for all aspects of environmental regulation is not new. Such agencies, usually overseen by a government ministry or commission, are operating in North America, Europe and the Far East. Countries with a national agency include Germany, Sweden, Denmark, Japan and even Hong Kong. The best known, the United States Environmental Protection Agency, had a 1991 budget of $6.1 billion and a full time staff equivalent of about 18,000. (This number is in addition to the tens of thousands of regulators working in state level environmental protection agencies, departments of natural resources or their equivalent.) Relating directly to the Office of the President, the USEPA fulfils regulatory functions, administers pollution levies, disburses grants (nearly $500 million to individual states in 1991) and conducts operational research. In addition, under the National Environmental Protection Act (NEPA) the United States assigns long term forecasting and strategic research functions to the Council on Environmental Quality. It was this body which produced the influential Global 2000 Report at the request of President Carter (Barney, 1980).

Other countries also maintain national councils of environmental experts and advisers. Germany has the Umweltrat and France a High Committee on the Environment which has more than 50 members, including representatives of environmental organisations and trade unions. Italy also has a national committee of scientific experts.

Countries vary in the way that policy control is exerted by ministries. However, not many place environmental protection, local government, housing and planning all within one ministry (as is presently the case with the Department of the Environment in Britain).

In Germany, the Federal Ministry for Environment, Nature Conservation and Reactor Safety was created in 1986. It has responsibility for water resources, waste regulation, air pollution, noise control, safety of nuclear reactors, nature conservation, environmental health and food safety. France has a similar national ministry, concerned with all environmental issues, including technological risks and natural disasters. In Denmark, the Environment Ministry does maintain a planning function, but keeps this administratively separate within a national agency for physical planning; other agencies include the national environment protection agency, the national food institute, the national forestry and environmental conservation agency and the geological survey of Denmark. Like Germany, Italy also created an environment ministry in 1986; this body deals mostly with pollution control and nature protection.

Based on our own abysmal experience in Britain and some of the more positive developments in other countries, it is apparent that the case for separating environmental protection (including regulation) from environmental management (including planning) at ministerial level is now overwhelming. At Cabinet level, it is clearly essential to have an environmental protection committee with representatives of key ministries (in France they call this the Interministerial Committee on the Quality of Life). It is also very clear that there are considerable advantages in setting up an independent agency responsible for monitoring and regulating environmental quality. Such an agency should remain accountable both to ministers and to the public but should relate to a commission or council of experts appointed by the minister responsible for environmental protection. The experts should include representatives of environmental and conservation groups, trade unions and local authorities as well as scientists, industrialists and environmental specialists. These structures are precisely what the Labour Party advocates and what I spelled out in a Fabian Society discussion paper, 'Labour's Environment Protection Executive', in July 1991.

But the creation of an Environment Protection Commission and Environment Protection Executive will not, in itself, be enough to change attitudes on the scale required. It is the essential framework for coordinated and coherent environmental regulation, but it is not the complete picture. We need to ensure proper support for scientific research; we need to improve the monitoring and assessments of environmental impacts, both of new developments and of existing private and public sector industry and services; and we need to increase public awareness of, access to and participation in environmental decision making. The free exchange of information is the key to all of this. And providing people with full information on environmental issues is an essential part of providing them with the freedom to decide what must be done.

Chapter 6

The greening of industry

Any politician who becomes a spokesperson for the environment receives countless invitations to visit factories and commercial operations where some aspect of good environmental management is being put into practice. There are companies in Britain which are adopting good environmental practice and the range of initiatives is wide – from installing multi-million pound combined heat and power systems to recycling wellington boots. Often, the total picture of a company's operations is not as green as the company would like to believe, but for many firms breakthroughs have been made in their way of thinking. A growing number of British companies are investing in energy efficiency, waste minimisation, pollution control and various other aspects of 'clean production', and it is heartening to see at first hand what can be done with commitment and a little creativity.

But time and again the same messages come through from business of a lack of a clear environmental lead from government and a fear that when decisions are taken industry is not sufficiently consulted, especially about the timescale of the introduction of new standards. More than once I have been told by firms that they don't mind tough environmental targets being imposed as long as they know where they stand, and are operating on a 'level playing field'.

Meanwhile, a green industrial revolution is underway in Europe, largely driven by EC legislation and citizen pressure. However, I must admit to a real fear that British industry is in imminent danger of becoming a victim of this revolution rather than an active participant. Due to the inertia, non-intervention and lack of investment in the 1980s, Britain has fallen badly behind, both in terms of its own practices and its ability to provide products and processes to help ourselves and other countries solve their problems. We are looking at a future in which our industry is forced to embrace better environmental practice by pressure from Europe rather than as a result of British initiatives. This is not conducive to good national performance and self-respect, nor, indeed, to our ability to export goods and services.

In a 1989 MORI poll of 500 senior managers from top UK companies, 82 per cent of respondents accepted that British business does not place a high enough priority on environmental protection. Nevertheless, there are many examples of British companies which have responded effectively to environmental challenges. These have been well documented by the Prince of Wales' 'Business in the Environment' initiative and the Royal Society of Arts 'Better Environment' award scheme. There are also a number of more formal publications which provide case studies of companies (usually well-known ones) which have been successful in one environmental sphere or another (Elkington and Burke, 1987; Clutterbuck and Snow, 1990; Elkington *et al.*, 1991). Examples range from extractive industries (e.g. gas, oil, minerals), through manufacturing to telecommunications and retailing.

The point increasingly made by those commentators and consultants who promote good environmental practice in industry is that it simply represents good housekeeping and good business sense. Managers who fail to recognise this are risking both legal liability and missing out on markets in an increasingly green-consuming world. Thus the message which goes out to business leaders is very much oriented towards the lead they must show and the investments they must make in order to safeguard or increase profitability. As Elkington and co-authors (1991) assert: 'If there is one single characteristic shared by every company that has successfully pursued environmental excellence, it is this: the lead has come from the top.'

One of the drawbacks of this approach is that it does tend to make the pursuit of 'environmental excellence' contingent on having a lot to lose or a lot to gain. While a large corporation is commercially successful and management time is devoted to environmental issues, improved environmental performance can be expected. But it must be acknowledged that, while some of the giant corporations have improved, there is considerable room for more improvement; and more than cosmetic changes, or changes in presentation, are required. Furthermore, the pressure for change through concern about public image has been much less keenly felt by small and medium-sized enterprises, with a lower public profile. Yet the future performance of these enterprises is of as much concern as that of the large corporations with a wider reputation to protect.

Another problem with the current message to business is that in requiring the board room to set the pace, it does reinforce present company structures and top-down modes of communication and organisation. These may actually be inhibitory to improving environmental performance in smaller organisations. Within large corporations there are usually formal channels of communication in order to maintain coherent objectives across a wide variety of operations. In addition, the more enlightened of the large corporations do try to ensure genuine two-way flow of ideas and information. Typically, these corporate communication channels are also used to proselytise the environmental goals of the company and develop in the workforce a spirit of enthusiasm for improving environmental performance.

However, even with these channels of communication, we can see that in too many companies this means that orders come exclusively from the top. And sadly, too many British managers are still locked into a defensive frame of mind on questions of environmental performance and impose this attitude on their employees (ultimately threatening redundancy if environmental regulation becomes too strict). These are exactly the same employers who have traditionally been sceptical on a wide range of issues involving the workforce – from health and safety to quality management. So if a lead has to be shown by management, it should be a commitment to change traditional board room attitudes in favour of more industrial democracy, genuine dialogue and cooperation.

As with most revolutions, Britain's green industrial revolution is one which needs to start from the bottom as well as the top. Government can provide incentives, but company directors and senior managers must recognise that their best chance of long term success lies in establishing a dynamic partnership with their workforce. The real greening of industry needs to involve every employee in every task they perform. It is not about one gesture or token measure to give a company 'green' credentials.

In its 'executive guide', Business in the Environment advised:

> Employees' creativity and enthusiasm can be harnessed to the benefit of the company if they are kept informed and involved in improving environmental performance. This is necessary for the success of environmental improvements, and also helps keep and attract good staff.

While this statement falls a little short of a clear exhortation to greater industrial democracy, it does illustrate that some enlightened business people now accept that improved environmental performance cannot be achieved through edict of the management alone.

Fortunately there is plenty of evidence to suggest that British workers are more than ready for the environmental challenge and in many cases they are well ahead of their managements. A number of trade unions have well-developed strategies for promoting employee involvement in company environmental policy. This fact was not registered by the Conservative government, which failed to mention the role of trade unions once in its White Paper *This Common Inheritance*. Given its ideological antipathy to trade unionism this was probably to be expected. However, in view of the potential for harnessing the organisational framework of trade union branches in the workplace, it is more surprising that the role of unions has also been overlooked by some key commentators.

As I argued in Chapter 1, concern for the environment is as natural for trade unionists as concern for health and safety and workplace rights. Indeed the issues are often linked. Even major corporations like DuPont, the US chemical giant, are now putting environment, safety and health together in company policy making. Today British unions are actively developing policies on the environment and making the connections between global environmental crises and the day-to-day rights of workers to live and work in conditions which are both pleasant and safe. These connections are not new.

When cholera ravaged the urban slums of nineteenth century Britain, it was partly fear of the early trade unions and other radical groups that drove the authorities to improve the state of

Britain's sanitary infrastructure. Edwin Chadwick (the so-called father of public health) wrote 'if a Chartist millennium is to be averted, the governing classes must free the governed from the spur of their misery by improving the physical conditions of their lives'.

And in the twentieth century, when major chemical and nuclear incidents have threatened environmental disaster, it is invariably the workforce which has been in the front line. In the nineteenth and early twentieth centuries, Germany was an undisputed world leader in chemical manufacturing. But in 1921 an explosion in a BASF plant resulted in 561 deaths, and a similar incident involving IG Farben killed 184 workers in 1948. As a result of these and many similar incidents over the years, the union representing German chemical workers initiated an environmental campaign with the theme 'doubly exposed, doubly concerned'. Even today, accidents involving pharmaceutical and chemical production, oil and petrochemical plants, and other chemical stores and production facilities are far from rare. No fewer than 97 were notified to the EC's Major Accident Reporting System (MARS) between 1985 and 1990. Fatalities occurred in 20 and significant environmental damage in 11 of the incidents.

In France and Italy, some unions began to recognise in the early 1970s that quality of life is as important as wage rises and as a consequence devoted as much attention to reducing the working week as they did to pay claims. In the United States, cooperation between unions like AFL-CIO and the International Association of Machinists (IAM) and environmental organisations goes back to the early 1980s. A large number of American unions now support nuclear freeze policies and diversification in defence industries. Joint campaigning has also covered issues like 'environmental right to know', air pollution controls, and toxic waste.

Meanwhile, British trade unions have been in the forefront of environmental campaigns against the sea dumping of nuclear waste, the use of asbestos and water privatisation. They have lobbied in favour of diversification of the defence industries into socially useful and environmentally sustainable production. And trade unions have long advocated greater investment in energy conservation, combined heat and power, clean technology and public transport.

Of course it has not always been an automatic reaction for trade unionists to embrace environmentalism. It took some time before the National Union of Mineworkers accepted the link between coal burning and acidification. And many workers in the nuclear power industry still see environmentalists as scarcely better than Luddites. But these defensive reactions are now the exception rather than the rule and, as the NUM discovered, the sooner the environmental arguments are taken on board, the sooner a case can be made for the sustainable, long term future of the industry. Furthermore, if unions take their health and safety policies seriously, then a number of logical conclusions follow for environmental policy too.

But there is more to modern trade union concern for the environment than the link between health and safety and environmental risks or indeed industry-specific campaigns. It is becoming increasingly clear that businesses which fail to respond to the challenges of late twentieth century environmental imperatives and which fail to invest in clean technologies and pollution prevention may lose competitiveness or, worse, may be fined or regulated out of existence.

Thus some unions have launched more general campaigns on the environment with a view to safeguarding the employment prospects of the present and future generations of workers. Several unions make corporate donations to environmental campaigns, and very many union branches are affiliated directly with environmental organisations. In May 1991, the Environment Action Group of the Trade Union Congress presented a report 'Industry, Jobs and the Environmental Challenge' to the National Economic Development Council. The report drew attention to both the opportunities and the threats posed to employment by stricter environmental policies. The greatest threat was of course the abysmal failure of the Conservative government to invest in clean technology research and development and of industry to lock itself into existing methods and take short term decisions. It was noted that German investment in the pollution control industry exceeds that of the UK by a factor of three. Germany now commands approximately 40 per cent of the EC market for pollution abatement technology. Continued poor performance in this area will inevitably lead to UK job losses. In contrast, it was recognised that stricter environmental regulation could lead to

significant increases in employment in environmental management industries, especially air pollution and waste management.

Concerns such as these have led individual unions like the
General Municipal Boilermakers and Allied Trades Union (GMB)
to initiate a 'Green Works' campaign which aims to establish
partnerships with management and 'green' agreements on a
range of environmental issues: freedom of environmental information at work, training, higher standards of environmental performance and environmental auditing. The Manufacturing,
Science and Finance union (MSF/STM) now calls itself 'the union
for green growth' and has produced a detailed action pack for
members explaining how to press management for
environmental audits and green agreements in the workplace. It
is not always easy, however, to enthuse managements on issues
like environmental training. One very well-known chemical company rejected MSF's proposal for time off work for environmental training in the UK despite having given exactly that
opportunity to its workers in Germany. Public sector unions like
The National and Local Government Officers Association
(NALGO) devote considerable efforts to environmental
awareness-craising among members. And recently, 27 British
unions formed a 'Trade Union Environment Team' comprising
senior officers who share experiences and conduct joint campaigns on a wide range of issues.

In years to come, the role of trade unions in securing and
protecting workplace environment rights will be crucial. There
must be many more opportunities for ordinary people to press
for better environmental performance in the organisation which
employs them, whatever its size and impact, and Labour governments should make these rights inalienable.

But as Britain moves into the post-industrial era, relying more
and more on small, flexible service sector units, as manufacturing
switches to more modestly sized, high technology companies, the
very nature of employer–employee relations will change. Power
structures and decision-making mechanisms will become more
diffuse and theoretically more accessible to ordinary employees.
Even the more traditional, larger scale industrial concerns should
come to recognise the benefits of including elected
representatives of the workforce on their boards in order to
improve information exchange and promote consensus. This

already happens in Germany, Sweden, Norway, the Netherlands and Austria. Pressure from these countries and the European Community will eventually ensure greater industrial democracy throughout Europe. Certainly, socialist and social democratic governments are already committed to fostering this trend, and a British Labour government must be in the forefront of moves at a European level to guarantee industrial democracy.

There will also be many more partnerships between local and regional authorities, the private sector and the voluntary sector in which employee involvement in management is an integral feature. There are innumerable examples of successful joint venture companies in France and elsewhere which are owned and managed by municipalities in combination with a variety of private sector interests. Typically, these include enterprises in the water and waste industries, and combined heat and power schemes providing low cost energy to local populations. In the United Kingdom, regional enterprise boards set up in the West Midlands, West Yorkshire, Merseyside, Lancashire and Greater London had, by the end of 1986, invested £35 million in 200 companies, indirectly supporting 14,000 jobs in the process.

As I have already argued, there is a strong ecological argument for regional government and regional control of water, wastes and land use. And what better way for a regional authority to enhance its local environmental quality and improve the regional economy than to stimulate employment in joint ventures with the private and voluntary sectors to prevent pollution, reduce wastes and segregate the remainder for recycling. In the United States, many county and state initiatives have already done exactly this, and, working with bodies such as the Institute for Local Self Reliance and private waste recovery corporations, have developed numerous local (often inner city) initiatives. These projects have created useful employment, improved environmental quality and provided real commercial opportunities in waste recycling and reuse. Effective source reduction and separation of wastes has led to significant reductions in waste streams and recycling rates of more than 30 per cent in some American cities and counties. This significantly reduces the need for new landfill or incinerator capacity for municipal solid waste. Schemes such as this are set up with the full involvement of local communities and trade unions, all sides benefiting both environmentally and economically.

Other employment models worth considering include employee share ownership plans (ESOPs). Again, these have proven very successful in the United States where they serve to balance the interests of shareholders and employees in small or medium-sized companies (Gould, 1990). ESOPs, like the more familiar co-operatives in the UK, are organisational structures which are designed to ensure greater employee involvement in decision making and which should feature increasingly in the British economy. They are also entities which lend themselves to greater environmental efficiency. Labour hires capital rather than the other way round, so there is significantly less likelihood of the kind of exploitative relationship with human and natural resources which often characterises traditional capitalistic enterprises.

Thus, in the next few decades, we should look forward to a decentralised economy, a diversity of productive organisational structures, and with a markedly enhanced role for employees and workers in all decisions affecting the growth, development and environmental performance of their enterprises. We must create the climate of controls and attitudes for a strong, decentralised and environmentally conscious network of pollution control, waste minimisation, waste collection, segregation and recycling operations, promoted by regional and local governments and accountable to local people and the workforces involved. But there is no possibility that this will occur without a clear lead from national government.

Of course there will always be some enterprises which because of either their size or the nature of their business require special forms of environmental regulation by national or supranational agencies. Multinational corporations with monopolistic tendencies present special problems because of their ability to switch production or waste disposal from countries with strict environmental standards to countries with lower standards. Such corporations need to be made accountable through the application of international standards and their enforcement by agencies acting in coordination, not in isolation. For example, it is relatively easy to force US-based companies to behave responsibly with respect to the import or export of hazardous wastes, because the US Environmental Protection Agency demands full documentation in both directions. It is much less clear whether such strict requirements have been observed by US subsidiaries elsewhere –

particularly in less developed countries, although in the UK too we have had problems with waste originating in the USA which has slipped through the control network. And although some multinationals claim to meet equally high standards of environmental performance in all countries in which they operate, the evidence suggests otherwise. Indeed, it is revealing that many corporations stop short of claiming to apply US or EC standards in Latin America, Africa or Asia – merely that they observe the national laws and regulations in each country in which they operate.

Another form of enterprise which requires special attention (this time at national level) is the natural monopoly which concerns local resources. In this category we may include the gas and electricity utilities, coal mining and – of particular interest to me – the water industry. There is no doubt that such monopolies are in a privileged position, with respect to both price setting and resource consumption. This privilege is in grave danger of being abused, especially by those recently privatised industries concerned with energy production and water supply in the UK.

I have already described what I think is a potential danger with the privatised monopoly industries – that of unholy alliances for inappropriate investments. But of much greater concern to me is the danger that some 'investments' may be made for reasons which have nothing to do with improving services or protecting the environment and everything to do with maximising consumption and maximising profits.

The water industry provides perhaps the most glaring example of a resource-rich enterprise which is now as likely to make a strategic investment decision for purely commercial gain as it is for the reasons of improving drinking water quality or cleaning beaches. Why else would the newly privatised water companies now be diversifying into areas such as solid waste disposal, hazardous waste incineration and even television franchises and hotel management? The arguments about domestic water metering have especially highlighted the water industry's commercial aspirations.

Everyone is by now aware that global warming is going to change weather patterns in the UK as everywhere else. Rainfall is likely to become more intense and more seasonal; meanwhile summers are going to get hotter and drier. Regional imbalances in water availability will become more acute, with the South East of England being especially vulnerable to diminishing sources, through low river flows and declining underground aquifers.

The response of some economists and conservationists has been to argue passionately for water metering as a means of restricting demand. They do this from a real concern for the long term security of drinking water supplies and vulnerable aquatic habitats. In contrast, a variety of consumer and public interest groups consider water metering a real assault on the needs and welfare of the old, the young and the poor. My own view is that those favouring domestic water meters have not been able to prove their case. In countries with meters water consumption is often higher than in Britain. Moreover, while the level of charging for water is important, it is inevitable that the area where increases in consumption will occur in future will be in luxury uses, not ordinary family consumption. People who can afford swimming pools will fill them whatever the cost.

But what was most interesting throughout these debates about water metering was the attitude of the water companies. At the time of privatisation, most of the water companies showed a real interest in metering which indeed could bring them advantages; and, moreover, in some areas meters were introduced for new consumers and made compulsory for non-residential properties from scout huts to small businesses. Regardless of the cost of installing meters (estimated at more than £2 billion) and the fact that this investment would not improve anyone's service but simply redistribute charge burdens, the companies felt the investment might help their plans to turn water into a marketable commodity. However, one year after privatisation, and with profits soaring nicely (even in the absence of metering), the companies had all but lost interest in the idea of compulsory universal metering. This left the conservationists high and dry. Even if their arguments had been right, they would have counted for nothing with the water industries given the overwhelming commercial priorities.

Clearly this is no way to exercise control over such a vital resource as water. And it is the most powerful current example of the socialist case that there are some industries which are simply too important to leave to free-market principles of management. Water privatisation was ideologically driven, and took no account of public opinion, public health, environmental priorities or consumers' rights. There can be no doubt that the only logical move for a Labour government inheriting such bizarre animals as the private water companies is to ensure their return to public control in the shortest timescale possible. The price paid by consumers and the environment will be much greater in the long run if such action is not taken, although obviously there can be significant achievements in advance of such a step by the greater use of regulatory mechanisms – both on charging policy and environmental controls.

It is not just in the public utilities that priorities must change, and it is not just government that will exert pressure. A survey carried out in 1989 for the Scottish Equitable pension fund found that 96 per cent of people interviewed would not want to invest in some areas for 'ethical' reasons. The area of concern most frequently raised by respondents was pollution of the environment. This was mentioned by 74 per cent of people compared with only 51 per cent who were concerned about South Africa.

In response to growing environmental concerns a whole series of 'green' unit trusts have been launched over the last few years. In 1991, Pensions Investments Research Consultants (PIRC) listed 18 funds with a total value of £190 million. While this may be a very small proportion of the total unit trust market, it is growing rapidly.

There is also a growing trend on the part of pension funds, which hold about 30 per cent of company shares, to take environmental performance into account when making investment decisions and to put pressure on companies in which shares are held to improve standards. This is a positive development, but there is a danger that many individuals and funds are investing with good intentions but with absolutely no knowledge about the validity of the 'green' claims being made by some corporations.

In fact some of the so-called 'green funds' have little real interest in the environmental record of the companies they buy – rather they see a chance to increase profits in a new sector. These funds buy what are known in the jargon as 'green opportunity stocks'. This means companies which are well placed to make money out of tighter environmental legislation – particularly companies in the waste or water treatment businesses.

A good example (cited by Anne Simpson in her book *The Greening of Global Investment*) is a large and well-known corporation – a precious metal dealer and smelting company which is included in the James Capel Green Book (their list of green stocks) because it has a prime position in the market for platinum – a key component of catalytic converters. The company is poised to benefit from new EC laws making catalytic converters obligatory on all new cars by 1993 and this is the basis for its inclusion, not its own environmental performance. However, the environmental impact of smelting is far from green; indeed it can be extremely harmful to the environment.

Some funds are more rigorously screened and an effort is made to include companies from different sectors which are genuine in their commitment to the environment or which make a positive contribution to environmental protection. But the criteria for inclusion in the green funds are in the main extremely vague and give no real basis for comparison between companies. Ultimately the confidence which an investor can have in the environmental record of the companies included will largely depend on the quality of information which analysts are able to or choose to obtain.

The difficulty which investors experience in obtaining information from British companies underlines yet again the need for far greater freedom of environmental information in Britain. It also highlights the need for a benchmark against which companies' green claims can be judged. This is not a uniquely British problem, but elsewhere shareholders are increasingly using their financial powers to force companies to adopt more sustainable and responsible policies. For example, The Valdez Principles form a code of corporate environmental conduct which was launched by shareholders who had assets of $350 billion in the Exxon Oil Company after the major spill from the Valdez tanker in Prince William Sound, Alaska, in 1989. In this country, the Fisons Peat campaign is a good example of joint action by environmentalists and active shareholders to put pressure on a company to improve its environmental performance.

However, all the evidence suggests that environmental awareness is still at an early stage among shareholders and companies in Britain. In a survey carried out by Touche Ross in 1990 a majority of European companies thought legislation would have a 'major impact on all aspects of their business', but in Britain a majority thought their industries would not be seriously affected.

Some UK companies said their activities had no impact on the environment, a claim made nowhere else in Europe. Thus, there might be a green veneer to much advertising and public relations, but there is little evidence that the majority of British companies are really convinced of the need to take a critical approach to their whole operation from top to bottom.

Inevitably, this whole area will have to become a matter for government intervention. Indeed, because of the intimate linkage between green claims, green investment and fair trade, any national regulations will also have to tie in with existing and future European Community policy on everything from the Single Market to ecolabelling.

I have already described the value and importance of environmental auditing and impact assessments as mechanisms for improving freedom of environmental information in the community and in the workplace. Such techniques should also serve to provide quantitative factual information on which investment decisions may be based, whether at the individual or pension fund level.

The case for making regular audits of environmental performance a mandatory requirement is now overwhelming, at least for all large and medium-sized companies. European Community proposals for a directive which would have required such audits were overruled, but it is inevitable that consumer pressure and the need for real comparative information by investors will force companies down this road in any case. Socialist governments in Europe should respond by introducing mandatory national schemes as soon as possible; then by force of example and by exerting pressure through the structures of the European Community, they should ensure that environmental auditing becomes an integral part of free and fair trading within Europe.

In Britain, a logical first step for many companies should be the adoption of formal environmental management systems. A scheme has been proposed by the British Standards Institution which, if successful, would provide a starting point for those companies really wishing to demonstrate their commitment to sound environmental practice. Moreover, companies which obtain BSI or similar accreditation for environmental management should have nothing to fear from any UK or EC system for mandatory environmental auditing. There are now a large number of consultants working in this field who are capable of assisting commercial companies in the execution of audits (though there is a need for an accreditation system). And organisations such as Business in the Environment, the Trade Union Congress and the Confederation of British Industry all provide publications, guides and checklists which give advice to companies embarking on their first environmental audit.

Interestingly, the system of environmental management proposed by BSI is similar to another standard which has worked very successfully in British industry concerned with quality assurance (BS 5750). Companies which attain BS 5750 must demonstrate a high level of commitment to quality assurance of products or services, and this commitment must extend throughout the organisation and every stage of production. It therefore depends a great deal on employee motivation and involvement. The parallel with good environmental practice is obvious. Ideally a commitment to overall quality management should automatically result in the minimisation or reduction of wastes at source (whether as a result of loss or spoilage of products) or simply through increased efficiency in production or supply and energy used. Such improvements have a direct environmental benefit as well as improving profitability.

The environmental management system proposed by BSI may ultimately extend throughout the commercial economy, since it could also result in small companies having to meet environmental performance targets introduced by their 'customers', i.e. those larger companies who wish to apply the same rules to their suppliers as to themselves. Large and medium-sized companies conducting environmental audits will increasingly apply principles of 'life cycle analysis' to their products and processes and this will place greater responsibilities on suppliers to provide environmental information on raw materials, e.g. details of energy consumption, sustainability of source and so on.

As environmental auditing spreads and as formal accreditation schemes gather momentum, it should become simpler for investors to make real judgements about the comparative environmental performance of commercial companies. Governments must ensure that schemes are nationally and internationally consistent, and in the UK there is a strong case for involving agencies responsible for environmental protection in the accreditation process.

This brings us to perhaps the most important question of all: how to make industry itself less polluting. The consultancy group Ecotec have estimated that the European pollution control market will expand from $33 billion per annum (US) in 1989 to $47.2 billion per annum in 1995. Much of this growth is of course driven by stricter environmental legislation from the European Community. Just one new directive – the Municipal Waste Water Treatment Directive – will precipitate expenditure of over $100 billion throughout the EC over a period of 10–15 years. But in the UK, lethargy on environmental standards has meant that we have fallen behind in developing clean technologies and clean production techniques. The sad fact is that many pollution control technologies have been invented in Britain but gone abroad to be developed, manufactured and sold. Typically, such technologies are marketed by companies in countries where stronger regulations force industry to clean up.

For example, British industry has conceded to Sweden much of the development and marketing of fluidised bed combustion technology which is a considerably cleaner way of burning coal than conventional combustion techniques. The development of anaerobic digestion technologies for the treatment of industrial wastewater was promoted in Germany, Holland and Denmark far in advance of its adoption by the UK. The catalytic convertor was invented in Britain but has only become a standard item on cars manufactured in more progressive European countries.

The point hardly needs emphasising that in the long run lax standards do British industry no good if, meanwhile, other countries are pressing ahead with environmental improvements. A report from the Department of Trade and Industry, 'Markets for Environmental Monitoring Instrumentation', accepted that British manufacturers of pollution monitoring equipment have been hampered by the slow development of environmental legislation in this country. In fact the UK's share of EC exports of air pollution control equipment fell from 63 to 40 per cent between 1975 and 1985 (Elkington and Burke, 1987). In 1988, ICI and Shell Chemicals spent less as a proportion of sales on environmental protection than BASF, Hoechst and Bayer of Germany, Ciba Geigy of Switzerland and Enimont of Italy. Meanwhile, in the USA, public and private expenditure on environmental protection is around $100 billion per annum.

European, international and domestic pressure means that stronger environmental protection is inevitable. For British industry this should be seen as an opportunity and a challenge rather than a threat.

However, as I have already argued, there is a very long way to go before British industry is able to benefit fully from the opportunities created by the green industrial revolution. It will require investment in research and development on a scale orders of magnitude greater than the few millions of pounds presently devoted to the Department of the Environment and the Department of Trade and Industry. But 'eco-opportunism' is only one side of the equation. British industry can and must develop clean processes and technologies which ameliorate or eliminate environmental pollution altogether and these should be marketed and exported with an equivalent vigour to that exhibited by companies based in Germany, Switzerland, Scandinavia or North America. But there are sound ethical and economic arguments for British industry adopting better environmental practices regardless of the type and derivation of technologies which may assist in the process. At a fundamental and ethical level, UK companies should be playing their part in ensuring that Britain's economy moves on to a more sustainable footing, that natural resources and raw materials are conserved and that wastes are minimised or eliminated altogether.

The term 'clean technology' is one which is open to a variety of interpretations. For example, there has been a tendency in many quarters to consider 'bolt-on' or 'end of pipe' solutions as an adequate response to immediate problems of industrial pollution, whether of air or water. As increasingly strict environmental quality objectives have been adopted, so tighter limits have been placed on chemicals discharged from power stations, incinerators, factories and wastewater treatment plants. This has led industry to introduce filters, scrubbers, precipitators and sedimenters into effluent streams in order to reduce the concentration of pollutants to within limits judged acceptable by regulatory agencies. Such an approach has been convenient to adopt in Britain – especially in those cases where negotiated 'consent' limits have been the favoured means of regulating the amounts and concentrations of individual pollutants which a plant may discharge into the environment. However, in recent years both the philosophy and the practice have been found wanting.

In the first instance, 'end of pipe' solutions often serve merely to redirect the environmental impact from one medium to another. The use of lime to reduce acid emissions from power stations necessitates the quarrying of limestone from areas of scenic beauty. The removal of contaminants from liquid effluents by sedimentation and precipitation creates sludges which must then be landfilled or incinerated. This may result in the transportation and disposal of potentially toxic materials either into the atmosphere or to the land. Secondly, in the absence of adequate policing and enforcing mechanisms, companies can risk breaching consent limits on a frequent basis, for example if filters become overloaded or if they are operated in an inefficient manner.

Some industries use the municipal sewage treatment works as their 'end of pipe' technology. In an unholy alliance with the water industry, they pay a fee for the privilege of discharging wastes to the public sewer which then contaminate sludges produced by sewage works. This renders them unsuitable for use as agricultural fertilisers and soil conditioners. The sad thing is that those industries which are not presently connected to public sewers but which discharge direct to rivers or estuaries are now actively encouraged by the National Rivers Authority to connect into the sewers in order to alleviate surface water pollution. This perpetuates the system of pollutant transfer between media and completely fails to break with Britain's traditional 'dilute and disperse' mentality which implies that ultimately the environment is a free good. Policy failures of this kind have led many commentators to place less emphasis on end of pipe solutions and instead to encourage the more holistic concepts of 'clean production' and 'pollution prevention'.

Clean production implies the inclusion of all aspects of procurement, processing and distribution in the environmental balance sheet. It also means that environmental performance is not judged simply on the plant's record of compliance with emission standards. The minimisation of energy consumption and wastes, and the reuse or recycling of byproducts (including packaging), all become important factors in the equation. Many industries have demonstrated that by adopting a clean production strategy they have been able to 'close the loop' on certain forms of pollution and waste thereby totally eliminating some environmental impacts. And most importantly from the companies' point of view, they have quickly recovered investments, saved money and improved public esteem into the bargain. The US Environmental Protection Agency's Office of Pollution Prevention maintains an information clearing house with computerised access to hundreds of contacts and case studies which demonstrate exactly these points. John Skinner of the USEPA (1991) quotes various cases of process modifications leading, for example, to an 81 per cent reduction in hazardous waste output in the chlorinated solvents industry; to a reduction in waste generation (with $150,000 increased revenues in fertiliser sales) from ammonium sulphate wastewater treatment; and large reductions in wastes and an annual $30,000 saving in costs through an internal waste minimisation programme in a laboratory operation.

There is a well-known saying 'where there's muck, there's brass'. Roughly modified for today's environmental vernacular, this should become 'pollution prevention pays'. This indeed is precisely the message of the 3M corporation in its strategy for promoting best environmental practice. Of course it is always more cost effective, for the whole of society, for firms to avoid pollution and waste than to eliminate or dispose of them later; and it can also be more cost effective for the companies themselves. But it must be recognised that for many industrial processes, this will necessitate a period of transition during which substantial innovation and investment will be required. This is where government must play a decisive role.

It would be ludicrously optimistic to expect industry to change the philosophy and practices of decades overnight, simply because government willed it. Clearly, there is plenty of scope in the regulatory mechanisms of pollution control to enable government to force industry to reduce emissions of pollutants to air, water or land. And given the integration and enhancement of UK administrative structures proposed in Chapter 5, I have no doubt that a British Labour government would ensure much stricter enforcement of industrial emission standards to protect the quality of the environment. Market opportunities may also induce some companies to embrace aspects of clean production, as may persuasion, education and dissemination of examples of good practice. But when it comes to such issues as waste minimisation at source and energy efficiency, it is very difficult to dictate to an individual company what should happen within its factory walls in order that it moves rapidly towards best environmental practice. It may be possible to set targets for entire industries or sectors, but how is this to be translated into action at the company level?

All the evidence of the last few years shows that pollution control legislation, identification of market opportunities and dissemination of examples of best environmental practice are not, in themselves, adequate to ensure significant progress towards waste minimisation and energy efficiency. Thus if British industry is to be properly galvanised into clean production, some irresistible inducements and substantial amounts of technical assistance are going to be required.

One proposal which could be useful is a specific energy levy for industry, the proceeds of which would be used exclusively for the promotion of energy conservation by the provision of grants and technical support. This could fit into a system of integrated pollution control which included energy conservation standards which had to be met prior to obtaining planning consent for new factories or authorisation for new processes. In addition, there is a strong case for the introduction of levies on all forms of waste disposal (notably incineration and landfill), the income being devoted to research, development and the application of clean production techniques – in particular the elimination, minimisation, reuse or recycling of wastes. Any such levies could commence at relatively modest and painless levels. But the intention must be to raise sufficient money to make a real difference to the industries concerned and provide significant incentives for industries to apply for grants and technical advice, to plan investments and, ultimately, to minimise their own costs. Such a policy could achieve dramatic reductions in industrial energy consumption and waste production over a period of 5–10 years. Side benefits would include substantial reductions in national carbon dioxide emissions, reductions in pressures on landfill sites and incineration facilities, and overall improvements in the efficiency and sustainability of British industry.

Specific percentage waste reduction or recycling targets for different industries may also be valuable within the context of national and regional plans, but care will need to be exercised in order not to penalise those industries and individual companies which have already made significant progress. This will require a comprehensive knowledge of long term trends in the composition and volumes of waste streams. It would be helpful if industry was required to draw up and publish waste reduction plans on a plant-by-plant basis, providing details of specific commitments which could be measured and compared over a number of years. In the United States, this is now a requirement under the Pollution Prevention Act. The Labour Party is already committed to variations in the rate of Value Added Tax for products which incorporate a minimum quantity of recycled materials, penalising the unsustainable use of virgin raw materials. But an all-encompassing levy on waste disposal would serve to move the entire economy into a pollution prevention and waste minimisation philosophy.

In the United States, some county sanitation departments have increased municipal solid waste landfill costs by factors of three and more in recent years to more than $100 per US ton in some cases. This has allowed best environmental practice to be combined with the promotion of reuse and recycling schemes which allow for significant proportions of wastes to be eliminated from the waste stream. In 1990 and 1991, the state of California planned to invest a staggering $600 million in waste reduction and recycling schemes. This also allowed it to postpone or cancel plans for a number of 'mass-burn' incinerators. There is absolutely no reason why the principles behind these strategies should not be applied to industrial wastes, whether of a hazardous or non-hazardous nature.

A similar philosophy of levies and incentive charging can be applied in the pollution control field to supplement the effect of tighter emission standards and environmental quality objectives. In Germany companies which invest in pollution abatement technologies receive reductions in levies. Elsewhere, for example in France, there are tax breaks and long term, low interest loans available to companies wishing to improve their environmental performance.

In the long term, reductions in energy consumption and waste production will bring tangible benefits to the national economy. By reducing the need for importation of fuel and other raw materials and by improving production efficiency, both the balance of payments and the competitiveness of British industry will improve. Useful and worthwhile employment will be created in energy conservation and in waste collection, sorting and recycling. The level of technological innovation and technical assistance provided by bodies such as the Department of Trade and Industry's Warren Spring Laboratory will be markedly enhanced, and much of the government's contribution to this effort can be met by the levies and charges associated with environmental protection.

We need a body, like the French Institut National de L'Environment Industriel et des Risques (INERIS), which is capable of advising and leading the way on clean production research and development. The only body in the UK capable of fulfilling this role is the Warren Spring Laboratory. And, as happens in the case of the Office of Pollution Prevention in the US Environmental Protection Agency, the Warren Spring Laboratory should be given a leading role in assisting private industry, local government and the non-governmental sector to set up demonstration projects in clean production techniques, waste minimisation, recycling and reuse, energy reduction and clean technologies.

Together with Labour's Environment Protection Executive, Warren Spring could be charged with sorting out the problem of contaminated land sites, and with maintaining an emergency response capability in the event of incipient or actual direct threats to human health or the environment in the United Kingdom or overseas.

Given political commitment and strategic intervention by government, opportunities should arise to commercialise and export British expertise and technology in clean production. Instead of importing toxic waste, we should export our technology. Britain could still become a key player rather than a bystander in the green industrial revolution. The last 13 years of sterile, unthinking dependence on market ideology has, quite simply, proven disastrous. British industry has missed commercial opportunities and the economy and the environment have both suffered. We need the vision to help British industry invest in the technology and processes that will ensure its efficiency and success into the next century. There is no better example of why a Labour government is needed to improve the long term prospects of British industry for the soundest practical, ethical and environmental reasons.

Undoubtedly we shall require a national plan for waste with strict targets for waste minimisation applied to each industry and sector. We will need to agree regional targets for municipal waste reduction, for recycling and recovery rates. And governments at every level will have to ensure that by their own procurement policies and interventions, strong markets are created for recycled goods like paper, board and plastics (glass and aluminium markets are already quite robust). The water industry will have to ensure the reduction of industrial waste inputs to sewers in order to safeguard the quality of sewage sludge. Many places, for example Paris, New York and Orange County (USA), have demonstrated that by applying vigorous trade effluent controls, dramatic reductions can be achieved in levels of toxic metals and organics discharged to public sewers. When this is done, all sewage sludge can be reused as a safe, natural fertiliser and soil conditioner in agriculture, horticulture or forestry. National targets should be set for this too. It may be necessary to encourage compacts or trading agreements between individual industries and regions in order to secure national goals in the most cost effective way.

We shall also require a national plan for energy conservation, in private industry as well as in the domestic and public sectors. Again, government must set strict and enforceable targets and be prepared to provide significant incentives and to impose sanctions in order to make rapid progress.

All of these measures imply intervention and overriding of the so-called free market. But anyone who has collected newspapers for recycling, only to find that the newspaper industry cannot be bothered to create any demand, will know perfectly well that some markets need to be carefully nurtured. Long term environmental gains must be underpinned by short and medium term strategic investment. We should not be afraid to intervene in this way when it is ethically, environmentally and economically the right thing to do.

But even if all of the above steps were taken and if, as well, the whole of British industry moved rapidly and efficiently towards clean production techniques, many intractable problems would still remain, as a legacy from the past. Industrially and agrochemically contaminated land, for example, concerns many people, not least because of the great difficulty we will have in identifying who may be responsible and how they may be made to pay for past mistakes.

In the United States there are more than 1,200 sites on the National Priority List for clean-up under the so-called Superfund Legislation. This legislation was enacted in 1980 following the 1978 scandal of New York's 'Love Canal' where toxic wastes, including dioxins, were discovered seeping into the basements of residential properties. Originally budgeted at $8 billion, the fund was raised by a tax on the oil, petrochemical and chemical industries. But it is envisaged that, by 1993, at least $300 million will be added to the fund each year as a result of successful litigation against those responsible for the contamination of land and groundwater resources.

We are only just beginning to recognise the extent and severity of the contaminated land problem in Britain. Local authorities have been asked to compile registers of potentially contaminated sites. However, no-one has any idea what the final bill might be for cleaning up these sites – it could be hundreds of millions of pounds per annum by the end of this century. So we urgently need to put in place a mechanism for ensuring that remedial work goes ahead, without being delayed by the very time-consuming and sometimes wasteful efforts which the United States presently devotes to litigation on the problem.

There is no doubt that we shall discover many horror stories. Poorly managed toxic waste landfills, decommissioned gas works, coke works and power stations, farm waste dumps and abandoned military bases will ensure that Britain has its fair share of land and groundwater contamination problems for many years to come. Agrochemicals, heavy metals, poly-chlorinated biphenyls (PCBs), solvents and radioactive substances will be among the cocktail of contaminants we shall have to deal with.

We have no option but to take urgent action to identify sites, to assess the magnitude of immediate threats to public health and the environment, to rank contaminated sites in order of urgency of remedial action and to get on with the job. There is some logic in insisting that all those who have been involved in the creation, transportation, treatment or disposal of hazardous wastes should ultimately pay for the clean-ups, ideally on a full polluter pays basis. Indeed, it is to be hoped that the EC will enshrine the

Superfund concept of 'strict, joint and several' liability for polluters in its proposed legislation on the subject. But we may as well recognise now that in many cases no polluter will be available to sue and hence some kind of general fund will need to be raised in any case.

Also we will need to consider how to avoid the problems of industrial, agrochemical and military contamination of land in the future. In one sense, regulating and inspecting the hazardous waste treatment and disposal industries is the simplest part. If companies involved in those industries also develop some form of mutual fund or insurance policy which guards against an individual company going bankrupt on the discovery of a single major contamination problem, that will help solve any future difficulties concerning liability or ability to pay for clean-ups. But it is a very different matter policing activities and averting contamination of land when the responsible party is the civil nuclear power industry or the Ministry of Defence.

Indeed, when agrochemicals continue to be scattered in small and diffuse quantities on remote farmland and when mining and refining industries are bound to conduct their activities in inaccessible regions, it is difficult to envisage what kind of pollution prevention strategy will be most effective.

There is a strong case for following some aspects of the US system, and attractions in their use of a rolling fund of clean-up reserves based on a levy imposed on the main industries concerned (power, mining, petrochemicals and agro-chemicals). Such a fund could be administered by trustees who would include representatives of the relevant industries. Although past errors would necessarily result in early demands on the proceeds of such a fund, progress in clean-ups and better environmental practice in industry, agriculture and the armed forces would gradually result in a diminution of demand. Where specific culprits were identified, it would be worth taking all possible steps to recover costs directly to replenish the fund. But it would be vital to ensure that court proceedings did not delay remedial action on contaminated sites.

It almost goes without saying that all practical, political and ethical considerations argue against the importation or exportation of hazardous wastes across national boundaries – save in very exceptional circumstances: for example, where help needs to be provided in the event of disasters elsewhere. The Basle Convention will result in significant reductions in the transboundary shipment of such materials for routine treatment and disposal. As socialists, our objective should be to outlaw such practices altogether, except where there is a proven, environmental reason. Waste is best eliminated or treated as close to the source of its creation as possible. That should apply as much to nuclear waste as to toxic or other hazardous residues. There is nothing like the visible and embarrassing fouling of one's own nest to force good housekeeping and the devotion of maximum efforts to pollution prevention.

We need to establish a comprehensive inventory of all toxic or harmful substances arising from industrial, agricultural, military or similar activities. There should also be a system for tracking and auditing all movements and disposals of hazardous waste. Naturally, all of this information should be available to local communities and local environmental health departments who are in the immediate vicinity of hazardous waste facilities and the movements of dangerous materials. This will enable public pressure to be exerted on hazardous waste producers, treaters and transporters to provide sound reasoning for their waste policies and clear safeguards for the integrity of their operations.

In conclusion, there are innumerable preconditions which must be met in order to improve prospects for the greening of British industry. These include attitudinal, cultural, organisational and financial reforms. We need a government which will create a framework for pollution prevention and waste minimisation which rewards best practice and penalises lack of progress; a government which will raise and deploy significant amounts of money to provide incentives to industry to adopt best practice, in the context of a tight, regulatory framework of controls.

Wastes should be dealt with as close as possible to the source of their production and, in any case, reduced, recycled or reused to the greatest extent possible before treatment and disposal options are considered. Types and quantities of wastes need to be understood and defined with respect to time and changing economic circumstances. Trade in wastes, whether hazardous or non-hazardous, should be blocked whenever possible, and any move by economic or political institutions such as the EC or

GATT to define this as a restriction of free trade should be rejected.

Our obligations to people and planet require us to ensure that every member of the workforce, every trade union, every manager, every board member, every trustee of a pension fund, every consumer and every investor considers the environmental implications of each and every economic decision they make; but the key must be a positive lead from government.

Chapter 7

Economics for our future

Environmental protection is inseparable from the other functions of government. Most notably, energy, trade, agricultural, industrial and transport decisions all have an environmental impact; so environmental policy, if it is to be effective, must be integrated into the policies of all these departments. Even more fundamentally, environmental protection must be integrated into management of the economy, which tends to be regarded as the central task of modern government, and which sets the parameters for the operations of other departments.

For the most serious environmental problems – from acid rain and pollution of groundwater to global warming – are caused by economic activity. Economic policy, which already seeks to control the scope and nature of that activity, is therefore the area that above all others needs to be addressed if we are to enhance and safeguard the environment.

But while it is clear that economic activity gives rise to all the problems, it is very far from clear that economists, as academics or practitioners, have all the answers. Economics is a very inexact science, and most ordinary, intelligent people regard the projections and statistics of economists with a large degree of scepticism. Indeed, it is often said that if civil engineers made as many mistakes as Treasury economists, there would be hardly a bridge left standing in the country! In fact, if one considers how far engineering or medicine have advanced in the last 200 years, the advances in orthodox economic analysis seem very small indeed.

J. K. Galbraith (1979), in *The Affluent Society*, noted the staying power of 'conventional wisdom', showing how received ideas can remain in circulation long after their explanatory force has been rendered null and void by new developments in the real world. Once a broad framework of ideas is accepted, learned professors may make their reputations through passionate skirmishes about the details, but few will venture to challenge the basics: those who do so will be written off as harmless eccentrics or dangerous radicals.

From an environmental point of view, if from no other, much conventional, economic wisdom long ago reached its sell-by date, and the basis of the framework needs to be re-examined. Among the first to reach this conclusion (and therefore regarded as an eccentric in many quarters) was the maverick economist E. F. Schumacher, who 20 years ago was arguing that infinite economic growth is not possible in a world of finite resources. In the three decades since the end of the Second World War, he pointed out, more industrial activity and consumption of resources had taken place than in the entire previous history of humankind (Schumacher, 1973). This could not continue exponentially and indefinitely. Indeed, it couldn't continue for very long at all.

Socialism, for Schumacher, was 'of interest solely for its non-economic values and for the possibility it creates of overcoming the religion of economics'. This is an interesting, but rather odd remark, implying that 'non-economic values' are an appendage of socialism rather than (as I argued in Chapter 1) lying at its very core. Schumacher warned that if socialism agreed with capitalism on the central thesis of human welfare being best served by an increase in general prosperity and consumption, then it had no future. Yet, while acknowledging the danger, we need not feel too threatened by this: clearly, we are not simply interested in increasing material consumption. But if ours is a broader concern for the quality of life and the quality of people's environments, it certainly remains true that removing poverty and deprivation is essential to improving the quality of life of very many people, both in this and in less developed countries.

One of the skills that enabled Schumacher to swim with such relative success against the tide of conventional wisdom – to the extent of soon becoming something of a guru to (predominantly young) people disillusioned with 'materialist' values – was his talent for putting new and complicated ideas remarkably simply. Typical of this was the title of his collection of essays, 'Small is Beautiful'. But in fact this was an oversimplification. Small is not always and in all cases beautiful. The transference to new, clean technologies will not always mean a reduction in the scale of operation: I myself was recently asked to and did formally to 'open' a new, industrial boiler that was larger than the boilers it was replacing but which, because it used clean coal technology, was also considerably less wasteful and less polluting. In wider, overseas development terms, the viability of many useful and necessary projects depends upon the installation of energy and industrial plant on a scale that would deeply offend any *a priori* commitment to smallness.

This is not to deny the originality and importance of central features in Schumacher's case. His critique of Third World development models remains relevant, if interpreted broadly as an argument for socially and environmentally appropriate technologies in place of haphazard attempts to imitate Western 'progress'. And he was perfectly right to identify and challenge the assumption of continual growth, from a perspective of desirability as much as from one of physical possibility.

These ideas have enjoyed slowly increasing influence, but there has been considerable resistance to them from some socialists. Two important factors shed light upon this: firstly, the refusal of socialists to abandon a vision of social progress, and the linking of this notion to the eradication of poverty, always evident enough to make talk of halting growth seem ridiculous; and secondly, the pernicious influence of Thatcherism in the 1980s.

The many and bizarre accolades to Thatcher that we have heard since her demise obscure the simplicity and the logic of what she in fact achieved. Schumacher was fond of quoting Keynes, who in a particularly gloomy moment, in 1930, declared that 'Avarice and usury . . . must be our gods for a little longer still. For only they can lead us out of the tunnel of economic necessity.' This was the bottom line defence of twentieth century capitalism: only greed gets people going. And this, clearly, was Thatcher's *idée fixe*: selfishness works; selfishness is good; selfishness is socially responsible. Keynes sounded like a tired and unhappy man in the middle of a Great Depression; Thatcher sounded jubilant.

It was a repulsive idea, which set all the political clocks back several decades. In the late 1960s and 1970s, many socialists had been looking seriously at the realities of life on the shop floor, questioning the rationality of condemning women and men to mindless labour, subordinate to machinery in order to manufacture machinery in order to acquire the purchasing power to buy machinery. Marx' theory of alienated labour was one of the main talking points on the intellectual left, while practical socialists were thinking about new models of industrial democracy and looking at ways (like those being pioneered by Volvo, who restructured their production process so that tasks were no longer broken down into simple, repetitive functions) of making the experience of work more creative. Schumacher and socialism were, in fact, getting very close.

Thatcher put a brake to the progress of all such idealism. She brought all the arguments right back to a more materialistic level, for she re-invented the crudities of capitalism, and the free, unfettered market. The entire labour movement was thrown on the defensive, as unions came under attack, public services were dismantled and unemployment deliberately allowed to rise. Concern for the quality of the working environment and the value of material consumption suddenly seemed a luxury or a distraction from the more pressing business of defending jobs, services, and even manufacturing industry itself.

But if this slowed down Labour's new emphasis on quality issues, the 'no growth' platform of many early, environmental lobbyists did much to prevent their case being listened to. Doyen of the Green Party, Jonathon Porrit, came close to accepting this in a recent interview:

> 'Sacrifice' is a concept that runs like a steady throb behind a lot of green literature – we're going to have to sacrifice because the Earth or the Third World demands it. I'm not sure that you can sell a whole, new political worldview on the strength of a sort of masochistic inclination.
>
> (*New Ground*, 29.)

Asking upper and middle income consumers to make sacrifices for the sake of others or for the sake of the environment may in itself be hard enough; but to tell pensioners, the unemployed, the low paid and the Third World that the good times are over and they cannot expect any future increase in living standards is not just hard, it is totally unacceptable. Labour Party members have, almost by definition, always been aware of the needs of the less privileged: it is the feeling that such needs should and could be met that draws them to the Party in the first place. So they are hardly likely to warm to a view that, by ruling out growth, also appears to rule out improving the lot of the many who remain needy.

But the fundamental debate about environment and growth has shifted significantly over the last two decades, in no small part precisely because of the insistence of socialists on attending to the material needs of poor people in both developed and developing countries. The no growth lobby has retreated to the inner recesses of the Green Party. The new focal point for discussion is not how to halt growth, but how to regulate it, and how to reconcile it with environmental protection. Framed in these terms, we can begin seriously to re-examine our attitudes towards economic development without discounting from the outset any possibility of increased production and wealth creation.

It is quite clear that the philosophy of capitalism is in a very much weaker position to make this kind of adjustment; for the individual pursuit of wealth, considered as the driving force of society, leads to degradation of the natural environment as inevitably as it leads to the exploitation of people. This is so not just because of the greed of the successful, but because of the logic of individual rationality itself, as has been recognised for several centuries in various formulations of what is known as 'the tragedy of the commons'. Taking the simplest model, we can imagine a pastoral society where individual families graze stock on common land. To maximise their gain, it is in the interests of each family to increase the number of animals they graze, although eventually this will lead to overgrazing, soil degradation, and ultimate tragedy for everyone. But even if some families recognise that collective disaster lies ahead, unless there is some agreed regulation of stock levels it is still in their interests to increase their individual production: because if they restrain their output on a purely individual basis, out of altruistic or ecological motives, they will have no guarantee that others will do likewise, and so will endure immediate sacrifice without saving the future either for themselves or for others.

This skeletal model shows the complete absence in a genuinely free market of any internal mechanisms for safeguarding either collective welfare or the environment itself. The much more complex reality of modern capitalism pits individual interest against collective interest in exactly the same way. It is in everybody's interests to stop the fouling of air, earth and water; but so long as this is only a matter of individual decision, it is in no individual's clear and obvious interest to do so, if others are unlikely to follow suit. This applies to production, where environmental costs have been considered 'external' to the cost of production, and where 'internalising' these costs on a voluntary basis – i.e., paying the additional costs of avoiding pollution – would, industrialists lament, merely make businesses uncompetitive. And the same unfortunate logic also applies to individual consumption: why should I personally give up the convenience of a private motor car, if no-one else is required to do likewise? I may well be left standing at the bus-stop in the rain, breathing in everyone else's exhaust fumes, unhappy in the knowledge that my sacrifice will have reduced our society's production of greenhouse gases by an immeasurably small fraction.

It is abundantly clear that a completely free market, in this sense, 'contains the seeds of its own destruction'. But the free market is in fact a chimera: a host of regulations of various kinds have affected trade and industry ever since the end of the feudal era. There is, after all, a distinction between anarchism and capitalist government, although this is not always apparent in the appeals of Conservative ministers to the 'market philosophy!' The implication of such appeals is that it is always best not to interfere with private economic activity. This is an obvious and dangerous nonsense. A regulatory approach, as pioneered by Labour since the inception of the party, and practised in other countries, is absolutely essential to environmental protection, as to all safeguards of collective welfare. However, it must of course be recognised that regulations can be used just to protect special interests, and so in themselves are no panacea: we need the right regulations, appropriate to achieving environmental objectives in a socially equitable way.

The first element of such an approach must be a lesson, drawn directly from business management itself, which Schumacher and many since have been right to insist upon: namely, the distinction between capital and income. A private concern, on any scale, will soon run into trouble if its capital is eaten away; and yet in our macroeconomic management we, and all industrialised nations, have for many years been 'borrowing environmental capital from future generations with no intention or ability to repay', as it was put in the Brundtland Report. More than this, the indicators that are normally taken to measure the income or wealth produced each year in a country – Gross National Product and Gross Domestic Product – include money generated by, for example, the extraction of oil or timber, without acknowledging the fact that these resources can only be used once, and once gone are lost for ever to future generations.

By analogy with a small business, this practice would be the same as producing annual accounts showing 'profits' that included, year after year, revenue from the sale of parts of the premises and other capital assets. The most junior trainee accountant would be quick to point out that these aren't profits at all: the whole future of the enterprise is being jeopardised for the sake of enjoying the cash now.

For these reasons, GNP has become the *bête noire* of many environmentalists. There has been much debate about ways to reform national income accounting to produce an annual figure that, unlike GNP, reflects resource depletion and pollution and so gives a truer picture of sustainable income – income that won't simply dry up one day when the capital is all used. Because of the importance of the issue, all plausible models for alternative indicators should be given serious attention. However, the complexity of quantifying and evaluating so many environmental variables is such that, even if a way to calculate a figure could be devised, it is highly likely that it would be rather sketchy and questionable.

It may well be, therefore, that a better way to proceed would be to retain GNP as a yardstick, but to be clearer about exactly what it measures: namely, no more and no less than the total economic activity in society, without the implicit assumption that economic activity itself is a true indication of income or lasting prosperity, much less of social well-being. It has usefully been suggested (e.g. Jacobs, 1991) that parallel, physical indicators of environmental degradation and resource depletion could be developed. These would be more straightforward than figures which attempted to put a cash value on environmental assets; and, for the sake of public awareness, could be published regularly in an 'environmental quality index' that embraced indicators of, for instance, air and water quality. France, Canada and Norway have already made progress in establishing national environmental databases of a kind that could provide a starting point for such an index. (For a discussion of developments in those countries, see Salah el Serafy's 'Natural resource accounting: An overview' in Winpenny, 1991b.)

Public opinion will, obviously, be a major factor in determining the nature and pace of environmental legislation over economic activity. Politicians should give a lead, but if they try to run too far ahead of public opinion they will not find themselves in power; and politicians who ignore public opinion while in power will not remain there very long. That is why I have argued at length for an improvement in access to and quality of environmental information and education, since an informed and educated public will exert the right kind of pressure on politicians. In the context of environmental and economic indicators, there is good reason to believe that physical indicators of damage and depletion would have a greater impact on public opinion than a highly complicated, reformed version of GNP.

An interesting comparison can be made with the way that we think about Third World development. Although GNP gives a rough guide to whether a whole, formal economy is expanding or contracting (not forgetting that there may be a very large informal economy which is not measured at all), everyone would readily accept that figures for child and infant mortality say far more about poverty or its absence than GNP per capita, which takes no account at all of income distribution. This is recognised, and emphasised, by nearly all professionals working in aid and development; which in itself shows that we are not, or need not be, so much in the thrall of GNP, as a unique and comprehensive tool, as some environmentalist objectors appear to believe. GNP can and must be put in context, as socialists have long argued in relation to distributional and welfare issues. We must now begin to consider not just the welfare context but the environmental context too.

Adjusting present economic indicators, or developing new indicators of environmental quality and resource depletion, will throw into sharper relief the question of preserving environmental capital, and the consequences this has for the kind of growth we can allow. We should not expect this to be a comfortable issue to confront. Successive generations have for a long time been led to expect a slow but steady increase in living standards. We have, broadly speaking, accepted until very recently that human society is constantly 'progressing', and although some sceptical voices occasionally questioned the nature of that progress, most people have assumed that future generations will be better off than we are. Certainly, looking back to the youth of our older relatives, the almost invariable message is that 'times were harder then', and this has seemed like confirmation of a general trend towards increased prosperity.

But facing up to environmental reality – which only recently began to impinge upon us – requires us to adopt a new attitude to future generations. We can no longer merely suppose that in the future people will be better off because of the mounting evidence that our own productive and destructive activity can result in permanent despoliation of the natural environment that provides the basis of all prosperity. This is a perturbing and completely new moral problem. It may well be that people in the past worried about what kind of world their children would inherit, in terms of social, political and military reality; but the new nightmare is that the children of tomorrow may inherit a world that, even if they have the resourcefulness and imagination to overcome all social and political troubles, is too damaged to support them. The irreversibility of the havoc that can be wreaked by disasters such as Chernobyl therefore places us in a wholly new relation to future people.

There is only one proper response to such an awesome responsibility. At its simplest, we must make sure things don't get worse; we must do everything in our power to make sure that future generations start off with at least as much chance as we have of enjoying a reasonable quality of life within a rich and diverse environment.

To say this is to assert the primacy of the ethical perspective. We should be quite clear that we are talking about a moral obligation, and equally clear that the obligation is irrefutable. To be sure, some people might ask, with a pretence at being down-to-earth, 'Why should we care as much about future people as about ourselves?' But in fact, of course, the onus is on such doubters to explain what is so special about them that they deserve more consideration than future people; and the truth will always be that they are not special at all. Just as any attempt at justifying egoism, racism or fascism has always stumbled at this first hurdle, so in these new circumstances we can see that there is no intelligible argument to support our greater right, against future generations, to consume the earth's resources.

In practical terms, all parents – and the overwhelming majority of the human race become parents – intuitively understand the wish to give our children at least as good a start in life as we ourselves had. Many of us have grander plans than that, which may or may not bear fruit; but I think we would all recognise a minimum responsibility not to leave our children worse equipped to face the future than we were. This applies equally to the great and the humble: from dynastic capitalists, who would be ashamed not to leave their heirs at least the same capital stock they started with, to unskilled labourers who strive to keep the wolf from the door. And this point is not a trivial one. The bearing and rearing of children is common to most peoples throughout history; it is deeply embedded in all of us and rightly shapes our priorities. We should not be embarrassed, therefore, to adopt something so unpretentious as the principles of parental responsibility in our formulation of national and global environmental policy.

But, grasping towards this truth, some in the early ecology movements concluded that we ought immediately to freeze all consumption and economic activity. In this we can recognise something of the panic shown by the man in the New Testament parable who buried his talent for fear of losing it. The difference, though, is that it is simply not feasible, let alone desirable, to call a halt to production, bury industrialism and retire to the hills, leaving the earth intact for the children of the future. Those who advocate such a course, although now in a small minority even within the environmentalist movement, have allowed their panic at the scale of environmental degradation to obscure all judgement as to what is practical. Furthermore they tend, in their anxiety to save the earth for the future, to disregard the claims of poor and oppressed people here and now, who don't need to give up a lifestyle of high material consumption because they have never 'enjoyed' any such thing. If we are not capable of doing right by such people now, we will scarcely be capable of doing right by people as yet unborn.

At the other extreme, reverting to the parable of the talents, there are those who argue that our duty to the future consists in maximising the technical and financial legacy we bequeath. How fortunate were we, they reason, to inherit a world where the wheel had already been invented, along with intensive agriculture, penicillin and television, so that we can enjoy the benefits of mobility, ample food, health and entertainment. And how even more fortunate will our children be, the argument goes, blessed with what we in our lifetimes can produce and invent. We should, on this view, invest our talents accordingly.

This perspective – really no more than a formal commitment to the belief in inevitable progress (led by greed) – is as dangerous as it is complacent. It ignores the fact that human creativity has not yet resolved the problem of extending the benefits of technological advance to all people. It ignores the fact that much of what we invent is not intrinsically desirable (nuclear, biological and chemical weaponry, cigarettes, food additives and child pornography, to name but a few) and that other products which initially seem desirable (generated electricity, motor cars, refrigerators) have environmental drawbacks that do not become apparent until many years after their introduction. This, in other words, is to ignore human fallibility. If our parents and we made a mess of the world, without ever intending to, what reason is there to suppose that from now onwards we will be immune from making similar, or even worse, mistakes if we continue to make decisions in the same way? We must, at least, take a precautionary approach to any new economic expansion, for the simple fact that we are not able always to predict the outcome of our actions.

Most crucially of all, an 'invest, and bequeath more' argument fails to account for the irreversibility of much environmental degradation. We may make giant strides in biotechnology, but we are a long way from being able to re-create the Dodo, or the North American passenger pigeon, or the thousands of other plant and animal species we destroy each year. This is direct interference with the opportunities and choices our descendants will have: straightforward robbery of the future.

Choice and opportunity are the key concepts here. It is these that we now have a responsibility to guarantee for future generations, and these that must inform our idea of what 'sustainability' or 'sustainable development' is. For it is clear enough that sustainability is the approach we must now adopt; but unfortunately it is not nearly so clear what this involves. Like many political concepts (such as 'justice', 'freedom' and 'democracy') almost everyone is agreed that sustainability is a good thing. But having a new buzzword in itself solves no problems at all. The real debate is between rival understandings of just what sustainability implies, and how it is to be achieved.

Perhaps the most influential (although by no means the most useful) current interpretation is that offered by David Pearce and the co-authors of *Blueprint for a Green Economy*. They propose a system of environmental protection, based on cost–benefit analysis and monetary evaluation of environmental assets, which has been well received on the right. It is, in effect, an attempt to reform and rescue rather than finally depart from the classical economic models, by creating a wholly artificial pricing system for 'goods' – like the atmosphere, the living landscape and the existence of whole species – for which markets never have existed. As such, this system has considerable appeal for those who have no deeper appreciation of value than the price at which things are exchanged; but it signally fails to do justice to future generations, most crucially because it is based entirely upon assessments made now, and so leaves out of account the preferences of people in the future. But despite the inherent weakness of this system, it has attracted considerable attention and so warrants detailed consideration.

Pearce *et al.* (1989) argue that a 'constant stock of capital' must be passed from generation to generation. This stock comprises the sum of natural capital (the atmosphere, rivers, forests and other reserves) and 'man-made' capital (technology, industry, agriculture, wildlife parks, etc.). It is, on this view, permissible to run down natural capital further, so long as man-made capital is increased proportionately. This rule is therefore 'consistent with removing the Amazon forests so long as the proceeds from this activity are reinvested to build up some other form of capital' (Pearce, 1991).

One immediate objection is that we are not to know the preferences of the next generation. Might not our grandchildren somewhat regret the absence of the Amazon forests if we chop them all down? And who are we to decide what kind of man-made capital, and how much of it, will serve to compensate them for the loss? We could, with the proceeds, develop a fantastic industry in personal submarines, and turn large areas of Antarctica over to a tourist resort and penguin park. But how are we to know that future generations would not prefer just to have the forests left intact?

In part answer to these objections, Pearce and his colleagues present environmental valuation as a way of enabling 'trade-offs' to be made between environmental and man-made capital. There is a certain logic in this. Differing amounts of two things can only be compared if they are measured in the same way. Man-made capital is measured in money. So in order to say that such and such an environmental feature (as an element of natural capital) can be traded off against an increase in man-made capital, we must take the simple step of deciding to measure those environmental features in terms of monetary value.

There are two kinds of technique for doing this. One involves studying actual behaviour in real markets, the other involves developing hypothetical models of what people would pay to preserve threatened environmental features, and thus of the implicit value they put upon them. The first methodology considers phenomena such as the lower market prices of houses under aeroplane flightpaths (so deriving a value for the peace of an aircraft-free existence) or the amount that people actually pay to travel for recreation to environmental amenities like clean beaches, hills and woods (so deriving an amenity value for these features). The second, hypothetical approach relies heavily on market surveys in which people are asked how much they would be willing to pay to preserve a rare orchid, a green field site, or a freshwater course.

In fairness, it must be said that environmental valuation techniques of this kind, however mad they may appear, have had a positive influence on some European and US environmental decision making. (See, e.g. the case studies collected in Barde and Pearce, 1991.) There is some evidence that cost–benefit analysis, as the principal formula for making planning decisions, will be less likely to leave the environment out of account if environmental valuations appear on the balance sheet. We can at any rate sympathise in principle with Pearce's claim that 'if the "true" value of the environment were known, we would not degrade it as much' (Pearce, 1991). It is good that this debate should be opened up, although unfortunately Pearce put it on the wrong tracks.

However, it must also be said that the first set of methods – those involving observed behaviour – has a much greater appearance of solidity, reliability and empirical verifiability. This is not surprising, because they are most like more established methods for calculating the total economic impact of new developments, and if these are thorough they will certainly take into account even quite remote consequences, such as the increased cost of restoring buildings when traffic is increased by new roads, and the effects on property values in the area. But these are based on 'old' criteria. Loss of leisure amenity can, perhaps, also be costed with reasonable accuracy, and it is proper that such costs be put in the balance.

But these apparently plausible methods are of little use in addressing the wider and more fundamental issues of environmental degradation. They clearly do not, for example, allow us to establish a value for the whole atmosphere, or for a measurable decline in atmospheric quality. Nor do they provide values for threatened wildlife or threatened species. In order to generate such values, the 'contingent' or hypothetical methods of evaluation must be used – asking people how much they would be prepared to pay. These methods have so far proved much less convincing, despite the best efforts of environmental economists to refine their methodology.

The proof of this is that contingent valuation has to date been used much less in practice than observed behaviour techniques. The authors of a study of the application of valuation techniques in the Netherlands report that:

> To be considered for acceptance into environmental policy, benefit estimates must have a core of 'hard' estimates, e.g., foregone repair costs to materials, foregone productivity losses etc. Willingness-to-pay estimates, especially if measured with the contingent valuation technique, are often much larger than hard estimates but are considered to be less persuasive. As a rule, they are not accepted by other Departments or Ministries. (Apart, that is, from the Department of Environmental Management.)
>
> (Kuik, Jansen and Opschoor, in Barde and Pearce, 1991.)

An example of just this difficulty in application is provided in the study. A willingness-to-pay survey conducted at random among Dutch households found that Dutch society as a whole would be prepared to pay 1.45 billion Dutch florins per annum to protect forests and heather from damage caused by air pollution. Yet the effects on timber production of continued pollution were calculated at only 13.1 million florins per annum. This latter is a 'hard' figure, based on the market price of timber. Such a huge discrepancy surely calls into question the usefulness or accuracy of either or both valuation methods. The environment ministry did not, in any case, use the results of the willingness-to-pay survey because, among other reasons, it would not prove acceptable to other ministries.

According to the authors of the study, such surveys may nonetheless have a role in awareness-building. And yet, revealingly, they later conclude that 'Assessment of damage in physical terms can be as useful (or even more) for public awareness building as monetary assessment.'

The problems involved in applying this kind of evaluation technique in Western Europe are even more intractable when the technique is exported to developing countries. It may seem plausible to ask a European, reasonably versed in market survey methods, how much she or he would be willing to pay to preserve a local area of woodland, or even how much she would contribute to the preservation of forests she may never see, in Amazonia. (The level of contributions to organisations like the World Wide Fund for Nature has, in fact, been cited as indicative of the 'existence value' that Europeans put on distant environmental assets.) But even in Europe, ability to pay has been shown – unsurprisingly – to affect willingness to pay. And it is not clear at all that any useful information could be gained by asking indigenous people in Amazonia how much they would pay to preserve their forests and, by implication, their whole culture and lifestyle. Wouldn't they find such a question nonsensical? And wouldn't that be more a testament to their good sense than to any lack of sophistication?

This kind of difficulty led James Winpenny, who was commissioned by the UK Overseas Development Administration to write a practitioners' guide to environmental evaluation in developing countries, to conclude that generally the most useful valuation techniques are the least novel (Winpenny, 1991a). These include costing the effects on production of new developments, calculating preventive expenditure for avoiding environmental damage, or replacement costs where damage is unavoidable; and calculating the costs, in terms of medical expenses and lost income, of damage to human health. Although he regards contingent valuation as 'a perfectly intelligible type of market research', he is sceptical about its application in developing countries.

The usefulness of the less novel, 'hard' valuations should not be underestimated. There are difficulties in calculating preventive expenditure or the costs of replacing environmental features, since we can seldom predict with certainty the environmental outcome of any intervention. But on the other hand it can, for example, be shown by the 'effects on production' technique that the economic benefits of preserving standing forest (in terms of renewable resources and products like oils, resins, bamboo, tannin, honey, beeswax and chemicals extracted from plants for pharmaceutical products) can outweigh the economic benefits (in timber and grazing land) of chopping it down. That should provide useful material for arguments with the logging companies.

But if this is the best that we can hope from environmental valuation, then the system loses both its mystique and its radical appeal. The Pearce Report was, after all, dubbed a 'blueprint', in what seems like deference to the radicalism of *The Ecologist*'s 1972 'Blueprint for Survival'. Yet if we expected a revolution from it, or even a significant advance in economic thinking, then we must be disappointed; for it turns out that, in the Netherlands as much as in Amazonia, the valuations that most count are still the 'hard' valuations, those that ultimately depend on market forces and market prices. Yet hasn't this very tendency – to consider environmental assets only for their market value – been one root cause of the problem all along?

Contingent valuation comes closest to offering a new way for determining values that are not based on market prices – the 'true' values that Pearce wants us to appreciate. Yet even if there were no practical difficulties in the application of this methodology, there are two fundamental objections to it that have not yet been satisfactorily answered. The first is conceptual. Is 'value' the same as 'monetary value'? We value friendship, we value walks in the country, we value inconsequential conversations with people in the street. But would we want to put a price on these things? Would it make sense even to try?

Professor Pearce is adamant that 'all decisions imply valuations', adding in an acerbic footnote that 'This elementary point appears to have escaped most of the critics of valuation.' (Pearce, 1991, Chapter 1). In a sense, he is entirely right. If a constituent of mine decides to go to the pub for a beer and some idle gossip, that decision clearly implies that he values the beer and the gossip more highly than the possibility of having a cup of tea at home and watching Jeremy Paxman on *Newsnight*. No doubt about it, he has made a clear value judgement. But I am sure that none of my constituents are so worldly or so daft as to have computed all this in financial terms. No-one in their right minds would rate an hour at the pub as 'worth' £5, compared with a mere £3 worth of value to be derived from an hour's television. (Or even vice versa, of course.)

Value judgements, be they grave or trivial, personal or universal, cannot all be reduced to merit valuations. It is, indeed, a sad reflection on the values of our age that anyone so distinguished as Professor Pearce should think they could; and surely it is the novelty, rather than the perspicuity, of his case that has brought it so much attention. Of course he is right to point out that a decision to build a motorway implies the value judgement (on the part of those who make the decision) that the benefits of such a scheme outweigh the noise, pollution and ugliness it will bring. But that does not mean that the judgement can be formally expressed in monetary terms. Reducing the value we place on the existence of animal species or an attractive landscape to a cash value is no less silly than trying to attach a cash value to the pleasure of beer and gossip.

Who but an economist would ever dream of supposing that economic value, or monetary value, is the only kind of value there is (or, at any rate, the only kind that matters in decision making)? Rather than trying to get the environment on to the balance sheet, might it not after all be better to ensure that environmental decisions are made off the balance sheet; to ensure, that is, that considerations other than purely economic or monetary considerations are taken fully into account after totting up financial costs and benefits?

But what if I am completely wrong? Suppose that environmental valuation is, in Winpenny's words, 'perfectly intelligible'
and that, even if it doesn't manage to reveal a fixed, 'true' value
for environmental assets, it does at least show the price that we,
as a society, are prepared to pay to preserve them or receive in
compensation for their loss. Even if this were so, valuation would
still not provide an adequate way for meeting our responsibilities
to future generations, or to the environment itself, for the simple
reason I have already mentioned: namely that, at best, valuation
can only tell us something about our values and our preferences
as present consumers. It tells us nothing at all about what people
in the future might want, and excludes from the start any notion
of responsibility to the environment for its own sake. Who are we
to decide on behalf of people in the future? Can we honestly trust
ourselves to weigh their interests equally with our own, immediate
interests? And can we be so sure that we have no responsibility to
the environment that is not reducible to making it serve either our
interests or those of people in the future?

The answer to the second question – whether we will weigh
the interest of future generations equally with our own – is almost
certainly no. This is reflected in planning criteria by a 'discount'
rate for future benefits: a gain for tomorrow is only counted as a
percentage of what that gain would be if it were realised today. In
practical terms, this way of thinking and of calculating benefits
counts against long term projects such as reforestation, because it
will be so long before the benefits are felt.

Given this general background it seems likely that the interests
of, for example, the grandchildren of present Amazonian forest
dwellers would not figure greatly in European or North
American willingness to pay for the preservation of the forests.
But even if this objection turned out to be groundless – even if a
deep seam of disinterested altruism revealed itself in the present
preferences of Europeans and Americans – the fact would remain
that we are choosing on behalf of future generations, and thus by
implication depriving them of the right and the opportunity to
choose for themselves.

To an extent, all action, including inaction, involves this
dilemma. Whatever we do will have direct consequences for the
future, and directly affect future opportunities. But it is reasonably clear that an approach to environmental protection based on

cost–benefit analysis and monetary evaluation, although it may in practice encourage weight to be given to the environment in planning decisions, cannot guarantee that the future will be provided for or maximise future options and opportunities.

A more explicit commitment to sustainability is required: one that emphasises the moral imperative of leaving open as many doors of opportunity to future people as is feasible. Such a commitment would take a precautionary view of 'trade-offs', insisting that the basic elements of 'environmental capital' are not negotiable, much less tradable, and seeking to leave that capital as intact as we found it. We can't just sell off the rain forests and hope that it won't matter, and that our children won't mind.

In practical environmental decision making, one of the frequently perceived limiting factors of pollution abatement and environmental enhancement is the cost of taking the necessary measures. This preoccupation is indeed implicit in the way that pollution has long been considered an 'external' cost of production – one that needn't affect the producer's profitability, and that can be passed on to consumers either in financial terms (where government has to intervene to render wastes safe) or in terms of suffering a degraded environment.

Much less often mentioned is the cost of not preventing or cleaning up pollution, but of failing to do so: the cost of neglect – not just accidents but wilful damage. In terms of our experience of a degraded environment, the cost is often obvious and very high. But the financial costs can also be high. Expenditure on operations to clean up Prince William Sound after the *Exxon Valdez* disaster, to minimise the damage in the wake of Three Mile Island and Chernobyl, and the lost income from ruined environments like the American Great Lakes and the Black Sea are all examples of the way that allowing environmental degradation to happen in the first place can prove very costly in the long run. And this will be felt even more directly and painfully if global warming does result in a rise of sea levels, with whole Pacific islands disappearing and low-lying coastlands being rearranged. In this sense, we have clearly reached a stage where environmental degradation can actually be a limiting factor on economic activity. There is therefore an overwhelming need to reverse the mentality which sees pollution as a transferable cost – to be paid somewhere else by someone else – and to realise instead that environmental protection will not just result in a better quality of life but can represent genuine savings too.

Environmental efficiency is therefore a key to the approach that we must adopt. Energy efficiency is an obvious example where the case is clearly proven. The great advances made in methods of energy efficiency in recent years – although they have not all been put into practice – show how much can be achieved in this area. It has been estimated that our total consumption of energy could be cut by more than half if the best currently available energy efficiency technology were adopted in our homes, workplaces, generating industries and transport systems (Toke, 1990); and there is every likelihood that research and development of new technologies, stimulated by serious commitment to energy efficiency, would provide the possibility of even greater reductions in resource use and greenhouse gas emissions, without reducing consumer-end amenity. Even the most radical targets yet proposed for reductions in carbon dioxide emissions could be met without too much difficulty through energy efficiency measures on such a scale.

Needless to say, market forces won't stimulate this kind of change; and, unfortunately, privatisation of the generating industry was a decisive step in exactly the wrong direction. The private companies have a clear, vested interest in producing and selling as much energy as they can. Shareholders great and small are hardly likely to enthuse about efficiency programmes, or to encourage the companies to adopt policies aimed at reducing sales given the ethos at the time of privatisation.

If the energy utilities are to remain in private hands, they must be subjected to strict efficiency standards, and required wherever possible to meet new demand not by increasing the amount of fuel burnt but by increasing efficiency so that the same amount of fuel goes further. Legislation of this kind already exists in the United States. At the same time we must begin to invest in 'combined heat and power' plants (usually, small plants which, instead of allowing heat to disappear up chimneys, use it for heating local houses and public buildings); and we must sponsor research and pilot schemes for renewable energy resources, against the day that we can begin to reduce our total dependence on fossil fuels. If a small amount of the research expenditure devoted to the nuclear power programme had been spent instead on research into renewables we would now be much closer to meeting our energy requirements safely and cleanly.

It has been widely suggested that an energy tax is the best method of cutting energy demand, and some politicians have now accepted this view. Such a mechanism has an ideological appeal to non-socialists because it is 'market based'; that is, it attempts to influence behaviour by intervention in the market place rather than by direct regulation.

But the trouble with energy or carbon taxes is that they almost certainly hit the poorest hardest. Energy demand is relatively 'inelastic': that is, it is seldom a luxury item, and so increasing its price tends not to reduce demand significantly. We all need to keep warm in winter, and to light our homes; and many of us are dependent to a significant extent on private cars for personal mobility, getting to work, etc. So if we have to pay more for electricity or petrol many of us will, reluctantly, do so; but this would clearly create major problems for those who cannot afford the difference. The wealthy will be relatively unaffected, with the fairly marginal reduction in demand being squeezed out of the poor, who almost invariably have the worst insulated houses and least efficient forms of heating, and who have less flexibility in the way that they use energy. People who are unemployed or dependent on state benefits cannot reduce their fuel bills by installing solar panels or buying a new, more energy-efficient car (if they have one at all).

A more promising approach would be to set up a programme of home insulation and energy efficiency, to introduce efficiency standards for construction and manufacturing industries and for energy-consuming goods (such as domestic appliances and, most importantly but most problematically, vehicles). Reducing consumer waste – unnecessary car journeys, and leaving house lights on all night – should be undertaken on the basis of public information campaigns rather than coercive indirect taxation. But, as I have argued at length in earlier chapters, general appeals to promote more environmentally conscious consumer behaviour must be backed by government action – to introduce product labelling schemes, for example, which must include information about energy efficiency, so that the choices of individuals will really make a difference.

This is not to say that financial incentives or market-based mechanisms have no role at all: we should not be as blinkered by dogma as the government has shown itself over the last decade. But, broadly, it may well be better to use financial incentives to encourage energy-efficient consumption rather than to punish inefficient consumption. For example, it would certainly be worth considering exempting particularly energy-efficient devices from VAT. This could be linked to efficiency standards, so that goods well above the minimum required standard enjoyed exemption. An exemption of this kind would operate not just as an incentive to green consumption, but as an incentive to green production too, since it would improve the competitiveness of 'environmentally friendly' products.

It is generally accepted that much could be done to improve energy efficiency in a relatively short space of time, using existing technologies and well-defined policy instruments. Our use of energy is itself a fundamental environmental issue, but the example is of importance not just in signposting necessary changes in energy policy but as a model for our whole approach to environmental management. (Jacobs, 1991, sets out a detailed case along these lines.)

For it may well be possible, following the course suggested, to bequeath to the next generation the same level of net energy capital that we now have available. In the literal sense, this will appear implausible: a barrel of oil burned today is gone for ever. But supposing we at present have known reserves of n billion barrels of oil equivalent, which under current technologies could generate x billion units of energy. More efficient technologies, already within our reach, would slow the rate of resource depletion and increase the amount of work done by each barrel of oil (or equivalent) consumed. So we might, even if no new reserves are discovered, be able to ensure that while gross reserves decline, the amount of work that can be done by those diminished reserves remains equivalent to what we can now achieve with present stocks under present conditions. In other words, we can not actually leave behind us the same stocks as now exist; but we could make sure that what is left is able to do as much work as x billion units of generated energy could do for us today. Future generations would therefore have an equal opportunity to generate and use energy (and an equal obligation to pass on the same potential).

A simpler, imaginary example shows how this could work in practice. In a world of 1 million families, where each family burns 2 tonnes of coal every year in open fires, there will be an annual energy demand of 2 million tonnes. Total coal stocks of 100 million tonnes would be enough for just 50 years on the open fire system. But, on this system, most of the heat from the fire goes up the chimney. If each family were able to acquire a simple stove, which produced the same amount of heat using only 1 tonne of coal per year, annual demand would drop to 1 million tonnes. So, after 50 years, there would be a remaining stock of 50 million tonnes: enough for another 50 years on the simple stove system. It would then be necessary, if it had not been done already, to develop a new stove that produced as much heat out of only half a tonne of coal a year, at the same time as investigating alternative ways of generating heat.

Here we have sustainability. It is not stocks that are sustained, but the ability of people to keep warm. Opportunity remains constant. Technology is not reviled as some kind of science-fiction nightmare, but it is put fairly and squarely in the service of people, rather than vice versa.

The pit, of course, is not bottomless. The day will come, in a world of a million people or in a world of more than 5,000 million, when declining reserves of fossil fuels, however carefully used, will no longer meet total needs. Twenty years on from Schumacher, we should be well aware of this, and so have no excuse for ignorance. Hence the need for investment, research, development and, hopefully, gradual transference to wind, wave and solar power. For sustainability also requires an eye to the future: an appreciation of the present outlook together with a sensitivity to long term trends and possibilities. In other words, it requires intelligent planning of resources.

From this model of energy efficiency, resource substitution and investment in alternatives, we can derive principles that should govern our use not merely of energy but of all environmental goods and services. I am not just talking about resources. Our use of air, earth and water as dustbins for the byproducts of production and consumption relies upon their absorptive capacities which in many cases have already been pushed beyond reasonable limits. This has created a situation of environmental stress, which works in two directions: the environment itself is stressed (and none of us can actually say with any certainty how much more abuse it can withstand); and people too are experiencing stress as a result of environmental degradation. But if we make our industries and our consumption less polluting, reducing current levels of environmental stress, then we may be able to bequeath a constant surplus of environmental capacity, so that future generations with less polluting technologies will have the same opportunity as ourselves to produce and consume. Once again, opportunity will remain constant.

A programme that operated on this principle of maintaining environmental opportunity at a constant level would require us to make an informed analysis of existing resources, environmental capacities and the scope for development of alternatives and replacements. Extraction of certain critical resources, that are severely depleted or irreplaceable, should be stopped immediately. Nobody could object to such a decision if it was made on the basis of a full assessment. Supposing, for example, that English broadleaved woodlands were included in the 'severely depleted or irreplaceable' category: this would imply a complete moratorium on economic activity affecting them. Assessment of critically affected environmental capacities might also suggest immediate curtailment of certain kinds of production. This sounds drastic, and therefore highly improbable: but it should be remembered how quickly the production of CFCs was controlled, once it became fully accepted that they cause critical environmental damage; and this illustrates the scope for a new agenda of pro-active control.

In the main, however, maintaining environmental opportunity would imply reducing pollution levels rather than completely banning certain activities. We can't simply ban the private car: but we can make ourselves less dependent on it (through investment in public transport), and we can make the machine itself less wasteful, less polluting. Meanwhile we should also be supporting more research into alternatives to the internal combustion engine.

Pollution abatement can best be achieved by setting targets, based on the principle of maintaining opportunity and informed by sound, scientific understanding of what the environment can tolerate. This must be the basis for agreeing targets, rather than considerations of how cheap and convenient it would be to meet them; and targets should have a strong, precautionary element, erring, if at all, on the side of underestimating the earth's capacities.

Once again, this sounds dramatic, and painful. But, as in the case of energy, we actually have much of the necessary means substantially to improve environmental efficiency. What is required is the political foresight and commitment to implement solutions that are already known about. So although greater control of industrial production is necessary, this is not inconsistent with maintaining, and even expanding, current levels of production itself. Provided each unit of production is made more environmentally efficient it is technically feasible to sustain growth at the same time as reducing total use of environmental capacity and reserves: indeed, in the short term, opportunities for developing pollution abatement technologies, plus opportunities for employment in waste minimisation and insulation industries, and in the construction, operation and maintenance of treatment plants, etc., could stimulate a small green boom.

Reconciling growth with environmental protection has long been held by many environmentalists to be the equivalent of squaring the circle: but it is certainly not a logical impossibility and, if we are imaginative and inventive enough, it need not be a practical impossibility either. The extraordinary advances made in industrial and materials technology during the last 50 years are a testament to human creativity, and therefore a great source of hope; with the important caveat that such creativity must be put at the service of well-defined environmental criteria.

To keep the economy in line with pollution abatement targets a number of active government interventions will be necessary. In selecting policy instruments, we should not become preoccupied by a sterile debate about the rival merits of 'market-based mechanisms' as against direct regulation. These are often presented as the favoured instruments of right and left respectively; but while it is true that the right is generally fearful of anything that seems overtly regulatory, the ideological distinction between the two kinds of approach is in fact hollow. Regulating what industry can and cannot do has a direct effect on the market place; and intervening in the market place directly affects what industry does, and refrains from doing. Both are valid forms of intervention, and the choice between them must in each planning decision be made on the basis of what is most likely to achieve the desired ends, with due regard to cost effectiveness, ease of administration and social impact.

There is no doubt that there will have to be a strong, basic framework of regulations. Direct regulation has a substantial policy record, as a clear cut and straightforward way of achieving objectives, and it is foolish to claim that further intervention of this kind is in principle undesirable or irreconcilable with profitable production. Health and safety legislation and regulations governing the food and water industries are solid examples of measures which are indispensable to public health, and which could not be achieved in any other way. They are not perfect, but they have got us as far as we are. There is an overwhelming case for direct regulations governing energy standards, pollution and waste control, and that those regulations must be more stringent than at present.

Any claim that increased regulation would reduce the competitiveness of industry should be judged in the light of the fact that in many respects British manufacturing has lower environmental standards than those maintained by our European partners. If other countries can improve their environmental performance and continue to manufacture goods competitively, then so must we. Indeed, there is growing awareness on both sides of industry – among both management and unions – that improved environmental performance will be one of the best guarantees of competitiveness as we approach the end of the century. The pressure of more environmentally demanding markets, both at home and overseas, threatens to leave Britain behind in a way that is not just damaging to our prestige. For if we can't conform to the higher standards of other countries in terms of what we produce then our market share will decline; and if we can't conform to higher standards in terms of how we produce then our industrial technology itself will become increasingly out of step with other countries and unable to benefit from innovation at international level. The further we get behind in these areas, the longer it will take us to catch up.

Market interventions through financial incentives or disincentives are often considered appealing because they do not require creating a watchdog body and because they have the appearance of being less coercive than direct regulation. But of course if intervention was far reaching enough, this noncoerciveness would soon prove illusory. By way of illustration, we may consider the government's recent recycling credits scheme, a main element of which requires that savings made by authorities on landfill space have to be passed back to the authorities who made the savings possible by setting up recycling schemes. Although in principle sensible, and in appearance attractive because it provides an incentive to recyclers without the government – or anyone else – having to stump up extra cash, the scheme falls short of what is needed because the mechanism fails to address an underlying problem, which is that landfill costs in this country are relatively low, and it is too easy to opt for the short term solution. The savings from landfill space as re-cycling initiatives gain pace will therefore not be significant: and nor, therefore, will the cash incentive.

In a report on the credits scheme prepared for the Department of the Environment, Touche Ross Management Consultants (1991) tip their hats in the direction of Conservative ideology with the puzzling sentiment that 'The purpose of the credit is not to bring the market up to a certain level of activity, but to allow it to achieve the economically efficient level of activity through the effect of market forces.' If that means anything at all, it means that recycling is to be encouraged only to the extent that it is economically viable. Yet the purpose of the credit system was elsewhere described as being able to facilitate reaching the government's own target of recycling 50 per cent of recyclable household waste by the year 2000: a clear case of bringing the recycling market 'up to a certain level of activity'. So which was the real purpose: to reach the target or to encourage an 'econo-mically efficient' level of recycling which might, of course, prove to be lower than the target?

So here we have a market-based mechanism which was pre-sented by its advocates as being cheap and painless (as well as being ideologically attractive to them). But none of that will be any good if it doesn't actually work; and there must be serious doubts as to whether a mechanism of this kind will achieve the desired target. If some practical means were introduced of mak-ing it work in market terms, such as setting a minimum landfill charge (and hence credit for savings), then it would no longer look painless. And as to being cheap, a Department of Trade and Industry official remarked at a recent conference on the subject that the way that each local authority was left to make its own *ad hoc* arrangements was in fact costing more than if the government had devised a proper, national strategy.

More far-reaching market mechanisms – such as an energy tax, as already discussed – would not escape the appearance of coerciveness at all. A tax of this kind would almost certainly be unpopular and would be very hard to justify, especially as it is doubtful whether it would actually succeed in significantly reducing fossil fuel demand. Indeed, the best argument for it is that it would provide a source of public revenue that could be reinvested in efficiency schemes, and used to compensate the lower income groups who would be hardest hit by the tax. (Although hypothecation of this kind will always be resisted by the Treasury.)

But we must not reject financial incentives or market mechanisms out of hand. Clearly, some such incentives can work. Charging returnable deposits on bottles, for example, is a long established mechanism for ensuring maximum reuse, and one that drinks manufacturers would do well to revive and extend. Perhaps there is a lesson here, that the simplest mechanisms are those which are most likely to get results. Certainly, simple measures such as differential VAT rates can have a useful role. The lower tax rate for lead-free petrol has set a useful precedent here. Equally, selective taxes could be placed on goods with a high environmental cost (such as conventional batteries and peat-based composts) where more benign alternatives exist or can be stimulated (rechargeable batteries, waste-based compost).

I regard the more complex and grandiose incentives with a large degree of scepticism. To an extent, the silver lining of being so far behind some other countries in environmental policy is that we can learn from their experiments and experience. We should, for example, be closely studying American and European experiments in tradable permits and pollution charges, where it is made illegal to pollute, but permits to do so are sold, and may be exchanged between companies, thus, in theory, operating as an incentive to all firms to minimise pollution levels. I am not particularly hopeful that such a byzantine approach to environmental management will produce the desired results. There is something intuitively unsavoury about setting up markets in pollution – for that is effectively what is being done – because it makes pollution, or the right to pollute, itself a resource that is in demand. What would we think of a new breed of 'pollution-brokers' who made a living in pollution futures markets out of buying up and selling tradable permits? This would certainly give a novel meaning to the phrase 'filthy lucre'; but, more seriously, there must be some danger that a potentially powerful grouping would emerge with a vested interest in perpe- tuating the trading system rather than in minimising pollution – thus proving again that the only way for real progress to be made is for government to intervene and establish a strong regulatory framework.

The results of this novel kind of system might well be highly unpredictable in other ways, and it is hard to see the practical attraction of trying to achieve, in so convoluted a manner, what could be achieved by direct intervention in line with planned targets. (Although, as in the case of monetary valuation, the real attraction is in many cases undoubtedly that of 'dealing with' environmental problems in a way that subsumes them into the principles of market operations, rather than seeing in them proof of the limitations of the market.) However, as I have said, we are in the position of not having to prejudge this kind of effort: we should study it, and make our minds up on the basis of the results. Meanwhile, the market mechanism with most straight-forward appeal is the application of selective charges or levies, which may be useful not as policies in their own right – aimed at forcing innovation to reduce pollution – but as a means of raising revenue to fund environmental protection in the public domain.

Clearly, substantial investment will be needed in research and new technology, to replace scarce or damaging materials, products and processes with less wasteful and less harmful processes and products that have greater potential for reuse recycling. There can be no question but that environmental protection and pollution abatement will, at least in the short to medium term, cost money; and it would be foolish to pretend that this will not affect the public purse. There is a particular need for increasing government expenditure in public transport, investment in infra-structure and the utilities, and research. For government as much as for private companies, investment of this kind is an expense which will bring tangible as well as qualitative returns.

Much of this investment can be funded by redirecting existing expenditure and diverting resources: reassessment of expenditure on roads, for example, may well provide the wherewithal for investment in public transport. There is also a clear and strong argument to be made for investing any 'peace dividend', arising from progressive reduction in weapons capability, in environmental protection: we are, after all, talking about defending ourselves and the future against the common enemy of environmental ruin. (Another, interesting congruence here is that the monitoring skills of modern defence techniques overlap in some important respects with the kind of monitoring techniques we need for environmental surveillance.)

Any further, net increase in public expenditure need not be met out of general taxation. Indeed, this would violate the 'polluter pays' principle: even where the consumer as well as the producer is considered to be a polluter, those forced to pay through higher taxes would include at least some who were not contributing to the pollution, or who were contributing proportionately less than they were forced to pay.

There is certainly a case for looking at ideas such as additional public expenditure on pollution abatement being funded from specific charges to polluters. For example, an additional levy on petrol could be used to bolster investment in public transport. This might appear to sit uneasily with opposition to a general energy tax but it differs in three, important respects. Firstly, the purpose would not be to reduce demand, but to provide revenue, and so the tax would be set at a level which was sensitive to the needs of people genuinely dependent on private cars for personal transport. Secondly, improvement in public transport would be a direct compensation, in terms of providing a realistic alternative, to all private car users. Thirdly, the largest part of the revenue would come from the thirstiest and most used vehicles, which tend not to belong to our poorer citizens.

Charges could also be levied on industrial polluters. This would allow an environmental fund to be set up to provide subsidies and soft loans to utilities and industrial concerns, allowing them to spread the cost of investment in new technologies over a number of years, and to deal with a backlog of past problems such as waste sites. Although it might appear odd to take with one hand what is given back with the other, an arrangement of this kind will almost certainly be necessary to force the pace of change.

It might be argued that industry could, on a voluntary basis, 'tax' itself in order to reinvest in more benign technologies; but at this point we run up once more against the harsh reality of the 'tragedy of the commons'. Voluntary mechanisms, and the role of persuasion and public information, should not be discounted: there may, indeed, be a critical threshold of public concern beyond which the 'greening' of individual companies becomes a commercial necessity. But if we are serious about setting environmental targets based on environmental necessity, we cannot simply wait for the market to reform itself. (Which is the logic of complacency and conservatism.) Unilateral action always carries the risk of self-imposed penalties, in terms of reduced dividends, which few firms would be willing to incur without guarantees that their competitors would do likewise: although, again, it must be emphasised that those industries that begin to invest in environmentally improved technologies now will soon reap the benefits in increased competitiveness. However, charging polluters is also a simple method for 'levelling the playing field' obliging all those affected to seek ways of improving their environmental performance; and providing loans and/or subsidies is a simple method for providing the means to make that improvement.

There is no doubt, however, that in the short term environmental protection will cost money if we stick to the old, limited system of accounting; even though neglecting the environment would, in the long run, cost a great deal more. Winning the argument against ill-advised, short term 'savings' will depend on the extent to which we can offer a new quality of life in return for new investment.

During the 'phoney election' in the autumn of 1991, and before the Prime Minister had finally allowed his intentions to be whispered in the ears of selected newspaper editors, commentators had already exhausted their best, most telling line: 'At the end of the day, the decisive issue in this election will be the economy.' The same is said every election time, in the same tone of profound insight. In fact it is in part a rather meaningless remark, and in part an insulting one. Meaningless, because 'the economy' embraces so much of domestic policy that it cannot be considered a single issue at all – although the commentators, in fact, often reduce economic issues even further, to a matter of who is going to tax what and by how much. Insulting, for the insinuation that people will always vote with their minds fixed firmly on their purses.

I believe this is a simplistic and narrow analysis. I believe the electorate has a great respect for straightforwardness and plain speaking; and I also believe that people are not motivated solely by short-term personal gain. There is widespread, intuitive understanding of the value of both individual and collective welfare, and that the quality of life does not consist solely in maximising private consumption. We must take this understanding, make it explicit, and argue candidly for a new quality of life based on the enhancement of collective welfare. The widespread public concern about threats to the National Health Service suggest that people will in fact be receptive to this argument.

In environmental terms, this means putting a higher priority on achieving cleaner, safer and more pleasant surroundings. The further we move in this direction, reorienting economic activity to meet newly perceived needs and interests, the less acquisitive and consuming a society we will become, and the less we will threaten the prosperity of our descendants.

In the long term, this does suggest new values, and may bring new patterns of consumption. There is no need to fear this, and no need to see in it an argument for returning to the caves. For in fact many of our profoundest social ills are directly linked to a misconceived quest to satisfy human needs through owning goods. The riots on Tyneside last year, for example, reportedly began when police attempted to arrest a pair of young 'joyriders'. The irony of this should not be lost on us. In our culture, private cars are the most potent symbols of personal freedom, power and prestige. Much ingenuity is devoted to their manufacture, and extraordinary artistic and creative talent is devoted to advertising and marketing them. Despite the increasing havoc wreaked by cars, in despoliation of the countryside, congestion and atmospheric pollution, we are still clearly addicted to them. And if it is plain enough that this addiction is not good for us collectively, it should also be plain that for unhappy and underprivileged individuals, without income or the prospect of driving legitimately, the addiction is a festering sore. Itching to drive, itching for the unique thrill of power and freedom, they steal cars and crash them. They, the people they steal from, and the people they maim when they crash the cars are all in different ways victims of the great car economy so beloved by Margaret Thatcher.

We all know that possessions alone do not make people happy. But every Christmas, wanting to express love, many of us work overtime or extend our overdrafts to buy more. The purest impulse of the parent, to bring joy to our children, has in our culture come to be mediated through the toyshop. This is ridiculous, and all parents know it; all parents, at any rate, who have been pressurised to buy, at outlandish prices, Teenage Mutant Hero Turtles, Bart Simpson, Euro Disney toys or whatever the latest craze might be. It is incredible that we should have allowed this to happen. Incredible that we should have allowed 4, 3, even 2 year olds to be seriously targeted as 'markets', and to have covetousness deliberately instilled in them by the ads between the Tom and Jerry cartoons. And appalling that the toys and electrical goods in many a British 8 year old's bedroom are worth more than the total possessions of whole families throughout the Third World. And should we be surprised, in so acquisitive a society as ours, when some of the children who get left behind, whose parents couldn't afford to buy them all that stuff, turn into juvenile car thieves?

In the long term, these acquisitive values must change; but politicians won't change them by simply invoking a moral crusade. Instead, we have a responsibility to give a lead by taking practical steps to safeguard the future, on the basis of preventive expenditure which will not only greatly enhance our quality of life – thereby reducing the pressure for people to seek fulfilment in material goods – but also avert much greater costs, and possible tragedy, that will occur if we fail to act now. Clearly, there is an ethical dimension to this: because it involves the decision to reassess and pay stricter attention to the needs of future generations, as against our own short term gain (which, properly considered, is not gain at all). And clearly this dimension embraces not just people who are remote in time, but the people in the developing world who are geographically remote from us: because the global economy can only be made genuinely sustainable if their needs are addressed – which is the understanding that we must take with us to the 1992 UNCED Conference. But these decisions are not rooted in high-minded altruism so much as in simple common sense, and the realisation that the environment, more than anything else, reveals the true community of interests between all peoples, now and in the future. These are choices we can't avoid. Inaction is a policy in itself: and an extremely dangerous one. Better by far that we should now seize the opportunity, in a constructive way, of choosing our future.

Bibliography

1 The environment and the socialist ethic

Boys, P. (19XX). Cholera, Class and Empire in the 19th Century, in *Science for People* No. 54.

Brockway, F. (1980). *Britain's First Socialists*. Quartet, London.

Galbraith, J. K. (1979). *The Affluent Society* (1958) in *The Galbraith Reader*. Andre Deutsch, London.

Hay, A., Hurst, P. and Dudley, N. (1991). *The Pesticide Handbook*. Pluto, London.

Levitas, R. (1990). *The Concept of Utopia*. Philip Alan, Oxford.

Marx, K. (1974). *Selected Writings in Sociology and Social Philosophy*. Penguin, Harmondsworth.

Owen, R. (1991). *A New Vision of Society and other Writings*. ed. and introd. G. Claeys. Penguin, Harmondsworth.

Poulsen, C. (1984). *The English Rebels*. Journeyman, London.

Repetto, R. (1985). *Paying the Price: Pesticide Subsidies in Developing Countries*. WRI, Washington.

Thompson, E. P. (1977). *William Morris: Romantic to Revolutionary*. Merlin, London.

Williams, R. (1983). *Towards 2000*. Chatto & Windus, London.

Winpenny, J. T. (1991). *Values for the Environment*. HMSO, London.

2 A global perspective

Bernstein, H., Crow, C., Mackintosh, M. and Martin, C. (eds) (1990). *The Food Question: Profits versus People*. Earthscan, London.

Black, G. (1981). *Triumph of the People: the Sandinista Revolution in Nicaragua*. Zed, London.

Coote, B. (1987). *The Hunger Crop: Poverty and the Sugar Industry*. OXFAM, Oxford.

Hancock, G. (1985). *Ethiopia: the Challenge of Hunger*. Gollancz, London.

Hardoy, J. and Satterthwaite, D. (1989). *Squatter Citizen: Life in the Urban Third World*. Earthscan, London.

Hecht, S. and Cockburn, A. (1990). *The Fate of the Forest*. Penguin, Harmondsworth.

Jacobs, M. (1991). *The Green Economy*. Pluto, London.

Ponting, C. (1991). *A Green History of the World*. Sinclair Stevenson, London.

Redclift, M. (1987). *Sustainable Development: Exploring the Contradictions*. Methuen, London.

Redclift, M. and Goodman, D. (1991). *Refashioning Nature*. Routledge, London.

Sage, C. (1989). Drugs and economic development in Latin America: a study in the political economy of cocaine in Boliva, in Ward, P. (ed.) *Corruption, Development and Inequality*. Routledge, London.

Shiva, V. (1990). 'Biodiversity: diversity or perversity' in *Third World Guide 1991–92*. Instituto del Tercer Mundo, Montevideo.

Sivard, L.S. (1991). *World Military and Social Expenditures 1991*. World Priorities, Washington.

Stevenson, (1991). Chemistry in Britain.

Winpenny, J.T. (1991a). *Values for the Environment: A Guide to Economic Appraisal*. HMSO, London.

Winpenny, J.T. (ed.) (1991b). *Development Research: the Environmental Challenge*. Overseas Development Institute, London.

World Commission on Environment and Development/G.H. Brundtland (1987). *Our Common Future* ('The Brundtland Report'). Oxford University Press, Oxford.

World Water/World Health Organization (1987). *International Drinking Water and Sanitation Decade Directory*. WHO, Geneva.

3 Making individuals count

Association of County Councils/Association of District Councils/Association of Metropolitan Councils (1990). *Environmental Practice in Local Government*. ACC/ADC/AMC, London.

Barwise, J. (ed.) (1991). *Local Authority Environmental Policy – A Framework for Action*. University of Surrey, Guildford.

Department of Education and Science (1991). *The Outdoor Classroom: Educational Use, Landscape Design, and Management of School Grounds*, Building Bulletin 71. DES, London.

Young, K. (1991). *Using School Grounds As An Educational Resource*. Learning Through Landscape Trust, Winchester.

4 Public perception and setting the agenda

Boyle, S. and Ardill, J. (1989). *The Greenhouse Effect. A Practical Guide to the World's Changing Climate*. Hodder and Stoughton, London.

British Medical Association (1990). *The BMA Guide to Living with Risk*. Penguin, Harmondsworth.

Brown, J.M. and White, H.M. (1987). The public's understanding of radiation and nuclear waste. *Journal of the Society of Radiological Protection* 7(2), 61–70.

Clark, B. D. (1991). Environmental Impact Assessment. United Kingdom. In *European Environmental Yearbook*. DocTer International UK, London.

Crump, A. (1991). *Dictionary of Environment and Development*. Earthscan, London.

Department of the Environment (1989). Digest of environmental protection and water statistics. No. 12. HMSO, London.

Department of the Environment (1991). *Drinking Water 1990*. A report by the Chief Inspector Drinking Water Inspectorate. HMSO, London.

Dudley, N. (1987). *This Poisoned Earth*. Piatkus, London.

Elsworth, S. (1984). *Acid Rain*. Pluto, London.

Elsworth, S. (1990). *A Dictionary of the Environment*. Paladin, London.

Forrester, S. (1990). Business and environmental groups – a natural partnership. Directory of Social Change, London.

Ghazi, P. (1990). Breath of blighted life. *Observer Supplement*, 3 March 1991, 32–5.

Gould, B. (1989). *A Future for Socialism*. Cape, London.

Harpham, T., Lusty, T. and Vaughn, P. (1988). *In the Shadow of the City. Community Health and the Urban Poor*. Oxford University Press, Oxford.

Hecht, S. and Cockburn, A. (1990). *The Fate of the Forest. Developers, Destroyers and Defenders of the Amazon*. Penguin, Harmondsworth.

Johnson, W. (1985). Old drains and diseases. *New Statesman*, 1 March 1985.

Jowell, R., Witherspoon, S. and Brook, L. (1987). *British Social Attitudes; the 1986 report*. Gower/Social and Community Planning Research, Aldershot.

Myers, N. (ed.) (1985). *The Gaia Atlas of Planet Management*. Pan, London.

Patterson, W. (1983). *Nuclear Power*. Penguin, Harmondsworth.

Pearce, F. (1982). *Watershed*. Junction Books, London.

Porteous, A. (1991). *A Dictionary of Environmental Science and Technology*. Open University, Milton Keynes.

Robens Institute (1988). Public attitudes to water quality and water privatisation. University of Surrey, Guildford.

Rose, C. (1990). *The Dirty Man of Europe. The Great British Pollution Scandal*. Simon and Schuster, London.

Simmons, I. (1989). *Changing the Face of the Earth. Culture, Environment, History*. Blackwell, Oxford.

United Nations (1990). *Global Outlook 2000. An Economic, Social and Environmental Perspective*. UN Publications, New York.

World Health Organization (1989). *European Charter on Environment and Health*. WHO, Copenhagen.

5 Knowledge, information and freedom

Barney, G. O. (ed.) (1980). *The Global 2000 Report to the President of the US. Entering the 21st Century*. Volumes I and II. Pergamon, New York.

Barwise, J. (ed.) (1991). *Local Authority Environmental Policy – A Framework for Action*. University of Surrey, Guildford.

Benn, A. (1974). *Speeches by Tony Benn*. Spokesman Books, London.

Benn, A. (1986). *Office Without Power. Diaries 1968–72*. Hutchinson, London.

Carson, R. (1962). *Silent Spring*. Penguin, Harmondsworth.

Central Office of Information (1990). *Britain 1990. An Official Handbook*. HMSO, London.

Gorz, A. (1975). *Ecologie et Politique*. Editions Galilee, Paris. Reprinted as *Ecology as Politics*, Black Rose Books, Montreal, Canada (1980).

Hennessy, P. (1990). *Whitehall*. Fontana, London.

Hobsbawm, E. J. (1990). *Industry and Empire*. Penguin, Harmondsworth.

Jenkins, C. (1990). *All Against the Collar. Struggles of a White-Collar Union Leader*. Methuen, London.

Labour Party (1964). Let's Go With Labour for the New Britain. The Labour Party's Manifesto for the 1964 General Election. Labour Party, London.

Natural Environment Research Council (1991). Corporate Plan. Environmental Sciences Towards the Twenty First Century. NERC, Swindon.

Payne, G. L. (1960). *Britain's Scientific and Technological Manpower*. Stanford University Press, Stanford, CA.

Stretton, H. (1976). *Capitalism, Socialism and the Environment*. Cambridge University Press, Cambridge.

Sussman, M., Collins, C. H., Skinner, F. A. and Stewart-Tull, D. E. (eds) (1988). *The Release of Genetically-engineered Micro-organisms*. Academic Press, London.

Taylor, A. (1991). Labour's Environment Protection Executive. Fabian Society, London.

Turney, J. (ed.) (1984). *Sci-Tech Report. Current Issues in Science and Technology*. Pluto, London.

United Nations (1990). *Global Outlook 2000. An Economic, Social and Environmental Perspective*. United Nations, New York.

Wathern, P. (ed.) (1988). *Environmental Impact Assessment. Theory and Practice*. Unwin Hyman, London.

6 The greening of industry

Clutterbuck, D. and Snow, D. (1990). *Working with the Community. A Guide to Corporate Social Responsibility*. London, Weidenfeld and Nicolson.

Elkington, J. and Hailes, J. (1988). *The Green Consumer Guide*. London, Victor Gollancz.

Elkington, J., Knight, P. and Hailes, J. (1991). *The Green Business Guide. How to take up – and profit from – the environmental challenge*. London, Victor Gollancz.

Skinner, J. (1991). Hazardous waste treatment trends in the US. Waste Management & Research 9, 55–63.

Trade Union Congress (1991). Greening the workplace. London, TUC.

Trade Union Congress (1991). Industry, jobs and the environmental challenge. London, TUC.

7 Economics for our future

Barde, J.-P. and Pearce, D. (eds) (1991). *Valuing the Environment: Six Case Studies*. Earthscan, London.

Galbraith, J. K. (1979). *The Affluent Society* (1958) in *The Galbraith Reader*. Andre Deutsch, London.

Jacobs, M. (1991). *The Green Economy*. Pluto, London.

Pearce, D. (ed.) (1991). *Blueprint 2: Greening the World Economy*. Earthscan, London.

Pearce, D., Barbier, E. and Markandya, A. (1989). *Blueprint for a Green Economy*. Earthscan, London.

Schumacher, E. F. (1973). *Small is Beautiful: A Study of Economics as if People Mattered*. Blond & Briggs, London.

Touche Ross Management Consultants (1991). Waste Recycling Credits: Systems and Mechanisms. London, Touche Ross & Gibb Environmental Services.

Winpenny, J. T. (1991a). *Values for the Environment: A Guide to Economic Appraisal*. HMSO, London.

Winpenny, J. T. (ed.) (1991b). *Development Research: The Environmental Challenge*. Overseas Development Institute, London.

Index

For Product Safety Concerns and Information please contact our EU
representative GPSR@taylorandfrancis.com
Taylor & Francis Verlag GmbH, Kaufingerstraße 24, 80331 München, Germany